A
JOHN LAFARGE
READER

A
JOHN LAFARGE
READER

Selected and Edited by

THURSTON N. DAVIS, S.J.

JOSEPH SMALL, S.J.

Introduction by

Harold C. Gardiner, S.J.

THE AMERICA PRESS: NEW YORK

1956

Imprimi Potest:

Very Rev. Thomas E. Henneberry, S.J.
Provincial, New York Province

Nihil Obstat:

John M. A. Fearns, S.T.D.
Censor Librorum

Imprimatur:

 Francis Cardinal Spellman
Archbishop of New York
January 8, 1956

COPYRIGHT, © 1956, BY THE AMERICA PRESS

PRINTED IN THE U.S.A. BY H. WOLFF

LIBRARY OF CONGRESS CATALOG CARD NUMBER: 56-7626

69211

CONTENTS

Acknowledgments

Acknowledgments are due to the following publications for permission to use their material: *Confluence* ("Religious Temporal Action"); *The Catholic Mind* ("Thoughts on a Catholic Elite"); *Jubilee* ("Christianity and the Negro"); *Liturgical Arts* ("Catholic Religious Art" and "Private Opinion and Church Authority"); *Social Order* ("Christian Humanism"); *The Voice of St. Jude* ("The Basis of Interracial Peace"), as well as to the America Press for other published material.

I should like also to express appreciation to my secretary, Mr. William H. Dodd, for his aid in typing material, and to my colleagues, Father Davis and Father Small, for their patient work in selecting and editing it.

JOHN LaFARGE, S.J.

New York, January 1, 1956

Foreword

" 'Tis love and love alone that rules for aye," proclaims the old song, and 'tis true, agrees the present writer.

The statement is much truer than ever the author of the song dreamed. How much more true can be seen illustrated and made concrete in this collection assembled from the written work of Father John LaFarge, S.J. For, if there was ever a man who has known the rule of love, it is "JLF," to use the familiar initials we have got so used to seeing on copy and proof pages during Fr. LaFarge's thirty years on the editorial staff of *America*.

But what love is it that has ruled Fr. LaFarge for the "aye" of his seventy-six years and especially for the "aye" of his fifty years as a priest and a Jesuit?

On the afternoon of December 8, 1955, some 250 friends of Fr. LaFarge gathered at New York's Roosevelt Hotel to pay him tribute on the occasion of his unique double golden jubilee. The group was made up mainly of those who had worked through the long years with Fr. LaFarge in the various organizations he had founded or guided. The very listing of the organizations shows the catholicity of his interests and his apostolate. Represented were: the Catholic Interracial Council; the Catholic Association for International Peace; the Liturgical Arts Society; the John Boyle O'Reilly Committee for Interracial Justice; the Alumni Race Relations Committee; the St. Madeleine Sophie Retreat Group; the Catholic Laymen's Union; the St. Ansgar's Scandinavian Catholic League; *America*.

But it was when Fr. LaFarge rose to acknowledge the tributes paid him that the afternoon's celebration fell into a pattern and took shape—and the shape and pattern was one of love.

This does not mean that love had not long before inspired all who were present. It had, and it was a deep love for the jubilarian. But

it remained for the jubilarian himself to make clear to all just what
the real basis of that love had been all through the years.

My dear friends, said Fr. LaFarge, have you ever thought—but
of course you have—what a powerful motive love is? It rules the
world, we hear sung. And that is true, but what love really rules
the world? Well, to be frank about it, it is not human love, the love
of man and woman, the love of parents and children, or the love of
friends. It is the love of God. That is what has drawn us all together
this afternoon and held us together all the years I have had the great
honor of working for and with you. I love all of you and hope that
all of you love me, but beneath and around and above that love
glows and shines the love of God. We would just not be here together unless we all loved God together. More than that. All the
parish churches in the world would be closed and boarded up unless
the love of God, treasured and manifest in the millions who frequent
them, kept them open and filled to reciprocate His love. All the
chancery offices, the schools, colleges and universities; the hospitals,
the groups like yours, working for the betterment of your fellow
men—all would droop, paralyzed and moribund, unless the love of
God kept them pulsing with its life-blood.

This was no prepared oration, but the outpouring of one speaking
from the heart. Fr. LaFarge went on. The love of God is not an
abstract, disembodied thing, he said. It comes down, descends, per-
colates into and permeates all our thoughts, our inspirations. It wells
up and flowers in our actions; it directs and guides us; it brings us
together in gatherings like this, from which it impels us to go forth
and spread that same love abroad.

This is something like what Fr. LaFarge said. These abbreviated
and printed words cannot catch the simple warmth, the humble joy
with which he said it. But when the gathering of his co-worker
friends received, at the end of the reception, his priestly blessing,
which came freighted with the love that Fr. LaFarge has experienced and transmitted over the years, there was not one present who
did not feel that he was being warmed with the love of God.

And what does all this have to do with the present book? It has
everything in the world to do with it, for the reader will soon realize

that every chapter under every heading is informed with this same
quality. Whether Fr. LaFarge is speaking with quiet wit and deeply
human sympathy of "The Absent Blacksmith," and drawing from
his absence the realization that "we need a rebirth of the creative
spirit joined to truly genuine, artistic craftsmanship," or pondering
the (perhaps) more profound problem of "Can We Cooperate with
Communists?" there is always the tone, the atmosphere, soon to be
sensed by the reader, that here a priestly voice is speaking. And if
the voice is priestly, what can it—what must it—be saying over and
over again save that these problems can be approached and ultimately solved only under a realization of the reality of the love of
God?

This is not by any means to say that this collection of the best of
Fr. LaFarge's writings is sanctimonious in tone. Far from it. Anyone
who has read *The Manner Is Ordinary* will not come to this present
collection unprepared for the urbanity, the charm, the quiet humor
and the fine literary taste that inform every page. Incidentally,
though it is a very important point, this *Reader* is an excellent com-
panion-piece to *The Manner Is Ordinary*, Fr. LaFarge's autobiography. In that story of his own life, Fr. LaFarge shows us what
we may call his instinctive reaction to issues and problems. The
Reader will reveal to the thoughtful reader the motivation of those
reactions, the intention that directed all of Fr. LaFarge's ideologies.
That intention can always be reduced, I feel, to precisely what we
have been talking about: the love of God.

Frank Sheed recently compiled an excellent anthology of pieces
on the saints and gave it the appropriate title *Saints Are Not Sad*.
Well, Fr. LaFarge is not sad, either, much as he may blush at the
suggested comparison. In the fifteen years I have been happy and
privileged to work with him on *America*, I have never seen him
discouraged by the way the poor world wags. International tensions,
slow progress in race relations here in the United States, the low
estate of ecclesiastical art, all these problems and more have never
made him say :"Oh, What's the use?" There is great use and only
one who knows the love of God can realize how great the use is.

This love we have been speaking of, as Fr. LaFarge has been

experiencing and manifesting it, is, to be sure, a love that demands great things, that is a challenge and a fire and a flame. To this challenge Fr. LaFarge has risen during his fifty years as a priest and a Jesuit. The following pages will attest to what an extent he has been warmed by the flame and illuminated by the fire.

If readers of this collection share in this, they will indeed be happy and blessed that in the *John LaFarge Reader* they have caught the lesson of love that Fr. LaFarge has learned and taught so well.

HAROLD C. GARDINER, S.J.

General Introduction

My associates on the staff of *America* are responsible for this Reader. To them it may have seemed obvious that you could scoop up a bunch of more or less permanently interesting treasures out of the storage-bin of past published or unpublished material. It once seemed a bit obvious to me as well, but I soon learned that most of what you fish out of past files and volumes has long since lost its punch. Whatever once flamed or crackled—or you thought it did— now only creaks.

So the best fare I could serve up for my associates was a few items culled hither and yon, samples in many instances of notions often repeated and variously embroidered. In any such selection most of the critical and reportorial material drops out, such as, for instance, the three very live papers that I did describing the assaults and outrages committed by the Nazis in Slovenia. How completely eclipsed were all these revelations drawn from first-hand sources by the later depredations of the Communist regime.

I was noticing that as the years advanced, more and more people are saying just what I had been saying pretty much in solitude, only they say it so much better with a vast apparatus of information and illustration applying to the present circumstances, such as I had not been able to command. What I then wrote would add little to what we now know, yet in pioneer days it was vexing and embarrassing to talk of things that are now common property.

Just for this reason I am—oddly enough—most happy with the stuff that nobody will remember precisely because others today are able and ready to carry the burden of arousing the public conscience.

That should be enough in the way of an introduction. Let me just add two or three further observations:

1. These are the reflections of one who personally was long a parish priest, not a specialist nor even a litterateur. They reflect his

concerns and interests derived from the school of hard knocks and from dealing with human beings.

2. The five or six categories under which these papers are grouped are only for convenience sake and obviously overlap, but the range of topics is sufficiently varied. So it is quite possible that if you are not particularly interested in one of these groups you might be attracted by another. I should feel happy if anyone were to note two or three papers in the whole collection that were worth glancing at a second time.

3. So much material that I have written on certain topics is readily accessible in book or pamphlet form, especially on the question of human relations and race relations, that I have included in this collection only three or four key papers. Those who are interested in my thoughts on these matters will find them in *The Race Question and the Negro* (Longmans, 1943); *No Postponement* (Longmans, 1951), as well as in a book now in preparation, *The Catholic Viewpoint On Race Relations* (Doubleday, 1956), and in certain chapters of my autobiography, *The Manner is Ordinary* (Harcourt, Brace, 1953).

4. However diverse the topics here included and the manner of treatment, the reader will, I trust, note an underlying common note, the note of hope. This is not an unreasoning nor fatuous hope, not a hope blind to the bitter and terrifying lessons of the dangers that threaten our country, our civilization and our very souls, but a hope based on an unshaken belief in God's providence in the troubled affairs of men, a hope that springs from faith in man as God has made him. It is a hope that derives its sense, its poignancy, from a priest's intense consciousness of the profound evil with which we must contend in these critical times, and it derives its undying strength from faith in what God has revealed to man, faith in God's grace if men will but use it.

I.
Art and Literature

Remarks about my father in the first two articles of this section were occasioned by the revival of his memory, attributable in great part to the devoted interest of some of his old friends, especially the art critic, the late Mr. Royal Cortissoz. They were a prelude to a more detailed treatment in several chapters of my autobiography.

I have always been, and remain, as fearful of discussing art as a cat is of wading in the water. Only two sorts of people can discuss art reasonably, those who know a lot, an encyclopedic lot, about it, or else the artists themselves: if, as is rare enough, they are sufficiently articulate to describe their own operations.

One who has grown up with artists is particularly diffident. But there are a few things which one can occasionally discuss in an unsophisticated fashion and the churchman has moments when he feels inclined to try to set certain notions right. If he will be lucky enough to be heard by men of the craft and by men of the cloth simultaneously he may do something to bridge over the gap which still exists between them.

You will find in these papers quite a bit about creation and creative power. This is easy talk from one who hasn't the remotest idea how to go about it. But the philosopher can always philosophize. If you wish to concretize your ideas you might some day observe, if you are around that neighborhood, the studio of Sister Thomasita at the Franciscan headquarters in Milwaukee, or the Benson studios in Newport, R. I. All I want is to start people searching. Liturgical art, incidentally, is simply art employed in the service of the Church's worship whether it be her ceremonial or the buildings in which that ceremonial is enshrined. There is nothing mystical in the expression. Unfortunately the liturgy, liturgical art, etc., suffer somewhat from semantics, but with time and intelligence that difficulty may be cured. I tried to clear up some of these perplexities in the paper

3

Catholics and Religious Art, *spoken in the sobering surroundings of the Boston Art Museum. (Hence the reference to Puvis de Chavannes, whom my father so admired.)*

About Sigrid Undset there was much to say. The little I have noted here seems all the more significant in view of the hardships this great good soul suffered after her return to her native country. If she had lived she had wished to spend her last days in Wisby, southern Sweden, serenely harvesting the reflections of the past and radiating still more of her spiritual insight. She was profoundly interested in the interracial question and all that was done to create interracial justice and formed several very real friendships with some of our workers in this line, both white and Negro, who in turn were charmed by her genuineness and simplicity. I have a happy memory of a couple of weeks previous to Christmas when night after night she sat up with the members of St. Ansgar's Scandinavian Catholic League busily packaging parcels for sufferers abroad. Her tragic experiences made her unreasonably bitter with regard to the Germans, especially since German pre-war visitors to Norway cruelly let her people down. But towards the end of her life she repented of her unforgiving attitude and the basic charity of Christ, so deep in her heart, won out in the end.

LaFarge and the Truth

MARCH, 1935

O NCE ON a stormy afternoon I undertook to explore what
was left of No. 30 Beach Street, in New York City, where
my father was born a hundred years ago this writing, on
March 31, 1835. Dodging among trucks emerging from loading
platforms, stepping over rain puddles, I found nothing at the end
of the quest that was even a remote reminder that once a dwelling
house had been there, or even a number thirty: it was merely a con-
jectural spot in the grim area of an immense brick warehouse. As
I made my way to normal streets and sidewalks, I wondered to
myself if it would be likely that John LaFarge's memory would in
a few years be reduced to naught but a few museum titles or cata-
logue references in the public libraries.

In one sense the question gave me no great concern, since if an
artist performed his work well while living, and managed the
affair of his own personal salvation, both of which I feel confident
that my father did, I see no reason or great bones about his artistic
immortality. There is good reason to believe that every genuine
contribution that any man has made to the sum total of thought,
beauty, and knowledge is never lost, but will rise again in the
great reconstruction of all things in the Word.

With all the more cause, therefore, there was reason to be impressed by the remarkable revival that LaFarge's memory has enjoyed within the last two or three years. Even such a group as
the Mural Painters' Society, at the height of its enthusiasm for the
"modern" in murals, chooses to number LaFarge among the living rather than among the dead. Royal Cortissoz has sounded his
praises unflaggingly in his writings and lectures for at least twenty
years past. Edythe Helen Browne writes a well-informed and ap-
preciative encomium of him in *Columbia*, March, 1935 and other
tributes appear.

At his overflowingly attended lecture in the Metropolitan Museum in New York City on March 10, 1935, Mr. Cortissoz reminded his hearers how LaFarge started his artistic career, as it were, from scratch. He had no precedent in this country. He had to create his own school, build his own artistic world by throwing a bridge across the Atlantic to link American art with the traditions of Europe. In this respect his work was unique. He was unique in another sense as well: by his extraordinary combination of a rich and varied intellectual life with an extremely active field of artistic work. Few artists are to be found with such a wide scope in both lines, of thinking and doing, since the days of the Renaissance. Old age brought newer horizons, new adventures of mind. As Henri Focillon (*Les Maîtres de l'Estampe*) says of an artist far greater than LaFarge: "Old age for him was not a decrepitude nor a decay, but the highest point of his existence." Uppermost in my mind was the question: with the apparent assurance of permanence to LaFarge's plastic creations, will aught remain of his thought?

An affirmative answer to that question would need to take into account two principal obstacles. The first obstacle is the method by which the thought was actually expressed. His inquiring mind explored the nature of art and the artistic process from numberless angles, historical, technical, metaphysical, moral. Elusive as was his subject, his speculations resulted in something that was lucid and solid in its intellectual texture. Indeed, his individual explanations are frequently of crystalline clearness, apt, pointed, and agreeably unpedantic.

His difficulty is rather the external one of a want of planned arrangement. This was due partly to his own aversion for the schematic and the formal, but also to the circumstances of the lecture method under which his ideas were conveyed. In an article, "The Mind of John LaFarge," in the *Catholic World* for March, 1935, I have tried to indicate briefly the logic by which his philosophy of art evolves, beginning with the contemplation of nature, and developed through memory, suggestion, intention, and personality. From a metaphysical point of view, there is distinct cor-

respondence between his ideas and that of the Thomistic concept
as expressed in Maritain's "Art and Scholasticism." Indeed, Maritain
and LaFarge illustrate each other reciprocally.

With all of LaFarge's insistence upon the primacy of the idea,
not of the emotion, as the basic factor in art, his philosophy is
flexible enough to leave room for the functional aspects of creative
art. Ideas to him are not mere speculations, but are intimately
bound up with the moral and emotional side of humanity.

Another possible obstacle flows from the fact just noticed, and
may be suggested by saying that the validity of the thought cannot be separated from the validity of the personality. No matter
how plausible, subtle, or eloquent be a man's reasoning, if he is too
utterly detached from our common human lot and from the standards of being as well as of doing, his thought will not permanently
stand up under the strain. Plato could not have made Socrates' argument survive the ages had he not depicted Socrates as a heart and
as a man. For this reason, however attractive may be the fancy in
itself, I do not think that LaFarge, *as a thinker*, is helped by a
tradition that he was quite a transcendent sort of individual, a sort
of mysterious, impassible being, made of different clay from the
rest of humanity, who managed to preserve an incredible equa-
nimity in the midst of every jolt of fortune.

It is true that LaFarge, in a sense, was many of these things and
much more. He created his own atmosphere, absolutely, in the
radio-active manner suited to *causeurs*. And he did remark that
the Trappist Order probably owed its origin to the needs of men
who were asked to explain their own jests.

It is true that politics did not exist for him, save that he occasionally voted the Democratic ticket as a matter of tradition; nor
economics. But everything discernible to the human eye did; and
no convention could stop him from prowling out of the house,
clad in purple kimono and straw sandals, at dawn of a summer
morning to observe the mist rising from the rocks upon the sea-
shore. Indeed, as was succinctly expressed by one of his former
pupils: "Mr. LaFarge sometimes got as mad as hell."

This LaFarge occasionally did, or very near to it. Moreover, it was necessary from time to time to make Mr. LaFarge as mad as hell, or thereabouts, if the immense enterprise of glass, paintings, murals, and lectures were to go on schedule and not sink under the relentless conflict of the Contemplative Mind with the Contingent Order. Much of this ignition process devolved upon LaFarge's own family, with some corresponding straining of patience. That one in that family never complained, but in some mysterious way through storm and stress saw only the humorous side of things, can only be explained by the grace that came to her with the wedding ring. The enshrinement of one's parent after twenty years in the dignity of the museum does not altogether obliterate the memories of these phenomena. Yet who would have him, or have had him, one bit different? Riotzo Awoki, today gray with years, who held all portfolios in the domestic cabinet of the West Tenth Street studio, and that gifted artist, Ivan G. Olinsky, whose skilled hand collaborated with LaFarge in much of his finest later work, still retain their affection for the irascible Master, as do all who knew him.

To keep the line of my argument: LaFarge's philosophic thought had as its support the validity of a very human man, an affectionate man who loved his family and his friends with a deep, even if cautiously expressed love. He had that peculiar faculty of loving even those whom he most complained of which Papini in his "Dante Vivo" notes as characteristic of Dante towards his fellow-Florentines, which is an attribute, perhaps, of the highly imaginative mind.

But a still more basic validation of LaFarge's thought lies in his profound moral sense. The irony and skepticism that so impressed the outer world was after all but a mask, a partly defensive one, and was laid aside by LaFarge when not in conflict with the business-inspired world that roared and buzzed about his ears. Alone with the Masters whom he cherished so humanly and sympathetically, with the universal rather than the particular mind, or with the young whose artistic efforts he so painstakingly seconded, so unselfishly admired, LaFarge was humble, reverent, simple as a child. The religious and moral tone which springs up in his writings was not a mere pose. It was the genuine LaFarge who counseled "the acceptance of suffering and of effort in patience, as part of the ordering of the world"; that we should "read habitually our Christian Bible in that meaning, not unmindful of the Sermon on the Mount"; that on the basis of the struggle of moral good "have rested the foundations of love and pity, of courage, of law, and of all the virtues." (*Considerations on Painting.*) Charged in his youth as an eldest son with responsibilities beyond his years, LaFarge developed early certain basic habits of thought, personal sobriety, and self-discipline, without which he could never have achieved a hundredth part of what he did. I think it significant that of his numberless friends I recall none of whom he spoke to me as a boy with greater affection than his classmate at Mount St. Mary's in 1853, Silas M. Chatard, of Baltimore, the future Bishop of Vincennes.

Mr. Cortissoz is correct in stressing the love of truth as the dominant passion of LaFarge's life and work. It was dominant, since it was the particular form that his moral sense assumed. It was responsible for many of his hesitations, qualifications, paradoxes, and apparent indirectness of approach to questions. This love of truth prompted him, rarely but nonetheless effectively, to keen and logical argument when occasion demanded it. But it habitually moved him to an incessant inquiry into the essences of things, as when he wondered whether, without some knowledge of geology, he could paint the mountain ranges that he viewed as he sailed by the islands of Tahiti.

LaFarge's concept of life had no illusions. He knew that any inconsistency between the artist's person and the truth of his work would infallibly betray itself in the end. "Let there be no misunderstanding"; he wrote, "art is not a lawless game: even want of power in the artist puts up unwillingly with incorrection, unless he be deceived by vanity. In his work the real man forgets himself and any small pride—clearly or obscurely feeling that to try to find originality is a sure way of losing one's path."

Art was greater than the individual or his ambitions:

Let us never be deceived by the slight rapidity of a few moments or a few years. In a supposed case, were a painter to devote all his life to one painting; could he do so; were he great enough to do so; to make a vase strong and fine enough to hold these feelings of his whole age— he would only have occupied a little piece of time, disproportionate in relation even to the continuous existence in time of the world he attempts to master.

His concept of life and art had no divisions:

As the creature represents in itself a record of the forces that have made it and made also the world, and as it is insofar an epitome of the universe, so the man who brings his mind to contemplate the creature, is himself communicating with the entire world. He is acting in the spirit of poetry, which touches us by establishing over and over again, this connection of ourselves with the universe; through our seeing how, in the poet's mind, some single thought, sometimes some mere fancy, some mere word, has ties with that we care for most, with the very foundations upon which we live.

The ultimate quest that arose from LaFarge's long brooding over the inmost values of life as of life's representation, was the quest of simplicity. When Henry Adams and LaFarge revisited Paris in 1892, this was dominant in LaFarge's mind. Writes Adams of himself:

At the galleries and exhibitions, he was racked by the effort of art to be original, and when one day, after much reflection, John LaFarge asked whether there might not still be room for something simple in art, Adams shook his head. As he saw the world, it was no longer simple and could not express itself simply. It should express what it was; and this was something that neither Adams nor LaFarge understood.

"The artist can hope," wrote LaFarge, "that in his fullest development he may become again as a little child: and that as he looks, or we look, at his work, it may be impossible to discriminate between the ingenuous statement of ignorance and the consummate synthesis of knowledge."

With all his outward complexity, I have known few men more inwardly simple than my father. He loved truth, because it reflected the Creator of the truth. He loved beauty, because it mirrored the truth. He strove to express this love in deed and word over a long lifetime of intense activity.

And that is about the essence of what anyone can say of John LaFarge.

Notes on the LaFarge Exhibit

MAY, 1936

THE EXHIBIT of John LaFarge's work given by the Trustees of the Metropolitan Museum of Art in New York City from March 23 to April 26, 1936 naturally afforded much pleasure to friends and admirers of LaFarge and his work, recalling the exhibit in Boston that took place shortly after his death in 1910. Among the seventy-four pieces displayed they recognized plenty of old favorites, such as the "Paradise Valley," the "Halt of the Wise Men," some of the best of the Samoan water colors and of the flower pieces, the gorgeous "Peacock Window" transplanted for the occasion from its relative seclusion in the Worcester Art Museum, etc.

There were also many that were less familiar, some of which, as Benjamin of the family, I personally had not seen before; others that I may have seen but did not recollect, as the delightful "Hilltop," loaned by the Boston Museum of Fine Arts, with its two figures of the late seventies resting under the pines in the twilight. LaFarges and LaFargeites, of whom the most eloquent is Mr. Royal Cortissoz, were generally happy about the exhibit, though there were some grumblings that there were not more of the artist's best drawings. The big lunettes for the Whitelaw Reid mansion, "Drama" and "Music," were naturally part of the show; but it was depressing to see some of their early brilliancy faded and other effects of time on these cheerful creations.

As one who is not an art critic, I have been interested to observe on what points the critics of my father's work appear to be reaching an agreement. The judgment of the present time, I should imagine, has a good chance to be the final judgment of posterity. We are far enough away—in spirit even more than years—from the nineties, when LaFarge most flourished, for the principal revisions in estimate to take place that necessarily occur after an artist or

12

writer has definitely taken his place in history—or in oblivion. Yet we are near enough to him to give a sober judgment, and avoid fantastic theories as to the man or his work.

For this reason I do not believe future generations will substantially differ from the conclusion of Henry McBride, writing in the New York *Sun* for March 28, 1936:

LaFarge has a definite place in our history as a teacher of art, creator of first-rate stained glass, and as a promoter of good taste. If the good taste he taught seems not to be too actively employed in present-day life nothing is static and lapses from the line of progress are frequent. Once the principle of good taste has been established it is definitely there and it is something in which the Prodigals, when iniquity gets too much for them, must return.

The critics are unanimous, so far as I have seen, as to the tremendous influence of LaFarge upon his generation; also as to the part that the intellect played in LaFarge's artistic work, quoting his remark to Mr. Cortissoz: "Painting is, more than people think, a question of brains." It is the predominance of this "cerebral activity" in a line of production which made a very brilliant appeal to the senses through form and particularly through light and color that has always made his art somewhat baffling for those who were not familiar with that "intention" upon which, in his writings, he laid great stress.

On the other hand, those who were more or less familiar with LaFarge's intentions, usually of a lofty and rather complicated description, find it difficult to stand away from the product in which these intentions were expressed and view his work merely as it strikes the eye. I, for one, am frankly unable to do so. Before most of his work I experience only a bewildering combination of matters about which I know my father was thinking—and usually talking—and the outward form that they finally took, which might or might not convey the idea, as circumstances or mood determined.

The difficulty with this intellectualism was that it occasionally became topheavy. A good deal of LaFarge's work seems to me to fall into three categories. There is the type of painting which the critics complain of, where the artist seems unable quite to lose himself in his work, with a consequent detriment to emotion, passion, concentration of effect. Such, for instance, is some of his later religious painting, which is represented in this exhibit by such figures as the two "Adorations." These grandly draped, exquisitely posed figures retain the atmosphere of the studio. They are either sketches for something more finished to come, or finished works that still recall the studio sketch that gave to them birth. These statuesque young men and young ladies—sometimes not so over young—properly garbed and winged—retain somehow a haunting memory of the vested choir of some very distinguished Episcopal church. They are finely executed commissions with a definite religious label.

Personally I love these old things for the memories attached to them and for what I knew he really had in mind. But I do not see that they will inspire many people to heroism, prayer, or even to contemplation. They will remain charming studio pieces, on a grand scale, for humble young art students of all times.

Indeed, I expressed myself to that effect to Father at sundry times and I think he saw the point, for he accepted it benignly. He gave me what was probably the correct explanation, that he was overburdened with the commissions he had undertaken, and that the disappointing effect was the result of fatigue as much of anything else. But I cannot quite absolve him on that point alone. I think that some of his admirers let him off too easy as to his integrity of performance. His persuasiveness and eloquence as to what he had in mind made them a little oblivious to the manner in which he carried it all out. And the epoch in which he worked, as well as the surroundings of a New York studio, were not such as to force that critical appraisal of spiritual content which another time or circumstance might have demanded. But the patrons were practically all non-Catholic, which was a spiritual tragedy for a deeply religious Catholic painter like LaFarge, and the numbing effect of this habitual relationship impaired the quality of some of his most ambitious work.

LaFarge, too, was always a little afraid, technically speaking, of the human form unadorned, which seems to have led him to a preoccupation with draperies. This, in turn, reacted to some extent upon the human warmth of his figures.

In the second and larger category, I should place those works in which the idea, simple or elaborate, is fully used with execution, emotion, or even passion. Happily there is no dearth of such. Among his religious paintings there are such deeply spiritual and emotional achievements as the "Nicodemus and Christ," which appears in three forms, one, a painting in the National Gallery of Art, in Washington, D. C.; another, a mural painting in Trinity Church, Episcopal, in Boston; the third, a window in the Church of the Ascension, Episcopal, in New York City; or the various scenes of the Wise Men and the Birth of the Saviour, where his inner ideals of reverence, love, and genuine devotion found unrestrained expression. Such, too, were the early illustrations as the "Fisherman and the Djinni," the portraits of children, and other events of his artistic youth which have always made us regretfully wonder what LaFarge might have been as a purely intra-studio creator had the heavy hand of decorative murals and glass not been laid upon his shoulders.

In this category, too, I should place his water colors of South Sea life. These have been hauled over the coals in recent years for not being Gauguinesque, for being too refined, academic, and what not. But I have never been able to accept the honesty of such criticism. Though I have never seen Samoa, and probably never could see a Samoa today like the unspoiled paradise of those vanished days, I am convinced that LaFarge painted directly what he saw. That he saw one thing and that the Gauguins and others even more revolutionary saw things much cruder and less pleasingly Homeric, is simply a fact, to which the pictures give evidence. Why is it such an artistic sin to see something delicate, fluttering, rhythmic, or statue-like among primitive peoples, when others behold only human clods and stumps?

To put it very simply, LaFarge *could* "lose himself," he could achieve considerable, even if not revolutionary or ecstatic fervor.

Where he failed, it was because LaFarge somewhat fell down on the tremendous job of being himself. If you doubt that, look at the four wholly spontaneous, youthfully fresh lunettes in the Minnesota State Capitol, done in the artist's last years.

In the third category I should place those many works, expressed in nearly every type of medium, which are not burdened with any serious idea extrinsic to the work itself, but which directly express his genuine passion for the marvels of light and color. Such are the ineffable flower paintings, which appraisal no one appears to gainsay; such, too, his most technically triumphant glass.

Here, again the recollection of the childlike enthusiasm with which these things were planned, plotted, and worked out enters into any personal appreciation of the exhibit. The flowers, for instance, were things lived with, not merely placed on a table or an easel study. The Lily Pond on the Ocean Drive in Newport where they were gathered; the black lacquer bowls that he had brought back from the East for this particular purpose; the particular spot in the house where the changes of reflection morning, noon, and evening might affect them; their buddings, unfoldings, and witherings, were part of one's life, that the painting itself might in turn be a living thing.

As to the intrinsic value of all this material I have only a vague idea. That rests with the critics, and the final estimate, in all probability, will be colored by the developments that society itself takes. No one knows what room the future has for the purely decorative. Only it is inconceivable that anyone could put *more* thought —if thought be of value—into that type of artistic process than did LaFarge.

One interesting question in conclusion. The critics are divided as to the prerogatives of the water colors and the glass. (Neither of these, curiously enough, have ever seemed to me to be quite the essence of LaFarge, but then most people achieve repute by things that are not quite their essence.) Such a decision would obviously depend largely upon the point of view.

If you examined the three decorative windows that were placed conveniently in hand-reach at the exhibit, you doubtless observed that they were real constructions, combining to high degree science, craftsmanship, and artistic feeling. They were not so much colored windows, so ordinarily understood, as mosaics of jeweled glass, fired, ingeniously moulded into flower shapes, welded together, juxtaposed and superimposed according to chemical formulae and industrial methods which LaFarge developed through several years of painstaking study in an obscure workshop in Brooklyn, and in subsequent years of experimentation. So too, on more architectonic, though less technically intricate scale, were his large religious windows. Glass, therefore, was his supreme achievement in a happy combination of intellectual research, skilful craftsmanship, and natural good taste. It also most strikingly exemplified his influence, since few American-made windows fail to recall the LaFarge technique in one way or another.

The water colors, on the other hand, were the work of the creative mind at play. They represented not a *combination* of gifts and enterprises, but a perfect *fusion* of mind and hand. Thus they appear to be more an expression of his purely creative self than the glass which expressed the craftsman, the organizer, and the student. Our preference, therefore, as to water colors or glass would seem to depend upon our interest in LaFarge as a purely artistic personality, in the more limited sense of the word, or as an organizer and director of a pioneer movement in American cultural life. Such a preference, I should imagine, would be always open to choice.

The Sociology of Art

MAY, 1936

WITH SERIOUS CONCERN over "cruelty to humans" and non-observance of the social Encyclicals whether in letter or in spirit, John J. O'Connor, in the issue of *America* for May 16, 1936, exclaims: "Catholic social-justice propaganda goes round and round. But nothing ever happens. We want *action*."

I am not prepared to grant that "*nothing* ever happens." Nothing like what ought to happens; but there are a few signs of life. I readily agree with Mr. O'Connor, however, that we need action, and cannot give too much thought or time to the problem of securing it.

Here and now I have no pretense to unravel this knotted theme. The modest aim of the few following lines is to suggest one type of action, which will by no means satisfy Mr. O'Connor, but may serve as a slight hors d'oeuvres temporarily pacifying his ravening appetite. It has the great advantage that it can immediately be engaged in, and with more effect than you are apt to imagine, while waiting for the major operations to begin.

Ideas in this connection were suggested by the theme that was assigned for a symposium, held under the auspices of the Catholic Poetry Society of America, at the College of Mount Saint Vincent, in the City of New York, on May 17, 1936. As soon as I learned that the conferees were going to take up the topic of the "Sociology of Art," it occurred to me that here was a vein where a little exploration might prove profitable, if we were concerned over the difficulty of arousing the Catholic social conscience to function, or to translate its dictates into action.

An expression like "sociology of art," labors of course under the indetermination which attaches to the word *sociology* itself. (Do not let us stir up the lions by asking what is meant by "art.") If we use sociology in what seems to be its most generally ac-

cepted sense, as a scientific study of the phenomena of human relationships—or group relationships, if you prefer—; then I suppose
that by the sociology of art you mean a study, in inductive fashion,
of art as it has been, throughout all epochs and regions, a manifestation of these human relationships; and, to a certain extent, their
cause. Such a study, of course, would be enormously varied and
attractive. It would take us back to prehistoric man, whom we
know of chiefly by his art, and remarkably capable art it was. In
fact, it would lead us through the entire field of human cultures.
The customs, the beliefs, the virtues and vices of humanity are so
intimately linked up with art that the story of art is simply the
story of mankind; and the sociology of art would be pretty much
the whole of social history, ethnology, history of religion, and what
else.

If we understand by the life of men their social life as distinguished from their purely individual life, and are concerned with
art as an influence rather than with art as a manifestation, then
one can subscribe to the definition which was provided by the authors of the symposium that "by 'sociology of art' is meant the
actual influence which art has in the life of men." "From the nature
of this influence," they added, "the social function of art might
be deduced."

With Mr. O'Connor's eye upon me, however, I confine myself
solely to the question of art as a means of securing social action.
Here, it would seem, a useful distinction could be made between
art as a means merely of exciting the desire for action, and art as
a guide to action; which may be illustrated by an example.

We have been deluged of late, in rotogravures and on the screen,
by photographic pictures of the horrors of war. Laurence Stallings,
as we know, added his pen to the camera in order to shock us. The
sight of these horrors naturally inspires in any normal individual
the utmost desire to act so as to put an end at once and forever
with such a curse upon the human race. (What they may do to
non-normal individuals is an unpleasant speculation.) Thus far,
the photograph has achieved its purpose. But has it achieved a
social function? I fear not, because the impression ceases with the

effectuation of that desire. There is no indication as to *how* one may act. None whatsoever, as long as there is a mere photographic record, and art has not come into play.

Let however the artist take hold of this theme, and he can immediately suggest—rightly or wrongly, skilfully or crudely—some method for dealing with the situation. It may be revolution, it may be prayer, it may be education, it may be the Kellogg Pact as the basis of the reorganized League of Nations, as Mr. Shotwell proposes; but the artist, if he wishes, can always provide some type of guidance. The classic example of this is the poster, as a means of exciting mass action, as when Howard Chandler Christie depicts for Mayor LaGuardia the Spirit of City Planning wafting the 50,000 old-law tenements into airy nothing as a gentle hint to New York's real-estate corporations; or the modern revolutionary mural which suggests the rough-and-ready methods of the torch and the barricade.

The function of art, then, is not only to provide a stimulus to social action but to suggest the method of action. It has likewise a further function, of a much higher nature, which is to instill an idea of the ultimate aim or goal of such action; in other words, to inculcate a philosophy of life as applied to social action. To the one person who is moved to actual violence by the revolutionary mural, poem, or drama, there are ten thousand who absorb from its flamboyant forms or lines the concept that man's destiny ends here below, and that his highest virtue lies in extinguishing those persons who would teach him allegiance to a higher Power. In this, rather than in its immediate excitement, lies the menacing function of anti-social art. If art, then, is to provide a partial solution of the problem of inspiring social action based upon Christian principles, it will imply by its very nature a philosophy of life based upon those same principles. But how is this to be accomplished with the same vigor and definiteness as is achieved in art that advocates destruction?

When such a question is proposed, I hear some persons say: Let us make our art spiritual, and it will inspire to lofty action. If the word *spiritual* implies a Christian philosophy of morals, this of course is true. But there is danger of a certain delusion in such a counsel, and this delusion lies at the root of many of the failures in the field of modern religious art. The mere fact that art is spiritual does not necessarily mean that it is inspired by a Christian philosophy of life. The most spiritual art that man has ever conceived is found in the great masterpieces of Buddhism, so brilliantly described by Laurence Binyon. Nothing more sublimated, more literally unearthly, has been delineated by the hand of man than those timeless, tenderly majestic figures of transcendent divinities. Yet their lesson of passivity and reincarnation is repugnant to our basic Christian ideas. And shall we not see in our times a birth of militant irreligious spiritualism? Indeed, not the flesh, but the revolting spirit shines out of the revolutionary production. As far as mere *flesh* is concerned, there is considerably more of it in Rubens or Veronese than in Gropper's cartoons. But for all their failings the Old Masters, while but falteringly *spiritual*, were deeply *religious*, while the spirit that breathes in Gropper appears to me the spirit that dissolves the social Christ.

The movement which aims to eradicate God and the supernatural from human life demands today an increasing moral discipline from its adherents, and emphasizes culture, which is a manifestation of the spirit. Following the pattern of famous heresies, the movement can perfectly logically step upward—for the present —rather than downward; and cultivate the spiritual life in the very interests of revolt.

To come to a definite proposition in answer to this call for some immediate Catholic social action: it seems to me that there is an extremely immediate task that lies ready for Catholics in every field of art, which is to embody at once the ideas and the ideals of the Catholic social program in the various forms of art which experience and psychology alike have proved to have influence on the conduct of men. I admit that this is a highly controversial task, and that the various attempts that have already been made to do so in the various plastic and literary arts have called forth storms of dissent; much of which may be well deserved. But we can only learn by experience, since no ready-made rules—outside of certain general precautions—are available in such a field. Unless, however, we are active and prompt, we shall find that our subtlest and most powerful arms, not those of the flesh but those of the spirit, of mystical, transcendant beauty, will have been stolen from us by the enemy. So France today is suffering from the inflictions of an André Gide.

When such emergencies are at hand, we find, as a rule, that Mother Church does not leave us unprovided. The art of the Church, termed liturgical art, as applied to the action of worship, will give us many a practical suggestion as to the application of art to the action of social reconstruction. It is but an ancient problem under a new form, and we have abundant resources with which to meet it, if we do not fall into the Rightist error of confounding spirituality with religion; or the Leftist mistake of blindly imitating revolutionary fashions. At any rate, here is some action that can be done at once, and that needs no synods or Church councils to initiate.

Religious Problems of the Catholic Artist

MARCH, 1938

CATHOLIC ARTISTS suffer certain difficulties in the practice of their religion. Some of these difficulties are of their own creation, it is true; for doubtless they should know better, They can go to Avernus like any other people through their own innate wickedness. But some Catholic artists whom I have known are like persons who have lost the thread of a journey at the beginning. They are not to be blamed if they use roundabout routes in the attempt to return to the path.

These few words are addressed chiefly to priests who deal with artists and to artists who deal with priests; but they may contain some profit for all good and faithful Christians. By artists I understand primarily professionals, who live wholly or largely by their art, men who primarily pursue beauty—in decoration, form or design—not so much craftsmen, whose first purpose is to produce something useful.

The root of the artist's spiritual difficulty is the sanctity of his art. This seems a strong word to use; but nothing else expresses so clearly the absorbing exactions of his ideal. The life of a genuine artist, not of a dilettante, puts as heavy a demand upon a human being as any other form of earthly activity. Somebody said that Saint Ignatius Loyola—and the same would apply to other great Founders—takes all there is in a man to give it to God. In a way this is true of the Muse. She claims the whole of man, because she demands of him the service of an absolute.

Wrote one artist to whom, among other things, I owe my existence:

"Genius," says the French phrase, "is a protracted patience." (*Le génie c'est une longue patience.*) It can only keep up its life by continuous effort, often by work so exclusive as to make all other ideas of life disappear. But we must remember that we are so enslaved by the idea of time which we measure in small instalments, according to other necessities, that we do not perceive that these efforts are really one single act—the act of life. . . .

Be it a short moment or a term of years, it [the artist's work] has cost the same thing, i.e., the whole man. (*Considerations on Painting*.)

As the pursuit of holiness has two aspects, one the ascetic, the other contemplative and mystical, so has the artist's life. The ascetic aspect is that of his craftsmanship, for, as the same writer said: "In all of the greatest artists there is a humble workman who knows his trade and likes it." No operating room, with rows of sterilized instruments, gauze and floodlights, is more rigidly consecrated to the last item of technical excellence than is a true artist's studio. The laws of craftsmanship are the laws of the Medes and Persians. All trifling, all play of emotions ceases when the long grind of training and practice commences.

Even more exacting is the mystical or contemplative side of the artist's life, for this demands not only concentration of physical and nervous activity, but concentration of his inner faculties: a tense focussing of the mind and imagination upon a form or synthesis that he has chosen to embody out of a hundred impressions and ten thousand memories.

When the artist lays aside his brushes or his chisel, pulls off his smock, hauls up the curtains and closes the door of his studio and steps into the outside world, he cannot escape from his work-life as readily as a workman; not even as readily as a professional man, a lawyer or physician. To create works of beauty he has been obliged to *live himself into* a world of habitual contemplation and instinctive selection. In the exact, scholastic sense of the word he has acquired certain *habits*, lasting inclinations of mind and imagination, which are too delicate and too intimately personal to be laid aside as you lay aside books and tools.

The supernatural life, however, has its own absolute. It confronts the artist with a completely different set of objectives. These affect him as a man, in the entire sense of the word, not as an artist. Religion's failures and successes are gauged by different standards from those of art. He may lamentably fail to produce a single work at which a critic would so much as glance, yet achieve an eternal masterpiece of sanctification through the practice of his religion. He may do the job of a Phidias or a Leonardo yet totally fail to make good in praising, reverencing and serving God, for which purpose his Creator called him out of the void.

He may simply make the best of a bad job, and keep his art and his religion in strictly separate compartments; wrench himself as best he can out of his habitual turn of mind, and don the mask of the Philistine in the fulfillment of his religious duties. After all, will-power and a lively faith can overcome the severest obstacles. I believe that Saint Peter has a corner of the Kingdom reserved for Catholic artists, architects and musicians who for a lifetime managed, as it were, to inhabit two worlds, one of temporal and one of spiritual profession, and have somehow acclimated themselves to both, like the Mexican highlanders who travel habitually from the mountains to the shore.

If the practice of religion were merely *negative* towards matters imaginative and esthetic, this procedure would present less difficulty. No more than other people do artists desire to live perpetually in a world of beauty. Indeed, plainness is somewhat of a relief for a too sensitive mind. Possibly less than other mortals are they troubled by certain uglinesses in our modern urban life, since they can more definitely escape from it. The real difficulty lies elsewhere. Religion, for its own sublime purposes, also makes use of those inner faculties of contemplation, imagination, sentiment which the artist brings to play in his professional life. It even makes use of the same external tools, sound, harmony, imagery. Most of all it calls upon these faculties and uses these tools in relation to the central and most sacred point of all our religion, the Holy Eucharist Itself. Our Saviour expects us to compensate, as it were, for His own personal unobtrusiveness by the dignity and splendor with which we surround His Presence.

Thus the artist who has been projecting his own ideal decorations, constructing his own architectural ideal, is obliged a few hours later to worship in a church where he is plunged into some other person's esthetic notions: another's music, or statuary, or murals.

If he expresses dislike or suggests reform, he is put down at once as a troublesome critic. Most church-goers feel a natural resentment against a person who takes seriously and professionally what for them is but an incidental emotional background to the practice of their faith. Still more resentment is felt by other professionals or semi-professionals with whose methods his own standards conflict.

The result in the artist's case is apt to be disastrous. He can easily become an habitual faultfinder, a sort of sublimated pest with whom pastor and congregation put up as best they can. Or, what is worse, he develops pessimism, believes that religion is not for him, slackens in its practice, loses thereby the light and strength conferred by the Sacraments, and so endangers his own soul.

Even his own art suffers a grievous wound. Though art has its own peculiar sphere, within that sphere it is deeply affected by the moral and religious orientation of the entire man. When the artist's own spiritual nature is cramped through isolation from the Source of life and light, his art, no matter how great his gifts, withers in the process.

Yet we obviously cannot solve the matter just by damning the artist. He has a soul to save like the rest of us. The Church does not tolerate artists alone; she honors them, and suffers serious loss if they cannot find a place within her walls. What, then can be done?

First, I think pastors of souls should themselves recognize the peculiar difficulties of the artist in the practice of his religion; they should bear with artists who are genuine artists and should sympathize with them. They should understand that certain deviations from the established norm of parish routine are not due to ill will, or to moral delinquency; not even to any personal eccentricity, but to the nature of the case.

The artist needs to have his life spiritualized through the very "sanctity" of his art; to utilize its professional discipline for the good of his soul and so effect a transfer of its "ascetic" character to his personal life. He should be able to bridge the gap between religious devotion and the mysticism of art. Artists, on the other hand, need to cure themselves of certain irritating misconceptions. They can learn not to apply too rigidly the standards of their art to the mere externals of religion, when they are not responsible for those externals.

But after all has been done to remove causes of friction, there remains a more complete remedy for the discord, which is the reign of *order* in our rubrical and liturgical life. Art gives to a thoughtful man a strong sense of *order;* indeed the two, as the philosophers explain, are most intimately related. The rubrics of the Church are not guaranteed to ensure beauty; but they do ensure order; not a rigid or fussy tidiness, but a simple and practical appropriateness, in which each object and each action falls into its place.

This order, as it were, is the portal to that ravishing inner beauty of the Church which reveals itself not to the merely external eye but to the eye of the soul. The artist, if he is a spiritually minded man, will sooner or later find that inner beauty revealed by the Church's order. It will amply recompense him for what he may suffer from displeasing assaults upon his outward senses.

If, therefore, we find among Catholic artists today a vigorous movement towards restoring, as far as a layman can help to restore, the spirit of order in the rubrical and liturgical life of the Church, let us not look upon them as carping critics. They are working for the only ultimate and lasting solution of a practical spiritual problem that has afflicted Catholic life for some four centuries. The Church seriously suffers from the difficulty that her artists find in fitting themselves into her rubrical and liturgical life. This difficulty arises not from anything in the Church or in her ordinances, but from our neglect of those ordinances. These breathe the wisdom, the moderation and graciousness of the Spirit of God, the inner harmony of God's own Blessed Mother, herself the Bride of the Holy Ghost. If this restoration of order is accomplished, we may live to welcome a few of those artist saints, who at present are seen only in stained-glass windows.

Sigrid Undset Visits America

SEPTEMBER, 1940

S O FEW Norwegian Catholics visit our shores, that the coming of Sigrid Undset, distinguished writer and lecturer, appears as somewhat of a novelty. The newest things, however, are sometimes closer to the past than we think. So that when Mme. Undset dropped in to see us at the editorial office of *America*, I was rather overawed by the thought that the very first woman who ever came from the Old to the New World was a Norwegian Catholic. There is actually a statue of that remote lady at the New York World's Fair, with her child, the first white child born in the New World. Further knowledge of her I have none, and leave the inquiry to the antiquarians. But it was the Norse Catholics who were the beginning of beginnings here and we have been waiting a long time for just such a representative as Sigrid Undset.

There is, however, a distinct element of novelty in Mme. Undset's case. She comes as an exile—for the time being—not as a wholly free seafarer. The peoples of the North, of Norway and Sweden, Denmark, Iceland, have been great wanderers by sea and land from the dawn of history. In their old pagan days they traveled as Vikings for adventure and conquest, and raised particular hell in England and Ireland. When the Irish monks and the Irish virgin Saint Sunniva returned the compliment by converting and civilizing the Norsemen, teaching them to read, bless themselves and confess their obstreperous sins, the Norsemen traveled for adventure, exploration and piety. They pilgrimaged to Rome, Jerusalem and other holy places.

Then, in our own times, after their forefathers had been robbed of their ancient Catholic Faith, they voyaged to this country in search of a different kind of adventure: the building of a new life across the seas. But wherever and whenever they traveled, they could, for the most part, go and come as they pleased in their native land. They were adventurers, not exiles.

Only in these last hours do we see the grievous sight of a Norse-woman who has done more than any living person to make her country known and respected through the world, obliged to seek refuge thousands of miles away from home. And home *is* home for Sigrid Undset. You need talk to her but five minutes to be convinced of that.

Mme. Undset can be sure of a warm welcome in this country for these and other very human reasons. But, I feel sure, she is much less concerned over the welcome to be given to her person than she is over the welcome for her ideas.

Her ideas will, I believe, bring considerable light to the American public upon matters that are beginning to concern us seriously in this country. I am not speaking of her literary judgments, which are numerous and penetrating, but of her deep absorption in recent years with questions of woman's role in the preservation of the family, which is naturally linked up with the influence of religion in a largely irreligious world.

These interests are not a mere private hobby of Sigrid Undset; they are matters which have come to a head more acutely in the Old World than in the New, and in the Scandinavian countries they reached a crisis, reflected in legislation.

Mme. Undset's first exploration, I imagine, will be the American home: the typical home, if there be such a thing. If she will read the *Saturday Evening Post* and some of the collateral family journals she will learn fairly well what most Americans think the home more or less ought to be. If she will drop into various family circles, which is easier here than in the Old Country, she will learn what it actually is. And if her habit of cool appraisal has not been lost on the voyage three-quarters around the world, she will probably conclude that here in America we had best be preparing ourselves fast for the acute shocks to our domestic self-complacency which are long familiar abroad.

We usually credit Henrik Ibsen and Ellen Key for upsetting certain fond delusions about the tranquility and automatic operation of family life. They were called realists and to a certain extent they were. But the true realist is not he who discovers *some* reality, but the person who discovers *the* reality or realities in a given situation. Like General Foch, they ask: "What is it all about?" Then they answer the question precisely.

Once upon a time Sigrid Undset was an agnostic. She and her associates saw in those days with painful clearness the inconsistency of a State Church which would permit divorce, in line with pagan principles; yet attempt to confer upon the divorced and remarried couple a Christian blessing. She saw that you cannot be pagan and Christian at the same time. She learned through her studies that this singular inconsistency was but one of many which came from the abandonment of the fundamental doctrines of the Catholic Church. And her position is today that it is a sheer illusion to expect to keep even the shell of monogamous marriage once the Catholic doctrine of sacramental marriage is lost. With no Christ, no Cana, there is no guarantee against the harem. Indeed, as she in one place conjectures, if marriage is actually deprived of its religious sanction and religious content, it might even be advisable from purely prudent and humanitarian reasons to revive the harem. In such a case, women would at least preserve a certain status when they are rejected. They would not be cast aside as a "stove-length of wood," as they are today by the whirring of the divorce mills.

The glory of America, as Mme. Undset will doubtless observe, is its incomparable Indian Summer, which makes us forget that the cold will ever return. She will likewise observe that family life and woman's status in this country share, too, some of the glory but likewise the illusion of the American Indian Summer. In Scandinavia they dreamed of a de-Christianized marriage which would somehow keep the sweetness of the Christian home but evade its tremendous responsibilities. But the fierce frost came of a dwindling population. They were casting about for remedies when the war seized them. In Sweden, the birth rate was found to be lower than in any other country of the world except, possibly, England. Only seventy per cent of the children necessary to keep a stationary population were being born, and soon there would be but fifty per cent, or lower. The same rude awakening has begun in this country. We begin to realize that the present drift is to destruction. We have lost our land and are losing our children. In the pregnant words of the economist, Dr. O. E. Baker: "The consequences of the loss of land ownership and of the decline in births will not appear as flashes of lightning and roar of thunder, like a summer storm; but, rather, they will develop slowly and silently, like the progress of the seasons. There will be warm days and cool days as in autumn, but with a steady drift toward winter."

What Mme. Undset has to tell us is not the tale of the winter, for we are growing aware of that already, but the much more important message of the new Spring, the resurrection which the modern world and the modern family must make in Jesus Christ. "It is impossible," she wrote in the Scandinavian Catholic weekly, *St. Olav*, "to advocate lifelong monogamy unless one believes that each individual soul is worth God's dying in order to save it. Nothing but such a belief can justify the Catholic idea of marriage. No other belief can give the people of our day the courage to live according to nature and to accept the children which God gives them: only this, to believe that every child has a soul which is worth more than the entire, visible, created world."

Sigrid Undset is exact in her judgment that there can be no lasting human welfare without a doctrinal foundation in the teachings of Christ. A neo-pagan or "after-Christian" world cannot hope to revive even the partial achievements of pre-Christian paganism. The Christless Yule of the Nazis will not even give us back, she remarks, the "Lord Frey" of the old pagan North.

But she is likewise unrelenting in her demand that Catholics practice to the very fullness, to actual heroism, the tremendous tasks of justice and charity which our Faith imposes upon us. She cannot tolerate the easy-going and worldly-minded Catholic, the person who seeks a comfortable spiritual minimum and accommodates himself to the established order of things for the sake of avoiding effort and self-sacrifice. The spiritual nuptials of the Church with her crucified Bridegroom, like the earthly nuptials of man and woman, impose a fearful responsibility that rests upon each member of Christ's Mystical Body. Painful as the task is, we are called to change the modern world with its cult of power and success.

There can be no compromise in any part of the world today with that power for evil which in a few short months has wrecked the peace, unity and much of the budding Catholicism of the Scandinavian countries.

Mme. Undset is quiet when you meet her. Were it not for her occasional swift changes to a childlike smile, you could call her impassive. The effect is heightened by her large stature. She seems more of a person to stay with and learn from than merely to converse with. But on one point she spoke passionately: her dislike for mere sentimentality, whether it be of the pious or of the worldly type. She is as opposed to fat angels and glass-eyed statues as she is to historians who fail to grasp the essential humanity of the Middle Ages. Sentimentality, in her view, indicates the death of true sentiment; and the sentimental peoples are those who feel the least deeply. And her next pet detestation is uncharitable talk. It is the Nordic peoples, she observes in one of her genially biting moments, who have invented all the social apparatus whereby women may gossip: five-o'clock teas, Kaffee-klatsches, women's committees, etc.

In a vivid description of the Saviour's Temptation in the Desert, Sigrid Undset warns the Catholic against the temptation to rely upon force, physical or political, as the God-ordained remedy for the healing of social or religious revolt. There is temptation in our day to hope for a glittering structure of politically reinforced Catholicism and to compromise with Fascism, as there was temptation in medieval times for the timid and pious to rely unduly upon the secular arm.

Regeneration in this day, as in all previous days, she expects to come through tremendous lovers of God and of suffering humankind. This is the lesson of the Saints whose lives she has so eagerly chronicled. In her own words, she wants people who will "pull the door wide open, so that Christ may enter and hold festival within." The poor and the outcast must enter and integral justice must be done for all persons and for all peoples, Christians, pagans and Jews. Only then, and by the work of such individual and heroic souls, does she expect to see the Kingdom of Heaven realized on our earth.

Private Opinion and Church Authority

AUGUST, 1948

THE FOLLOWING are a few considerations on the distinction between the official authority of the Church in matters of art and the opinions held by private individuals.

Art as such, *per se*, does not lie directly in the Church's province. The Church's proper commission is to teach the truth taught by Christ and to save souls by the means which He instituted for salvation. Art, however, can come under the authority of the Church accidentally, namely, when the Church uses art for its own purposes. The Church is not concerned with art as art, but the Church *is* concerned with art as a service of the worship of God. "The progress of the fine arts, those of architecture, painting, and music above all, has exerted considerable influence on the choice and disposition of the various external features of the liturgy." (*Mediator Dei.*) When art is thus employed in church buildings, church worship, the administration of the sacraments, for the purposes of public devotion, the Church permits only the use of such art forms as do not contradict its teaching or its pastoral authority. The teaching authority of the Church is solicitous about the doctrines which are expressed or implicit in the work of liturgical art; for instance, a representation of Christ, of the gospel scenes, or of the sacred personages. A doctrinal error expressed by a work of art would be foreign to the service of the Church; for instance, the famous Jansenist crucifix with the arms extended upward to indicate that Christ died only for an elect few and not for all men, or a mistaken representation of the Holy Trinity or of the Sacred Heart or of some other mystery.

The Church, furthermore, is concerned not only that the representations employed in its worship should be doctrinally correct, but that they should be suited to Christian life and worship, that they should create the proper atmosphere of reverence, "due ex-

ternal dignity," and respect and should partake in their own fashion
of the sacramental character of the mysteries to the use of which
they are consecrated. Hence in artistic objects related to worship,
the Church would require a certain degree of solidity, of gravity,
of beauty, and of harmony. The Church indeed remains the ultimate judge of their fitness for such a task; a function which in
turn is the office of the bishop as representative of the Church. The
bishop may, as he frequently does, employ a commission to advise
him in such matters and to help form his opinion, but his own
judgment would be the ultimate local responsibility.

The Church, nevertheless, recognizes the principle that art follows certain laws which are inherent in art itself, even when, as a
"noblest handmaid," it is put at the service of the Church. After
all, what the Church employs is not an abstraction but human art
with its limitations and its corporeal characteristics. This means
the employment of certain sense-gratifying (not sensual) attractions and certain rhythmic features without which art could not
exist. Also inherent in art itself are certain forms that possess innate
consistency with its own dignity and its own purpose. One would
not rightly expect, for instance, wood to act in the place of gold
or paint to fulfill the office of stained glass. The employment of art
and artistic skill by the Church implies from its very nature a
recognition of the innate consistency and dignity of the artistic
medium.

Such employment, furthermore, implies a recognition of tradition and progress alike as elements inherent in the very character
of art itself as a part of the whole drama of human culture. These
principles are beautifully brought out in the recent encyclical
Mediator Dei by Our Holy Father Pope Pius XII:

What We have said about music, applies to the other fine arts, especially to architecture, sculpture, and painting. Recent works of art
which lend themselves to the materials of modern composition should
not be universally despised and rejected through prejudice. Modern art
should be given free scope in the due and reverent service of the
Church and the sacred rites, provided that they preserve a correct balance between styles tending neither to extreme realism nor to excessive

"symbolism," and that the needs of the Christian community are taken into consideration rather than the particular tastes or talent of the individual artist. Thus modern art will be able to join its voice to that wonderful choir of praise to which have contributed, in honor of the Catholic faith, the greatest artists throughout the centuries. Nevertheless, in keeping with the duty of Our office, We cannot help deploring and condemning those works of art, recently introduced by some, which seem to be a distortion and perversion of true art and which at times openly shock Christian taste, modesty, and devotion, and shamefully offend the true religious sense. These must be entirely excluded and banished from our churches, like "anything else that is not in keeping with the sanctity of the place."

Keeping in mind, Venerable Brethren, pontifical norms and decrees, take great care to enlighten and direct the minds and hearts of the artists to whom is given the task to-day of restoring or rebuilding the many churches which have been ruined or completely destroyed by war. Let them be capable and willing to draw their inspiration from religion to express what is suitable and more in keeping with the requirements of worship. Thus the human arts will shine forth with a wondrous heavenly splendor, and contribute greatly to human civilization, to the salvation of souls, and the glory of God. The fine arts are really in conformity with religion when "as noblest handmaids they are at the service of divine worship."

When we turn, however, from liturgical art to art simply as a private matter, an expression of private sentiment, the Church's jurisdiction is no longer over that which is dedicated to its service but simply is included in the jurisdiction the Church has over all manifestations of human life and human conduct. The Church exercises no jurisdiction over the private expressions of the individual except, as the moralists say, *ratione peccati*, "by reason of sin," i.e., in matters which concern the individual's conscience. In such a field, therefore, the Church can directly censor only that which is evidently conducive to sin or is scandalous and disturbing for Christian life and Christian unity. She does not legislate in a positive fashion on private art as she does on liturgical art. However, the Church encourages the cultivation of Christian art just as the Church as part of her function encourages all forms of culture, as the passage quoted from the recent encyclical indicates. This is part, among other matters, of the temporal mission of the Church which does not leave temporal welfare out of consideration in the pursuit of the eternal. The Church, therefore, would encourage Christian art associations, the development of talent in the young, and the progress of art, especially that which is animated by a higher and more spiritual consideration than that which stems from a materialistic age. She likewise warns against the harmful effects of ideologies upon art, the subtle way in which art can be used for propaganda and for inspiring hatred and distrust of God and man.

Private opinion, therefore, in matters of *liturgical* art is free in matters of style as long as it conforms to certain doctrinal norms, such as the correct representation of the sacred persons and mysteries, and to certain pastoral norms, namely, the functional propriety of the object created or displayed and certain traditions which the Church cherishes as well as the general atmosphere of reverence and devotion. However, the mere opinion of an ecclesiastic is not the opinion of the Church. It has no particular value as the opinion of an ecclesiastic unless he speaks as an authorized spokesman of the Church. A bishop, for instance, may have his own personal likes and dislikes, which would be respected for his own personal worth, but unless he speaks *as a bishop* with regard to liturgical art in its own particular function, or as an interpreter of the decrees of the Church, the Holy See, or the congregations, his opinion would simply be a respected opinion but no more.

The same principle would apply to a personal opinion on *private art* as would apply to conduct of any kind, literature, acting, forms of human conversation, etc., namely, the general position of the Church with regard to faith and morals. The Church does speak on faith and morals, however, in all phases of human life. She is present in the market place, the NAM notwithstanding, she is present in the studio, she is present in the school and in the entire cultural field. In all of these she remains, nonetheless, within the limits of her own capacity. She is not concerned with the private opinions of people as long as these opinions are not in disaccord with Christian faith and Christian morals. However, the intimate relationship in the public mind between private art and liturgical art would seem to impose a certain restriction or caution upon private concepts and cultural manifestation.

In conclusion it is well to emphasize the need of a positive sense of responsibility on the artist's part, a realization of how far our own private acts do go toward moulding not only ideas but also policies and movements in the modern world. An irresponsible individualism, even in the expression of one's purely private opinion, is not in accord with a full and rounded view of the obligations that Christian charity and fellowship impose upon us as members of the mystical body of Christ and as citizens of a largely opinion-governed world. Our relation to the cultural movements of the day and to their implications for human dignity and human liberty has to be taken into consideration. These responsibilities do not differ in the field of art from those which are implied in any other form of human expression.

Catholic Religious Art

AUGUST, 1948

I N VIEW of the concentration of thought and discussion which
this conference represents, I feel I owe an apology for presenting to your attention a very inadequate treatment of a subject
that demands the hand and the skill of an expert. All that I can
offer are a few chance observations drawn hither and yon from
my experience which has extended into the pastoral world as a
priest on the one side and into the artistic world by inheritance
and contact on the other.

I do not wish to lose time by discussing the particular evil that
needs to be remedied. I assume that there exists a considerable
agreement on this point.

The fact that Catholic religious art in this country is as yet very
unsatisfactory, to say the least, that it certainly does not corres-
pond either in its content of thought and emotion or even in its
technical skill with the dignity and competence that our Faith
would demand is so much of a truism that it would only be weari-
some to labor the point. We suffer from the fact that we simply
lack artistic production and must be content either with repeating
the past through copies or else with empty and sterile mass production of entirely inadequate models taken from the present. Nowhere is this brought home in more startling fashion than when
you enter the halls of some magnificently planned and furnished
modern Catholic educational institution. Your eye meets a painful
contrast between the glory of the architecture and the weakness
and meanness of the paintings which ordinarily adorn the halls, the
parlors, or the chapel. However, I wish neither to emphasize nor
to analyze this particular point. Our concern is a practical one,
what may be a remedy for an evil which in one form or another is
quite generally acknowledged.

Of course there is a question as to how much real influence on
Catholic life paintings and statues do really exert. Holy souls spend

a lifetime in intimate companionship with atrocious works of art and yet find in them simply a mild stimulation to virtue or a means of fixing their attention on certain revealed truths, and are not affected for good or evil by the defects of the production. On the other hand, people can live amidst the most magnificent art and derive therefrom little benefit or even remain pure materialists. But allowing for all exaggeration, there must be nevertheless in the long run an effect on the Catholic mind. Associations and ideas are formed that gradually take root in the very concepts of our Faith. And so the matter is not one which can be safely ignored.

I believe that we can find our way out of the intricacies of the problem more easily if certain distinctions are kept clearly in mind. These distinctions relate to the different types of work of art, that is, the very purposes of the works themselves objectively considered, and again to the various attitudes with which these works are either projected or executed. Positive harm is done by lumping things together which really belong apart and if kept apart would greatly simplify our whole procedure. A few divisions would seem to be in order.

(1) There is religious art in the form of church decoration, where art is used as the background of worship, as an adjunct or a completion of architecture to such an extent that there is no absolute division between architecture and representative art. To this type of religious art may be applied the eloquent words of the encyclical, *Mediator Dei*:

Keeping in mind, Venerable Brethren, pontifical norms and decrees, take great care to enlighten and direct the minds and hearts of the artists to whom is given the task to-day of restoring or rebuilding the many churches which have been ruined or completely destroyed by war. Let them be capable and willing to draw their inspiration from religion to express what is suitable and more in keeping with the requirements of worship. Thus the human arts will shine forth with a wondrous heavenly splendor, and contribute greatly to human civilization, to the salvation of souls, and the glory of God. The fine arts are really in conformity with religion when "as noblest handmaids they are at the service of divine worship."

(2) Religious art again may be simply the work of the artist without any connection with any specific act of religious worship, work where he takes a religious theme. Such religious painting in the broad sense may decorate a private house, a public building, a school or a garden, or a tomb. It is clear that the norms which would govern this type of painting are simply those norms of propriety which should govern all works of art, and it is to be judged like any other type of expression, were it a poem, a novel, or a history. This does not fall properly within the scope of our liturgical and pastoral problem.

(3) On the other hand, what we may call the *ikon* is closer to the liturgical problem and the care of souls than is a "church art" which is merely used in a broad decorative and background sense. This is where the image or painting receives a certain veneration from the faithful and is so placed or planned as to aid directly in the concentration of worship, reverence, and liturgical ceremony, such as the image in a shrine.

But the fitness or appropriateness of a work of art needs to be discussed also from a subjective point of view, from the different attitudes or approaches which are made to religious art. Not only is the work's own purpose distinctive, but also that of the patron in having it executed and the artist in carrying it out. Here there is a wide variety of emotional approach, so much so that it seems unreasonable to demand of a work of religious art an emotional impact which it is not expected to produce.

It may be, for instance, our aim through the work of art to produce in the soul of the onlooker a sense of deep compunction, a consciousness of the tragic elements of created life and of the sublime tragedy of the life of the incarnate Word. Such, for instance, would be the crucifix; such would be the Pietà of the sorrowing mother, or other scenes from the passion of Jesus Christ; or representations of the four last things, death, judgment, etc. A splendid example would be the famous five-figured Pietà of Ivan Mestrovic, which aims to produce not only a deep sense of sorrow and compassion at the scene of Calvary, but also a sense of the agonizing struggles and sorrows of the artists's own Yugoslav nation.

Again, the aim of the artist may be to produce an intense consciousness of historical reality, so as to evoke vividly before the soul of the onlooker the very moment of some great event or mystery of God's dealings with man, such as the scenes of the public life of the Saviour, the Transfiguration, the Assumption of our Lady, the calling of the apostles, or the scenes of the divine infancy. As we know, the baroque art specialized particularly on that extremely actual sense of the moment in all its drama and its vividness. In this stress on the momentary aspect lie both the strength and the limitations of baroque art.

(4) Another aim would be that of contemplation, the work of art serving, as it were, as a pictorial meditation, producing an atmosphere of tranquility, or grandeur, or peace; a certain timelessness. One's vision is thereby freed from the hurrying vicissitudes of the present moment. Such is the temper of the decorations in this library by the great Puvis de Chauvannes. Though they depict scenes which are more or less historical, the atmosphere is not that of life with its restless hurrying moments, but that of eternity. And the same spirit of timelessness which we find in Puvis is the note of the great art of the Far East.

(5) The artist may seek to produce the sense of *awe and mystery*. His work may crystallize, as it were, the faith or the mysteries of the Gospel through some hieratic form, such as is found in the typical ikon of the eastern churches as well as in the early Christian mosaic decorations. Such productions may range all the way from the formally hieratic to the subjectively mystical and mysterious.

(6) Another and familiar type we may include under the general term of *devotional*, where the work of art aims not so much to produce a sense of historical reality or of awe or of contemplation but simply a sense of familiar companionship, as an aid to contact through prayer with supernatural realities and supernatural personages. The familiar term, "aid to devotion," would seem to characterize this approach.

(7) Again we have a pedagogical type, where the work of art is simply and frankly at the service of the catechism. It may combine many of the preceding elements, but its principal function is to explain; such, for instance, we find in many of the medieval pictured windows and in certain types of modern decoration that serve as a continuing visual catechetical lesson.

(8) Finally, there is the frankly symbolic type of art which cuts away from any direct representation and speaks in parables or symbols. These may serve to summarize great truths or may serve again to inculcate a sense of the mysterious and the divine.

As a practical measure, therefore, I think any judgment on a work of religious art should determine not only what is the objective function of the work, but what is the subjective aim in which we wish the artist to be engaged. If the subjective aim includes the notion of being pleasant, consoling, comforting, or uplifting, obviously the work of art is delinquent if it does not help in that direction. But if the subjective aim does not include any of the preceding, if it is meant to humble, to stir us and shock us, to make us realize the sinfulness of man, the terror of human existence, and the uncertainty of human life, then it would be a mockery to seek from it the more pleasing and comforting elements.

With regard to the pleasurability of religious art, I think we are affected by the current craving for immediate and palpable enjoyment. For eyes sated with the screen and the rotogravure and now with television, for the senses stormed by visions which are immediately and pleasurably exciting, it is difficult to assimilate something which demands a certain restraint, a certain abstraction. Hence the path is smoothed which leads toward a natural degeneracy; toward the pretty, the sensate, to use the well-known expression of Sorokin, the characteristic of decadent forms in late Greek and Roman art and great cultures of all nations.

But we know that where there exists a strong natural tendency to the abnormal and to the degenerate, it is spiritually normal and spiritually healthy to entertain a certain fear and hesitation as to yielding to that tendency. It is not normal or healthy to love the ugly and the displeasing or to turn aside from what is nobly beautiful. But a certain touch of austerity, a certain selectiveness, a certain preference for that which is not too immediate, too much of the Hollywood blonde, the college girl and college boy, the soft and the effeminate in religious art; as I say, a moderate sternness in this respect is only normal and a sign of genuine spirituality.

This does not mean, however, that we should allow ourselves to fly to the other extreme, into a revolt against beauty. As we know from its introductory clauses, the encyclical on the liturgy, *Mediator Dei*, attempts to establish an equilibrium or balance between the contending extremes which has developed in recent years in the matter of the promotion of the sacred liturgy. The same would apply not only to the liturgy itself, but to art as a handmaid of the liturgy. This is very simply and beautifully expressed in the encyclical's words:

What We have said about music applies to the other fine arts, especially to architecture, sculpture, and painting. Recent works of art which lend themselves to the materials of modern composition should not be universally despised and rejected through prejudice. Modern art should be given free scope in the due and reverent service of the church and the sacred rites, provided that they preserve a correct balance between styles tending neither to extreme realism nor to excessive "symbolism," and that the needs of the Christian community are taken into consideration rather than the particular taste or talent of the individual artist. Thus modern art will be able to join its voice to that wonderful choir of praise to which have contributed, in honor of the Catholic faith, the greatest artists throughout the centuries. Nevertheless, in keeping with the duty of Our office, We cannot help deploring and condemning those works of art, recently introduced by some, which seem to be a distortion and perversion of true art and which at times openly shock Christian taste, modesty, and devotion, and shamefully offend the true religious sense. These must be entirely excluded and banished from our churches, like "anything else that is not in keeping with the sanctity of the place."

I believe that in our attempts to judge how far works of religious art may fall under one or the other of these extremes, we are apt to lose sight of the power of association, which works, curiously enough, in quite contrary directions. Even sublime truths can be associated with quite atrocious artistic effort whether in the mystical or the pictorial line. On the other hand, through association and through practice and constant familiarity, those things which at first sight may be rather repulsively stylized and may seem to us as unduly symbolic or remote from the immediately pleasing may become extremely beloved and charged with a deep emotional content. Most of us in the western Church feel a sense of remoteness when we see the Byzantine ikons from Greece, Russia, or Serbia, and yet what is more familiar and more generally beloved than that thoroughly Byzantine ikon, Our Lady of Perpetual Help. Certainly the crucifix would be greatly disconcerting if we came upon it for the first time, and yet enshrined as it is with a thousand memories of adoration and penance and love, it glows with a sweet and radiant light. We must not underestimate the possibility of our Catholic people being trained through the schools, through education, and through practice to appreciate a certain more symbolic and less immediately and palpably agreeable type of art.

Yet no amount of defining and formulating will give us a sound religious art. Norms, standards, and motives are guides and safeguards for correct living, but of themselves they do not give life. They tell what ought to be, but not how it shall come into existence.

I think the day is past when we can afford to entrust the answer to this question to the care of a few chosen and sequestered groups. I do not look upon worthy religious art as a sort of Noah's Ark, preserved miraculously amid the floods and storms of a materialist age, and waiting for some happy times when the waters shall subside, and its passengers can once more walk upon the dry land. Certainly if art is to be an active concern to only a tiny minority and if the rest of the faithful are to be but passive spectators, or purchasers of ready-made, mass-produced statues and holy pictures, then surely our end has come, in a spiritual sense.

Our problem is not the hoarding of creative power, but that of its release; for that power dwells, I believe, in our Catholic communities to a much larger extent than we have been ready to recognize. The fact that we have neglected to evoke it does not mean that it is not there. When I say that the problem is that of releasing creative art, I do not mean that the creation which is released will all be of equal value, or even much of it of any value. If every Jack and Jill starts drawing and sculpturing, most of what they will produce will be just a reflection of Jack and Jill, of little merit, or imagination, or substance of any kind. Nevertheless, here is where I hazard a rather obstinately entertained opinion: I believe that where many Jacks and Jills *do* make such attempts, where there is a vast effort at production not in the brute quantity of what is produced but the quantity of souls who try to produce and who are interested in producing, then those sparks of beauty and wisdom that otherwise would remain latent will be fanned into flame; and the net result will be vastly richer and higher, even though the proportion of good work to poor may still be distressingly low. But of the latter, what difference does it make, if the net result is distinguished? A "folk art" in itself is but a limited thing, but all great art, if we are to judge by history, is rooted in some form of folk art. And why must all folk art be banished from American Catholicism?

To be concrete, therefore, let me say that I look not for some vague and childish leveling by which every Jack and Jill would prove themselves to be masters, but for a great multiplication of centres of really thoughtful and skilled production, not just a few dozen or more, but thousands and thousands of the same, in every town, in—broadly speaking—every larger parish of the country. All of these will not attain the same level of excellence, but all will be alert to better types of work. And their multiplication will put all our people into closer and more immediate touch with those who do create; and so, in turn, help to solve the ever vexing question of artistic patronage. Priests, religious, and people alike will profit by such close companionship, and mutual understandings and joint plannings will be the result.

Such a development is certain to take place in secular art. But why wait for it to occur in secular art when there are a hundred more reasons why it should occur among Catholics?

Of course, our Church has a vast wealth of glorious tradition. But this tradition is dead, it is a mere museum piece, if it rests but in the museums, and is not part of the working kit of widely spread and widely diversified popular artistic effort. In such an atmosphere, I believe, many of these artificial contests and tensions between so-called conservatism and so-called modernism will be resolved of themselves, because there will be a healthier and more normal state of both production and appreciation.

We are living now upon the final gleanings of a past artistic culture; upon a culture where art had become what it was not from the beginning: the chosen toy of a selected class, who in turn had spiritually drifted away from their noble origins in the days of faith. With E. I. Watkin, I believe that we shall profit little by continuing this gleaning, but that we shall do much better by looking forward to another spring, a spring in which religious art will penetrate and spread among the people as never before in Christian history; for it will be rich with the past while still richer with the promises of the future. "We should expect," says Watkin, "the autumn of one religion-culture to prophesy and prepare the spring of the next," and these words I am glad to make my own. Let us then know the aim of what we produce, vastly widen the base of production, and if we then, filled with the care of God and His Blessed Mother, labor together for this great end, we may see a new spring of religious art in America.

The Absent Blacksmith

JUNE, 1952

I N MY LAST few years as a country pastor, I use to take great
delight in visiting occasionally the workshop of a rural blacksmith, Johnny Wise. Mr. Wise shod no horses, but busied
himself with repairs to carriages and farm wagons and any sort of
metal working job that suited his skillful hands. He dwelt several
miles from the shop and walked to and from his work. Later he
rode an old bicycle.

No signs indicated the location of Johnny's shop, itself a nonde-
script wooden shed. It lay hidden in the trees a few hundred yards
distant from the narrow Three Notch Road that led through
interminable forest for forty miles along the high watershed of
the St. Mary's peninsula. Like all such places, it was filled with
innumerable scraps of iron and copper, bolts, screws, metal sheets,
wagon-wheel axles, rims and spokes, whiffletrees, discarded
carriage tops or shafts, etc. Like many of his trade Mr. Wise was
taciturn. When a customer appeared, he was accorded only a
curt nod, and was usually kept waiting while Johnny continued
with his work, so as to give the impression that the blacksmith
had more important things to do than idly to pass the time of day.
If your request seemed unreasonable, you received a short answer.
But if you really were looking for a constructive bit of craftsmanship, Johnny showed a controlled but unmistakable enthusiasm,
and neither time, trouble nor money counted. Though Johnny was
not my parishioner, but a vestryman of the local Protestant
church, he was keenly interested in doing work for my new
church of St. Nicholas: such as iron work for the altar and the
sacristy. I felt that God was very glad to receive the offering of a
man who loved his work, just as God had loved man in creating us.

The last time I visited Johnny's shop he was absent for the
day. He had left pinned to the door a notice printed in lead-pencil:

47

BLACKSMITH NOT HERE
WHERE HE IS GONE
NOBODY KNOWS NOBODY CARES

Shortly after that I left Maryland to take up my work in New York. Returning some years later for a visit, I learned that the blacksmith had been killed, struck by an auto on the new highway as he was cycling home one evening from his long day's toil. There were not many to mourn him: two old sisters, and a few rural neighbors. And with the transformation of the country-side, all reason for such a shop had ceased, and the shed was dismantled. Appliances now were bought from the great wholesale houses, and nothing more was made by hand. Yet I did care, and still think of the vanished blacksmith shop as I pass near its former location while motoring on the great new road.

The products of our liturgical art, too; the objects and images and utensils used as part of the fabric of our churches—these also are bought today from the commercial wholesale houses. The blacksmith is gone: the craftsman or artist who contributed the personal work of his hands, and saw that work enshrined forever in the House of God—a monument to his own love, a precious offering to God. Where he is gone, is it true that nobody knows and nobody cares? The purpose of our Liturgical Arts Society was to show that the Church very much does care: that honor and reverence to God, that the integrity of divine worship most assuredly demand a restoration of the individual artist's and craftsman's place in the scheme of our present great expenditures on religious construction. The obstacles to such a restoration are great but they are not insuperable, and those who work for this end are united with others of similar conviction all over the world. The commercial establishments have their function; they make available products that no amount of purely private industry could hope to construct or distribute in the present state of our economy. But there is a limit to their usefulness as well. Again, as I said, we need a rebirth of creative spirit joined to truly genuine, artistic workmanship. This is something for which both God and man must care.

II.
Religion

This entire book treats of religion, which in some form or other is the main business of life; but the seven papers here grouped concern more directly the spiritual—the inner-life. The four holy Doctors, Saints Leo, Gregory the Great, Ambrose and Augustine, discoursed inexhaustively thereon. On Christmas night each of them contributes a little homily to the Office of the Roman Breviary. Hence the Allegory. Pope St. Gregory (after whom the Gregorian chant is named) collected melodies and is said to have composed some three hundred of his own, which he taught to a group of selected choir boys. Ancient pictures show the saintly pontiff thus engaged, holding a stick with which he whacked any luckless lad who failed to pay attention or struck a wrong note.

When the Pope acted as choir master the pupil had to pay attention not only to the words, which came easily enough to natural Latin speakers, but also to the pitch and the rhythm as well. The Gregorian rhythm is "free," no drei-viertel Takt, but a rhythmic tone in accord with the rhythm of speech itself. This makes it highly interpretative of the Latin text and musically in line with the world's best folk melodies.

Must the lady with the dark locks remain forever outside? She suffered her harsh rebuffs. Remembering these, along with horrible cruelties in latter days, her soul was shaken to the depths. We are shocked at the bluntness of her refusal. But that bluntness does not absolve us from trying to understand how great are her fears. The way to understanding is bleak and difficult; it is impossible without patience, knowledge and love. Yet more souls have found their way, found it in sincerity, than most of us conceive, and their number will continue to increase. We are all guilty, and much too often we block the paths.

July 31, 1956 marks the 400th anniversary of the death of St. Igna-

51

tius Loyola, so for this Ignatian year it seems fitting to include some thoughts gathered in 1934 at the 400th anniversary of the founding of the Society of Jesus. These thoughts, which meant much to me at that time, mean still more to me at the present. A fitting companion to the fourth centennial of Ignatius is the account of a contemporary saint with whom I had the great privilege of speaking to twice during my life. The essay on Christian humanism is part of a symposium which appeared in Social Order *magazine, May-June, 1953. Two papers, that on the Schools and that on Inquirers, reflect the day by day solicitudes of a former country pastor who retained a pastoral point of view towards the world scene around him and in his contacts with individuals in the great city. They are the concerns and anxieties of the Church particularly in the United States.*

Finally, the report on the baptism of Catherine Frances was written to three of her older sisters, my own grandnieces, who stayed at home, and let Margaret—going on four—represent them. There is always more to say about baptism, much more than we usually derive from the rather summary treatment in the catechism. Baptism has faded too much out of the picture as a focal point for the great mysteries of our faith. We may reasonably hope that the present restoration of the dignity and timeliness of the mysteries of Holy Week and the Easter Vigil will help to bring out its significance. So, too, will the greater liberty now permitted by the Holy See for the use of the vernacular in the administration of the sacraments. Archbishop Edwin V. O'Hara, of Kansas City, has repeatedly pointed out what opportunities for instruction in the faith the use of English provides.

King Peaceful: an Allegory

DECEMBER, 1929

I WAS RATHER SURPRISED to meet Venerable Mother so casually. Merely turning off a side-street, I found her inside a little arched door, praying in the half-light of a Christmas-eve afternoon. She did not look at all venerable, with fair, fresh face, and her little gold crown planted on top of the demure nun's veil. (It was this odd contrast by which I recognized her, as distinguished from her older, dark-locked sister.) Only Venerable Mother's clothes seemed to waft an odor not so much of age as of eternity: like the keen out-door scent that another mother's fur cloak, long ago, brought to the fireside, when we children greeted her after her brisk walk home on a winter's evening. Though faint brown, like very old manuscripts, the folds flowed down in gold half-shimmerings, like the aurora in Antarctica. And four Holy Doctors stood at her side.

"I am glad you came," she began quite abruptly. "I hope you are not home-sick."

"*For it would be unlawful,*" said the first Holy Doctor, speaking before I could answer, in the measured tones with which, as Pope, he once spoke to Attila before Rome, "*it would be unlawful to be sad today, for today is Life's Birthday.*"

"To tell the truth I am—just a bit," I admitted. But the second Holy Doctor had his comment at once. "All the better," he said, "for if you are away from home, then you are like Christ, for *He was born, not in His Mother's House, but away from home. And this is a mystery, showing us that this our mortality into which He was born was not the home of Him Who is begotten of the Father before the worlds.*"

"And as long as you are here," continued Venerable Mother, "you might as well look at some of these grand old words that I shall sing on Christmas night."

"Mother, I appreciate your kindness," I replied. "But you know

53

I am not one of those medievalists. I am plain 20th century."

"Fiddlesticks!" said Venerable Mother. "I have a cupboard of specialties for the medievalists. But this is for everyone, and for your kind most of all." With that she pointed to a huge lectern, on which were spread out all the antiphons and lessons of Christmas Day, just as the priest reads them and the monk chants them in the Office or Breviary. And the Second Doctor (the father of free-winged melody) hummed gently as I read.

FIRST ANTIPHON. King Peaceful exceeded all the kings of the earth, and all the earth sought the face of Peaceful.

SECOND ANTIPHON. King Peaceful exceeded all the kings of the whole earth.

THIRD ANTIPHON. The days of Mary were accomplished, that she should bring forth her first-born Son.

FOURTH ANTIPHON. Know ye that the kingdom of God is at hand: Amen I say to you, it will not tarry.

FIFTH ANTIPHON. *Lift up your heads, behold, your redemption draweth nigh.*

"King Peaceful appeals to me," I remarked.

"Of course it does," answered Venerable Mother. "But the trouble with you people is that you try to concoct peace out of the world's poor elements alone. But you haven't all the makings. Brew peace all you want. It only turns to bitterness in the pot, without the herb of Divine Wisdom."

"Mother, you have said it," I groaned. "But where are *you* going to find peace? Isn't 'peace through the churches' just the thing all sorts of people are looking for today?"

"*Behold the beginning of* THE CHURCH," said the Third Doctor, whose voice resounded as it did once at Milan. "*Christ is born, and the shepherds watch, shepherds, to gather together the scattered sheep of the Gentiles, and to lead them into* THE FOLD *of Christ. . . . Only in One Fold, not in many, is peace.*" And the Fourth Doctor sighed in assent.

"Precisely," exclaimed Venerable Mother. "I was with the shepherds before even the Fold was first gathered. I crept with them to Bethlehem, and found there King Peaceful. I was but a child then;

and my older sister Synagoga was with me: before we had separated."

"Did you believe then that He was God?" I asked.

"I was but a witness without wit," she answered; "I saw without seeing, heard without understanding. Only at the first Pentecost, being confirmed with the name *Ecclesia*, did I understand; but I have remembered forever. Read!"

Borrowing then a little crystal lamp from the Fourth Doctor, who was scanning the Gospel of St. John, she flashed it upon the three great Responsories of the First Nocturn of Christmas Matins, and I read:

FIRST RESPONSORY. *This is the day whereon the King of heaven was pleased to be born to a Virgin, that He might bring back to heaven man who was lost. There is joy among the host of Angels, because eternal salvation hath appeared to men.*

VERSE. *Glory to God in the highest, and on earth peace, to men of good will. . . .*

SECOND RESPONSORY. *This day is the true peace come down unto us from heaven. This day throughout the whole world the skies drop down sweetness.*

VERSE. *This day is the day of our new redemption, of the restoring of the old, of everlasting joy. . . .*

THIRD RESPONSORY. *O, ye shepherds speak, and tell what ye have seen; who has appeared in the earth? We saw the new-born Child, and Angels singing praise to the Lord.*

VERSE. *Speak; what have ye seen? And tell us of the Birth of Christ.*

ANSWER. *We saw the new-born Child, and Angels singing praise to the Lord. . . .*

"But, Venerable Mother," I protested, "isn't that a somewhat old-fashioned idea that peace is something that comes down from Heaven? Isn't peace to be found in the collective enterprise of all humanity: the general pooling of all good wishes of all good men?"

"How can men give to one another what they have not of themselves, and have never received?" asked sharply the Fourth Doctor, lifting his lean, rather swarthy face. "The rapine and carnage that

I witnessed in Africa made me doubt if anything in man existed by which he could practice peace unaided by the enlightenment and the aid of divine grace. And the fifteen hundred years that have passed since I left Hippo for eternity, bear witness to the same truth. Peace must be *given;* and only He can give it, Who of His nature has the fullness of peace: Jesus Christ."

"And how has He that fulness?" I inquired.

"Because He is one with His Eternal Father," replied the Fourth Doctor, "being the Only-Begotten Son of God."

With a quick gesture, like that of a passionate orator, his arm shot out from under his mantle, and pointed to the Gospel of St. John.

"*Let some infidel Arian come forth,*" he exclaimed, "and talk of peace through humanism; of peace through mere human resolutions! Unless we believe that Christ is God's own Son, co-eternal and co-infinite with the Father, we cannot enjoy that full unity given us by the Redemption. But acknowledging that Divine Life, and being made one thereby with the Father and with one another, our human devices will be made fruitful."

"For on Christmas night," rejoined Venerable Mother, "He came to pass the verdict on war and death, which He was to destroy by the Redemption. Hence I sing at the entrance of the second Nocturn of Matins: *We have drunk in Thy mercy, O God, in the midst of Thy Temple;* and again: *In the Lord's days shall abundance of peace arise and flourish.*

"And at the end of the eighth Responsory, just before I close Matins by reading the beginning of the Gospel of St. John, I echo the glorious words—those words, good Doctor, which thou didst give thy life to fathoming—" Then, turning to the lectern, she proclaimed:

The Word was made flesh and dwelt among us. And we beheld His glory, the glory as of the Only-Begotten of the Father, full of grace and truth.

VERSE. *All things were made by Him, and without Him was nothing made.*

ANSWER. *And we beheld His glory, the glory as of the Only-Begotten of the Father, full of grace and truth.*

"Which of you," asked Venerable Mother, speaking to the Doctors, "remember how in the fifth century I sang these words in the Church of St. Mary Major, in Rome?"

"It was even after my time," replied the Fourth Doctor, "when your son Sixtus III was then reigning. And so grand was the vigil in which the Pope took part, that all other festivals in the Latin Church, except Easter and Pentecost, took it henceforth for their model."

"Yes," rejoined Venerable Mother, "and it was then that the great second antiphon of Lauds rose to the rafters of the first Church of Mary in Christendom:

"The Mother brought forth the King, Whose name is called THE ETERNAL; *the joy of the Mother was hers, remaining a Virgin unsullied; neither before nor henceforth hath there been or shall be such another."*

"Alleluia," intoned the Second Doctor, and sang the words of Isaias in the fifth antiphon: *"Unto us this day a little Child is born, and His name shall be called the Mighty God."*

"Alleluia," answered Venerable Mother. Then all grew dark.

Crib and tapers; lectern and the august figures that stood beside it faded away. And instead I seemed to stand upon the bare plain of Esdraelon, on the road from Galilee to Judea. All races, all nations of the world were crossing that plain; but I saw nothing of the multitude; I only dimly guessed their presence. For the first moment in history all war had ceased.

Nothing appeared but a lone, homely little man and woman; miserably clad; stricken; wandering as if they had come from an unutterably long journey. And then, far off, in a blaze of inaccessible glory, I saw that same Infant that had but a moment before been resting upon the straw. And a million voices chanted:

Thine shall be the dominion in the day of Thy power, amid the brightness of the holy ones: from the womb before the day-star have I begotten Thee.

Then I knew that only the Divine Son of God, true God of true God, could give life and peace to the world.

The little man and woman looked vaguely up, weary and uncomprehending.

Then again the voices sounded, but nearer and fewer, in more human tones:

The Lord hath sent redemption unto His people, He hath commanded His covenant forever.

As the figure of the Divine Child came ever nearer, the man said to the woman: "Let's go forward, Mother, and ask forgiveness." They knelt with bowed heads; and the nearer voices again sang:

Unto the upright there ariseth light in the darkness: the Lord is gracious and full of compassion, and righteous.

With the Lord there is mercy, and with Him is plenteous redemption.

"*De profundis,*" came from the wanderers' lips, that age-old plea for mercy, that the Church sings on Christmas night; that the first "King Peaceful," who had "exceeded all the kings of the whole earth," had learned of old from his father David, learned, and chanted in prayerful hope, and passed on to all future times, but then had forgotten. . . . And with its forgetting, peace—*sholôm* —vanished from Solomon's throne forever.

Stooping gently, the Christ-Child lifted up the penitent Gentiles, and showed them a vast and eternal Kingdom that He had come to found, and of this Kingdom there would be no end.

"*Of the fruit of Thy Body,*" sounded now the fifth antiphon of Christmas Vespers, "*will I set upon Thy throne.*" It was the second *Rex Pacificus*, the eternal and Divine, calling to the first King Peaceful, human and sinful, in the words of his father David.

Just then the sacristan came to light up the church, and I went out again into the street. Pushing through the crowded sidewalks, I saw that older sister, lost in the mob, with her dark locks firmly resisting the whitening years. Her eyes still witnessed to the memory of her ancient "King Peaceful," whose reign had turned to dust; and of longing for another Peaceful, who had not yet come, and who would *loose the bonds of the daughter of Zion.*

"Lord, remember David," sounded Venerable Mother's voice from afar. And the First Doctor read again the words of Isaias in the First Nocturn: *"Therefore* My People *shall know My Name in that day;* they shall know *that I am He that spake, behold it is I."*

The Philanthropy of Ignatius Loyola

FOUR HUNDRED YEARS of the Society of Jesus (celebrated on August 15, 1934) cause us to cast our eyes back to the Founder of that Society, and wonder what manner of man he was. Men are characterized by epithets, today most of all; though a little more moderately since the Emil Ludwig craze abated. Ignatius Loyola's coat of spiritual mail was always a magnet for epithets: glorious and chivalrous, ruthless and fanatical, strategic and military, etc. But attempts to depart from the conventional classifications of saints' lives, to describe Ignatius as a merely natural phenomenon and psychologize him accordingly, fail lamentably. An ingenious, synthetic product is the result; crude misconceptions are dispelled; history popularized; but the man does not live again whose spirit turned back the tide of Luther and flung out the battlelines for Christ.

Nothing is more baffling than the search for that central factor, idea, or spirit which polarizes the countless single traits of a saint, particularly a saint whose life was intimately woven into history. It is difficult enough to define in the case of any great personage; but in the case of the saint, an element enters in which no mere historical analysis can appraise: the direct intervention of God, especially in the case of the great founders and organizers of the Church. There is no clear demarcation between the man and the Divine plan: they are blended into one. You stumble on the finger of God where you congratulate yourself on opening up the mysteries of man.

As in his famous conversation with Father James Laínez concerning the revelations made to the founders of Religious Orders, Ignatius gave evidence of his having received the idea of his Society as a direct inspiration from above. With all allowance, however, for this element in his consciousness, we may still search for what

was most *immediate* to Ignatius as he surveyed the scene of God
and the world. The answer may be summed up in a word which
has woefully degenerated from its original high meaning, yet which
may again play its pristine role: philanthropy. Not "philanthropy"
in its current usage of humanitarian concern for the conferring of
material benefits; but *philanthropia*, the love of mankind, in the
sublime sense in which it was applied to God and to His Divine
Son, the supreme Philanthropist, by the Fathers of the Eastern
Church.

Every clearly defined character is aware of some special element
in the landscape of life. The naturalist strolls through the country-
side, and is keenly alive to its animal life; the botanist sees the plants
and flowers; the military strategist notices the heights and contours
suitable for fortifications or ambush; the politician thinks of the
voting power concealed in the homes that dot the roads; the painter
is alive to the interplay of light and shade; the archeologist to the
ruins of early structures; the parish priest thinks of the souls to be
brought to Mass and their Easter duty; the small boy notes in
summer the hills that will make a magnificent toboggan slide in
January. All of these view the same scene, but their disposition,
their training, their chief motivation in life, fixes their attention on
wide varied aspects. So the founders of religious orders: Bruno
sees the grave offenses against the Divine Majesty to be expiated;
Dominic, the multitudes thirsting for the Word of God; Vincent
de Paul, the havoc wrought by clerical corruption, by poverty and
social disorder.

All through the career of Ignatius, in all the phases of his unique
life, the object peculiarly immediate to his attention was the *condition of mankind*. Humanity's state, deprived of grace and the
Redemption, lay before him as a vision, summed up in his famous
meditation on the Incarnation in the Spiritual Exercises: humanity
"upon the face of the earth, in such diversity, in all kinds of clothing and gestures and types of countenance; some white and some
black, some in peace and some in war; some weeping and others
laughing, some well and some sick; some being born and others
dying"; humanity talking, swearing and blaspheming, fighting and

striking one another, and in the end losing their way on life's journey to the goal for which they were created. It was the European world made sick by the gaping wound left by the disunion of Christendom; it was the world of marching mercenaries, apathetic ecclesiastics, and warring sects. It was Luther's world. It was the Devil's world. It was the world Ignatius was thrust into as a poor soldier knight in the Basque country. But despite all that, it was God's world; to be reconquered for God.

Other good men of those times, or earlier, other saints, other founders, were aware of the condition of mankind and moved to the desire to remedy it: such men as St. John Colombini, St. Antonine of Florence, St. Anthony Zaccaria, St. Cajetan, St. Jerome Emiliani, St. Philip Neri, and others. Distinctive, however, of the Ignatian philanthropy were his *view of mankind*, and *his concept of the remedy*.

Ignatius' view of mankind is marked by three tenacious and fundamental traits: its transcendentalism, its universality, its realism. A word or two may make these ponderous expressions clear.

Ignatius' transcendental view of mankind and its destiny was absolute, and expressed in the device: *Ad majorem Dei gloriam:* "for the greater glory of God." He saw men as coming from God, as going to God, and he saw man totally in his Creator: "loving Him in all creatures and them all in Him, according to His most holy and Divine Will." In his entire life there was no weakening, no shadow of turning from this concept. Of the "A. M. D. G." says the historian Astrain:

This sublime thought, the most sublime to be found in heaven or earth, gives a marvelous internal unity to all those varied actions, at first sight so opposed to one another, which distinguish the life of Ignatius. All that he did, he did for the greater glory of God. Things high and low, great and small, congenial and foreign, spiritual and temporal, all were directed by Ignatius to the Divine glory.

The universality of his viewpoint impelled Ignatius to embrace in his zeal all mankind, without any limitation of race, country, or condition. At the death of Ignatius, in 1556, his Society was already solidly established in Italy, Spain, Portugal, France, Flanders, Germany, Brazil, Hindustan, Malacca, the Moluccas, and Japan. It had made entry into Ireland, Poland, Morocco, Tripoli, the Congo, and Mozambique. The universality of its extent was a reflection of the universality of the founder's vision. His concept was universal in another sense: he aimed at the restoration or cure of mankind *in toto:* the mind was to be re-educated, habits reformed, a new society built up, new social institutions created, a new man created, according to justice and the holiness of truth. His aim was not merely to relieve mankind, but to refashion mankind, according to the glory and splendor of the Divine plan that shone upon the brow of Adam as he adored his Creator in the Garden of Eden. Out of this vertical universality, if we may so call it, grew the educational program of the Jesuits.

In sharpest contrast, however, to that modern enemy of God to whom he has been ignorantly compared, Ignatius dreamed of no "mass man" as did Lenin. His eye was focused fully upon the individual. Each person's destiny was recognized as unique; and success in bringing back a single soul to its Creator was enough, in Ignatius' mind, for all the labor that might have been expended upon thousands. Even to prevent a single mortal sin of a single soul was reward enough for a lifetime. This trait of his philanthropy was seen in his treatment of the group of men who gathered with Ignatius at the foot of the altar in the crypt of St. Denis on Montmartre that Assumption Day, 1534.

Each one of these men, Xavier, the priest Faber, Laínez, Bobadilla, Simon Rodriguez, Salmeron, had been trained by Ignatius *separately,* without the knowledge of the others, for a couple of years or more, with infinite consideration of their individual temperaments. Certainly no easy task. Said Father Edmond Auger, who knew them personally: "I have heard tell of our great moulder of men, Ignatius, that the stiffest pastry he ever had to knead was this young Francis Xavier in his early years"; and the others presented corresponding problems. But after they finally had vowed themselves to their great enterprise, and had refreshed themselves with a frugal breakfast of bread and water, they passed the whole long summer's day in eager conversation "with great joy and exultation of soul."

Close akin to this preoccupation for the individual was Ignatius' realistic view of man. He had no illusions as to the stubbornness and complexity of human nature. His prudence knew no bounds. He knew that for the *exigua natura*, the small-minded man, there was no use going beyond his limits, and dazzling him with ideals which he was incapable of grasping. He knew that for the great hearts, for the *insignes*, enthusiasm to *brasser des choses grandes et hors des forces communes:* to "embrace great things and above ordinary powers," in the words of Auger, would lead into the swamp of egotism or disillusionment were the ground not prepared for the ideal by a radical purification of the heart. This purification, in turn, could be no general affair: no mere breast beating and cries of *mea culpa*. It must be specific, penetrating to the hidden roots of character weakness. "No one better than Ignatius," said Palmio, "could make the anatomy of a soul."

Ignatius' realism, his insistence upon discipline as a necessary corollary of this realism, his early profession of soldiering and his occasional use of metaphors of campaign, attached to him, in popular estimation, the terms *military* and *soldier minded*. This trait lends itself easily to exaggeration. As this writer once pointed out, it is not the Constitutions of the ex-soldier Ignatius, but the rule of St. Benedict, whose motto was *Pax*, which begins with a rousing call to arms and obedience for the sake of Christ. Father Leturia, one of the contemporary Jesuit historians who has kept closest to factual ground in the study of Ignatian origins, observes in this regard:

Without doubt the contour of the loyal and organizing captain lasted in St. Ignatius even under the folds of his Roman mantle. But united with the courage, the loyalty, and the centralizing strategy of the soldier, there lived and worked in his disposition other equally prominent traits which were in no wise military or militaristic in character.

Such were his fine psychological discernment of spirits, his power of tact and conciliation, as well as his affective and ecstatic flights which seized him in the presence of the majesty of the starry skies: "flights which found their mystical and supernatural crown in the intellectual visions on the banks of the Cardoner and the mysterious locutions of the Blessed Trinity."

Ignatius' concept of the remedy for man's condition was radical, tremendous, and enthralling. It was none other than the *Divine philanthropy*, expressed in the redemptive grace given to men by the Son of God. Ignatius, it is true, placed paramount the saving of the soul. Yet he profoundly departed from that obsession which had grown up in the later Middle Ages, obsession with the personal problem *of* salvation, rather than with the Divine plan of which salvation is the consequence. That obsession had driven Luther well nigh to insanity; it had impelled him to religious frenzy and finally to apostasy from the Faith. The madness of the times could not be healed by the contemplation of endless death's heads and pictures of souls snatched away by the evil spirit. As long as the eye was turned morbidly inward upon this single eschatological problem, the poison of despair stole over it as an opiate, while the passions retained their sway.

Ignatius bade his disciples lift up their minds, in all tranquillity, to the untroubled splendors of the Divine plan: to the glories of the creation, to the first man, perfect in body, serene in mind, joyful in the childlike worship of the Father. The complete restoration of that state in the life of the individual, *was* salvation. It was the work of the Divine philanthropy. Its complete restoration in society was the eternal Kingdom of the Son. Its moral restoration here below, through doctrine, penance, self-discipline, and the loving following of the loving and suffering and triumphant Christ in union with the sacramental life of the Church, was the guarantee, without further ado, that salvation would be achieved. Hence to work upon the building *now;* for if that is successful, all things future will care for themselves!

In the four centuries of its existence, the Society of Jesus, according to its capacity and the fidelity of its members to the ideals of their Founder and his first companions, has contributed its share to the Church's work in preaching, observing, and symbolizing this gospel of human reconstruction through the Divine. The tradition of despair, which plagued the world in Ignatius' day, has issued now in certain countries and certain classes of people in depths that Luther and Calvin never dreamt of. They cannot be met by palliatives. We Catholics have been standing still not because our remedy is inadequate, but because of the greatness of our hope. The anniversary of Montmartre, while the cause of humble thanksgiving for the followers of Ignatius, should also be an inspiration to all children of the Church to take fresh inventory of the riches of her spiritual program.

Religious Men Fear Secularized Education

JUNE, 1937

THE SPREAD of radicalism in this country has had this good effect: it has begun to arouse non-Catholics to the danger of a completely secularized education. It has put into sharper relief the illogical attitude of those who cling blindly to educational secularism as somehow connected with Americanism through the irrelevant middle term of "separation of Church and State."

It is only a beginning, but the beginning has already shown some effects, as is seen in a series of reports by the N.C.W.C. and the N.C.J.C. News Services.

Ministers and rabbis in Providence, R. I., became so concerned over the situation that on May 10, 1937 they held an informal conference at the Rhode Island College of Education to discuss religious instruction in the public schools, in which the Rev. Thomas V. Cassidy, Director of Parochial Schools for the Diocese of Providence, also took part. Extremely significant were the opinions expressed on this occasion.

The chief note sounded by the Protestants was that the Sunday school has proved itself entirely inadequate for religious instruction. Said Dr. James F. Rockett, State Director of Education: "Our children need education but they don't get it. The Sunday school went out with the kerosene lamp." Said a Presbyterian clergyman: "The average Protestant church school gives the pupil only fourteen hours of instruction a year."

But the non-Catholics appeared helpless when confronted with the problem of how to impart religious instruction, even if the opportunity were obtained. "Religion is caught more than it is taught," was a Congregationalist sentiment, leaving unsolved the question, from whom you were going to "catch" it.

A rabbi spoke, warning of tying up religion too closely with the

67

public school. As a boy, he found it "hateful" to be instructed in religion separately from the Orthodox and Catholic children in Poland; and "what a joy" later when in an "American" school he was not separated from anyone else.

The rabbi's attitude represented what appears like the crux of the problem in certain non-Catholic minds: the fear that if the rule of complete educational uniformity and conformity is in the slightest degree relaxed, for any cause whatsoever, it will mean that somehow the less "belonging" elements in our community will feel less at home; they will be subtly reminded of their differences. For such a mind it appears to be more important not to be socially set aside than to maintain one's own or any religion.

A Baptist clergyman, however, the Rev. L. Louis Aber, found no ground in his own experiences for such apprehension. Citing his observations in Scranton, Pa., Dayton, Ohio, Oak Park, Ill., and several other centers where religious instruction in public schools had been introduced, he said: "The plan worked successfully. I do not recall that in any of these cities this feeling of separateness described by Rabbi Goldman and Rabbi Braude entered into the situation. In the American set-up these objections are theoretical."

Another Jewish speaker found an insuperable obstacle in the fact that "in Jewish faith there is no central authority, no accepted standards of religious instruction. . . . We all love each other but we have ritualistic divisions. We should not be able to furnish adequate teaching." Hence, he concluded, religion cannot be taught properly in the class room. But such raising of difficulties does not liberate the non-Catholic from the problem; it merely accentuates his helplessness in meeting it.

A recent article in the *Christian Century* uttered almost a cry of despair.

As for elementary and secondary education, Protestantism abandoned those fields long ago to the public school. The children of the 25,000,000 Protestant families in the United States receive no formal education except one from which all elements of religion have by

political necessity been expunged. . . . Protestantism is now at the
point of discovering that its youth are adrift on the sea of secularism.

The Sunday school is little more than a ghost, Protestantism
"has no adequate medium of communicating to its own children its
concepts and convictions about God," and religious or moral truths.

The existence of such a collapse of Protestant and Jewish religious effort should make our non-Catholic brethren more alive to
the justice of the Catholic objection to discriminatory treatment
with regard to our own schools, where we are able to give to our
children the type of instruction whose absence the non-Catholic
deplores. As Archbishop McNicholas of Cincinnati remarked:
"This discrimination is fundamentally opposed to freedom of education. This state of affairs is not normal. . . . It is contrary to
fundamental justice to impose taxation upon a whole group without
conferring any benefits upon that group."

Recently Rabbi Morris Lazaron, of Baltimore, was quoted in the
Bulletin of the Thirty-third Degree Masons, Southern Jurisdiction, as expressing much satisfaction that a proposal was defeated
in the Maryland Legislature enabling transportation to be provided for children attending Catholic schools in Saint Mary's
County, Md., where nearly eighty per cent of the people, white
and colored, are Catholic. Such a state of mind seems incredible in
our day and times. These same Thirty-third Degree Masons will
go almost into hysterics over the ravages that Communism is making among Southern Methodist youth. No measures are too drastic,
to meet such an evil. Yet they become equally hysterical at Catholics who wish to preserve their own children from atheism, and
they raise the battlecry that thereby America's fundamental liberties are being endangered. They are appalled at the action of New
York State in authorizing free transportation to school for all its
children, regardless of creed; of Kansas for authorizing free transportation and textbooks alike.

But they can only maintain such a truly un-American position
at the price of fellowship with an ever-increasing and more repug-

nant body of educational radicals who will strike down in reality those liberties which Catholicism, despite all misconceptions as to its true nature, is bent upon maintaining. I believe that more and more non-Catholic educational leaders will come to see this point, and will eventually align themselves with Catholics in demanding some form of religious instruction, according to their several religious affiliations, for all children in the public schools, and a more just distribution of the burden of taxation for the benefit of parents who send their children to institutions where God's Name is held in honor.

Inquiring Unbelievers

MAY, 1939

FROM VARIOUS SOURCES a suggestion has frequently been made that the time has come for Catholics to emphasize those matters in which they disagree with the non-Catholic world around them rather than those things in which we agree. By so doing, it is claimed, our position will be more firmly established and we shall be rid of compromise, fiction and lessening of sacred truth.

The suggestion comes with especial force since we see that the unity of society cannot be built upon a watered-down version of Christian truths. The foundations of society, like the foundations of our own American Republic, are undermined when natural truths are not confirmed and clarified by supernatural Revelation; when natural morality is not aided by divine grace.

Let us lay squarely before non-Catholics our Catholic teaching on the Divinity of Christ and the Mystical Body, the Holy Eucharist, the teaching authority of the Church, and so on. Even if to hear of such truths is unwelcome, better that they stand the shock, and let the chips fall where they may.

If those who urge this emphasis mean that we have no reason for reticence concerning any point in Catholic doctrine; that we give a false view of the Church by confining ourselves solely to those things wherein we agree, or seem to agree, it deserves all approval. Moreover, the non-Catholic world of today at least in the United States, appears anxious to hear our most characteristic doctrines taught and explained. There exists a considerable natural curiosity about these teachings, and that we are unfair to ourselves and others if we refuse to gratify their desire for knowledge. A stream of inquiries that comes to the office of *America* from non-Catholic publications, organizations and individuals bears this out. The same

71

is the experience, as far as I know, of many other Catholic editors throughout the land.

Some of these inquiries are merely about ecclesiastical protocol, the difference between a Monsignor and a Canon, etc.; but many others are on essential points of religious difference.

A religious study club of Jewish young men and women in our neighborhood asked a local priest to talk to them on Catholic teachings. He chose the Sacraments and the Christlife; and learned from the long question period that followed that they were deeply interested in this topic as it was remote from their ordinary way of thinking.

Surely we should welcome a genius who could dramatize, in symbolic mystery-play or pageant form, one or the other great dogmas of the Faith, surround it with the best of the World's Fair splendor, and produce it on Broadway.

Father Joseph de Reviers, who designed the Pontifical Pavilion at the Paris Exposition, believes that popularity will soon turn her steps from the motion picture to the museum. Themes for the movies are running dry, and even historical themes will run short; while people crave the popular, psychologically construed exhibit, especially an exhibit of the progressive type, which leads you in logical sequence and imaginative interest from room to room. But what exhibit could be more absorbing than religion? No Soviet anti-religious exhibits can approach it in interest. People welcome in such an exhibit not only the statistical, cultural and ceremonial side of the Church—the Cloisters Museum in New York is a cultural exhibit—but the inner sanctum of Catholic doctrine: the Church as we see it, Christ dwelling and working in a world of souls.

There is, however, room for a very considerable error in all this plan for presenting to non-Catholics chiefly those things in which we *disagree*. It is erroneous to think that we can do so without also emphasizing very clearly those things in which we agree. Merely to challenge with disagreement and say nothing about agreement may be a picturesque pose. It may give the challenger a feeling that he is a brave, uncompromising soul, ready to take on every newcomer. It may inspire his own interior life. But it is subject to the fatal difficulty that words which spell nothing but disagreement are words spoken to deaf ears. Not only they are not listened to, but if listened to they are unintelligible, as were the vociferations of the Russian aviators to the fishermen on Miscou Island.

Most of those who have labored as parish priests in a religiously mixed community have seen, often to their sorrow, how little impression is made upon the average non-Catholic mind by the mere display of Catholic doctrine unless some bridge of common understanding is there to make intelligible the high formulae of the Faith. There are always some exceptions, some souls who are intuitively drawn, under the direct influence of divine grace, to a love even for those mysteries of the Catholic religion, such as the Mass and the Sacred Liturgy, which at first sight appear unintelligible. But these remain exceptions, and the majority of men crave some common ground of understanding.

Not of understanding alone, but of sympathy and interest: some sense that the unfamiliar truths are a *good* for them, is required. If the non-Catholic sees in what the Catholic propounds nothing but antagonism to his own person, particularly to what he himself holds sacred, rightly or wrongly, no matter how glittering and splendid that truth may be, no matter how passionate the conviction of the Catholic himself, there can be no initial approach.

Divine Grace, you say, will, or should, create such sympathy. But Divine Grace, which is the operation of the Holy Spirit, prefers not to create sympathy out of nothing, but rather to build upon and perfect that which is naturally present. We should and must work with the Holy Ghost, but we cannot just strut along our self-chosen pathways and leave to God what God expects us to do for ourselves.

The heart of this matter lies in a little-observed fact, that in the present-day American world, thanks in great measure to our de-religionized education and the poison drunk in from a capitalistic society, an immense number of those basic religious and moral truths have dropped out of the minds of our unthinking citizenry, which in former years did form a common ground or basis for conveying an idea of what we really believe. Due to this fact, our situation with them is not unlike a contact with the pagans. The situation, in some respects, is worse than with the pagans, for those truths which have dropped out have been supplanted by other positive rejections of basic Christian principles.

To express the matter in a more formal way:

Any declaration of Catholic teaching that we make to our fellow-man, whether or not he be of our own belief, will be based upon a syllogism. The major proposition of that syllogism is some general truth to which all religiously minded or at least reasonable men should agree. The minor proposition is some particular truth, which we can verify through some generally accepted source, such as the Gospels or the testimony of history. The conclusion is the particular point of teaching which we try to explain.

Thus we say, for instance (as a major proposition), that if Christ founded a Church, He must have endowed that Church with certain marks or signs which would make it known. The minor proposition reads: But the Catholic Church possesses such marks or signs; and the conclusion: Therefore the Catholic Church is the Church founded by Christ.

Such reasoning, if it could have got a hearing, could have brought conviction in Puritan Boston a hundred years ago. It brings conviction to many thousands of our non-Catholics in the United States at the present day who have retained a sense of the meaning of such a major proposition. But it is empty discourse to millions who have never heard of Christ; who know nothing about Him if they have heard of Him; who have not the remotest conception of what a "Church" is or might be, or why or how it might be "founded," or what difference it would make to anybody if it were founded.

If the "time has come," therefore, to speak to the non-Catholic world about the matters in which we disagree with them, the time has emphatically come to speak to them about the things in which we in some way agree with them, in order to speak intelligibly, let alone acceptably, of the truths we wish to convey. The Apostles themselves, following Christ's example, were careful to establish points of agreement with those to whom they spoke, recalling the Old Testament to the Jews, the Greek poets to the Athenians.

Suppose that I wish to confront, to challenge if you will, the non-Catholic public with the doctrine of the Immaculate Conception of the Holy Mother of God. Even after overcoming the usual gross misconception, that the Immaculate Conception of Mary means the Virgin Birth of Christ, how many "majors" need to be supplied to the man in the street of our times before he can accept either minor or conclusion! That there is a God, a God in Three Divine Persons; that a Person became man; that man is descended from First Parents; that sin exists; that sin destroyed the supernatural life for the first man and woman and their descendants; that this supernatural life is supreme good and its loss supreme evil; that it is connected with personal sin; that the God-Man had a Mother; that we are concerned about that Mother—and so on—this is merely skimming the surface of the "majors" that must evidently be supplied if we are to "challenge" the world with the *Immaculata*. But there are subtler yet, even more fatal omissions from current religious consciousness: the idea of worship, the idea of sin, or personal responsibility, of personal holiness, of the significance of anything spiritual, of the community—through time and space—of man and his generations, of permanence, of objective truth, of the validity of human reason—again, a long list.

Now acknowledging this is not defeatism. It is merely an attempt to substitute realism for romance. We can, and should, hurl the challenge of Catholic truth into the teeth of the modern unbelieving, materialistic world. But the "hurling" must be done upon the basis of those ideas that are already understood and are commonly acceptable, before our message can appear to the modern non-religious consciousness as anything else than sounding brass and tinkling cymbal.

Though the teaching of the Faith implies a syllogism, the world is not converted by syllogisms. Teaching of the Faith brings scant conviction unless accompanied by practice. If our lives demonstrate the Christian ideal of purity, personal love of Christ Crucified, uncompromising justice and superabundant charity, we shall have little difficulty in supplying "majors" for the argument.

Saint Frances Cabrini

NOVEMBER, 1938

THE CHURCH, on November 13, 1938, raised Mother Francesca Saverio Cabrini, foundress of the Missionary Sisters
of the Sacred Heart of Jesus, to the lofty honors of beatification. Her life was duly scrutinized by the usual exhaustive
procedure which must establish the heroic practice of the virtues
of faith, hope and charity; and Almighty God has seen fit to witness to His beloved by two miracles, incontestably proved. One of
these, the cure in infancy of the seminarian, Peter Smith, took
place in the United States, the field of a great part of Mother
Cabrini's apostolic efforts.

If we took Mother Cabrini's life as an answer, we should say
that sanctity consists in doing a great many most astonishing things,
all of which were evidently needed for the good of society and the
salvation of souls. But the definition does not fit, for other people
have established hospitals, schools and orphan asylums without
thereby winning the crown of beatification; while, on the other
hand, vast hosts of the Blessed have left not a line of writing, nor
a rule of foundation, nor a brick or stone behind to mark their
passage through this earth. They lived and loved, but they were
not creators of the visible and tangible.

In the case of Mother Cabrini, her *being*, in the full sense of the
word, thus her sanctity, was expressed in an extraordinary series of
tremendous activities, which shuttled her to and fro over half the
world and back again, month after month, year after year, planning, founding, building, in Italy, France, England and Spain; in
New York, Chicago, Seattle, Denver, Los Angeles; in Nicaragua,
Costa Rica, Panama; in Buenos Aires, Rio de Janeiro. She hurries
back from Brazil to New York and thence to Italy to arrange for
a foundation; stops off fifteen days in London and establishes a
house there on her way back to America. She is pre-eminently the

organizing type of saint; not the hidden contemplative, not the quiet teacher, not the world-fleeing penitent.

Her entire life is a steady, logical development of an initial principle, which fascinated her imagination as a serious, studious, cheerful thirteenth child of a well-to-do agriculturist in Lombardy. She grew to maturity in her rude experience as a country schoolteacher, when she had the strange experience of taking a vow of obedience to a more or less crazy and perfectly impossible spinster, not a nun; then to find her supposed superior immediately deposed and herself placed by the Bishop at the head of the little teaching community in her stead. Later ensued the following dialog toward the end of 1880 (she was then thirty years old, being born July 15, 1850); and it closed the long years of obscure labors and hidden crosses and misunderstandings which would have broken any less chivalrous spirit.

The Bishop of Lodi, the pious and zealous Msgr. Jelmini, called her to him and said:

"I know that you want to become a missionary Sister. I know no religious institutes of that character. Found one yourself."

Francesca Cabrini, reflecting a few minutes, then looked up at the Bishop and said in a firm voice: "I will look for a house, *Cercherò una casa.*"

Brief as this dialog was, it epitomized her whole exterior life, which revolved from that moment until her last breath around two poles: a complete authorization or commission for what she was to do; and then the search for a house—and invariably she found it. All her works she started in utter poverty; all of them she left in flourishing condition.

Her assurance in having obtained her commissions frequently dismayed the local ecclesiastical authorities. At first they were startled by the sudden appearance of this black-clad, blue-eyed figure who always had a perfectly clear idea of what poor, sick, orphaned Italians needed in the way of a residence or a school or a hotel to be transformed as she saw fit. But they soon became her warmest friends, and strong men were won by the dauntlessness of a woman, whose own strength lay not in any psychologic masterfulness but in any unshakeable faith in Divine goodness and Divine Providence.

The Archbishop of Rio de Janeiro found her with a broom in her hand when he visited her newly established house in his diocese. Pretending, in gentlemanly fashion, not to recognize her, he asked to see "The Mother General." She bowed, pointed to the parlor where His Grace would be seated, and soon reappeared minus broom and apron in all the dignity of a Most Reverend Mother.

The story of Mother Cabrini's wanderings and works is a vast epic. It is in the line of Mother Marie de l'Incarnation, in the seventeenth century; of Mother Elizabeth Seton, in the early nineteenth; of her own contemporary, friend and protectress in her early years of difficult foot-hold-seeking in Rome: Mother Marie of the Passion, foundress of the Franciscan Missionary Sisters of Mary; and, indeed, of the great Saint Teresa of Avila, with her famous "foundations," to whose joyous intercession Francesca Cabrini turned when traveling over desolate roads in Spain at one of the most trying moments in her long career.

Her life meant numberless voyages over a sea which she dreaded in her youth but loved in her later years as a moon-lit, limitless image of the strange, stormy yet all-bearing and ever-kindly Providence of God. It meant trips on mule-back at literally breath-taking altitudes in the Andes. It meant descending into the bowels of Colorado mines to give between blows of the pick a word of spiritual advice to Italian laborers. It meant hours spent in back-parlors of cheap restaurants of London; looking for orphan children in the suburbs of Paris; hot summer months in the east-side New York tenements of the nineties; talks on shipboard with Catholic Negro stevedores from Jamaica; rescuing bewildered Italians from being lynched by angry mobs; refusing the Queen of Spain's request to have two of the Sisters teach Christian Doctrine to the *princesas*—for fear lest the plain-minded Missionaries might become less plain-minded from contact with court life.

Then, too, it meant being architect and contractor and stone-mason and everything else when a twelve-month job of remodeling had to be completed in eight; it meant walking into the president's office of an Eastern college, who had never thought of selling the institution, calmly asking his price because it was what she needed for her work, and winning his consent at her own figure.

The most astonishing thing about Mother Cabrini's exploits is not their multiplicity and vastness, but the fact that they were carried out with a wretched physical instrument, a body shaken and torn by chronic malaria. Quivering with fever, Francesca Cabrini would set out to cross continents and oceans; yet never lost her tranquil, unalterable inner poise. As her gifted biographer, Nello Vian, remarks, she was a woman of essentials. Nothing could ever distract her from the work to which a boundless love of God and man impelled her soul: to bring salvation and comfort to the millions of Italian emigrants through the world.

The first Retreat I ever gave was to Mother Cabrini and her orphans and her Sisters and miscellaneous friends at West Park, in 1906. I remember that she rather alarmed me then; I had the feeling of meeting a relentless though pious *réalizatrice*, one who got stupendous things done, but made everyone rather uncomfortable in doing so. But as I analyze this recollection I see that most of that judgment came from the circumstances not from the person herself. The circumstances were the frightful spiritual and temporal conditions into which our own neglect and, be it said, contempt, had plunged the Italian emigrants who came to our shores; and those circumstances lent a certain harshness to any life which, as hers did, attempted not to pick out a few "nice" Italians from the mass, but to drag thousands and millions into light and health and salvation with one terrific pull of the net, tumbling the fish out upon the shore, helter-skelter, with scant guide or measure but the immeasurable love of God.

The harshness of her task was mirrored in the rather mournful garb of her Sisters; their rigid adherence to certain Old World customs as to heating and other concessions to human nature; and her own insistent pushing forward of her spiritual kingdom despite all obstacles.

On the contrary, the letters and the intimate outpourings of Francesca Cabrini reveal a most sweet and delicate soul. Most of all, they reveal the dazzling beauty of the inmost principle of her life, which made her say that while few are called to practice heroic austerities during their life, all are called to bear the "crucifixion of the spirit," which purifies and transforms the soul. The center of her life was not in dreams of outward achievements, but far within, in what she called the "mystic sleep of the soul," the utter oblation of the Spouse of Christ to her Lord and Lover.

It was in 1887 that the apostolic Msgr. Scalabrini, Bishop of Piacenza, proposed to Mother Cabrini to go to the United States. Leo XIII sealed her life's work with his succinct advice: "Not to the East—China and Japan—but to the West." In August, 1903, she acquired the old North Shore Hotel in Chicago, which was turned into the Columbus Hospital. At her death she had founded some thirty institutions in this country and abroad. Today, there are 3,584 of her Religious, with four novitiates and seven hospitals in the United States. The East did claim her in the end, for her Sisters came eventually to Shanghai, in China.

So the Sisters were right, in instinct, if not in liturgy, who had prepared the altar not for a Requiem Mass but for a white Mass of thanksgiving when we buried her at West Park in January 1, 1918. Her body had been brought on there from Chicago where she had died in December 22, 1917, the nuns praying every instant of the way. I had experienced more elaborate funerals, but not a more austere one, for the temperature was twenty-five degrees below zero, the chapel was unheated, and my companion and I had walked across the Hudson on the five-foot-thick ice from Poughkeepsie. Literally-minded, the three of us, headed by the Reverend Rector of the Redemptorist House of Studies at Esopus, insisted upon the usual "black Mass." But inwardly we felt we were beaten: those who knew her as none others knew her would one day see her glory emerge from her tomb as they assured us it would, and God would glorify to the whole world the humble schoolteacher of Vidardo who covered three continents and two hemispheres with the net of her passionate love.

Christian Humanism

MAY, 1953

THE FOLLOWING LINES are a fragment of what I might hope to pursue sometime at greater length. They may stimulate others to examine certain neglected aspects of Christian Humanism.

The pressure for an adequate statement of Christian Humanism arises from a multitude of different sources, bearing upon the position of the Church in the modern world.

Humanistic Problems of Modern Life

1. Social scientists are concerned with preserving the integrity of the home amid the immense dislocations of modern life: physical, cultural and geographical. The Catholic sociologist is confronted with the choice of showing how these conditions may be altered, for instance, by lessening the gap between rural and urban life; by changing our family-preventing housing shortage and materialistic real-estate policies, or by building up a moral resistance to these disruptive influences among those who must perforce submit to them.

It is still not quite clear just what elements in our modern urbanized and industrialized life are most hostile to Christian Humanism and to which of them we may eventually become adapted. Distributed ownership of property is a basic factor in the stability of the social order, yet the principle is not so easy of concrete application. In view of the high price Catholic social teaching sets upon the stabilizing effect of individual ownership, I was sometimes surprised to note the relatively small value placed upon it by the conservative rural population of Southern Maryland. The ownership of the land as a human factor did not seem to enter to any great extent into the lives of our rural Catholic people in that region:

into the lives of many of them it did not enter at all. Stable tenancy sufficed for their economic needs, and the permanence of the social milieu counted for much more than the mere soil.

A proper evaluation in the light of humanism of the disrupting conditions of modern life presupposes an evaluation of humanism itself. How far is it *human* to live in perpetual mobility—physical and social—and in contact with the thoughts and actions of mankind all over the world? How far can we survive, humanistically speaking, an increasingly standardized existence? Our answer to such questions will be determined by our concept of what balance and proportion in his life man is obliged to retain. With regard to our country population almost anywhere in the United States, it is often quite remarkable to see how much they have been able to retain of their traditional human values despite the incredible transformation worked in their lives by the change from the horse-and-buggy to the mechanized age.

Appeal of the Ideologies

2. Pressure, too, for the development of a Christian Humanism arises from the humanistic appeal of the totalitarian ideologies. Communist propaganda in this country among the minority groups does not bank solely upon their feelings of resentment. Recent studies of communism in Italy (cf. Panfilo Gentile in *New York Times Magazine* for December 7, 1952) note that the toughest strongholds of communism in the Italian peninsula are not the most socially disadvantaged areas, but regions like Tuscany which are relatively stable and prosperous. There is hardly any stop in the humanistic register which they have not at one time or another pulled out in their dealings with the American Negro: decency, respectability, love of home and family, peace, family stability, etc. Along with this is the totalitarian appeal to other and more dynamic elements of a humanistic nature: the love of adventure, of far horizons and mighty social changes, of universal fellowship, or else of sheer love of power for power's sake; the bait held out to the purged victims like Slansky and Clementis in Czechoslovakia.

It is imperative, yet not enough to combat the hydra-headed Communist conspiracy. Its tentacles grow as long as we offer no clear-cut Christian syntheses in response to its allurements.

At one of the weekly social forums of the Catholic Interracial Council in New York City, a zealous St. Vincent de Paul Society worker described how on his round of visits he had gone to the aid of an habitual drunkard. Himself a Negro, he presented to his Negro friend just two thoughts. One was the fact that he was interested in his neighbor simply for the love of Jesus Christ our Lord, whose image he saw in the drink-sodden wretch sprawled upon a bed in filth and squalor. He told him likewise that Christ Our Lord was offering him the gift of a new integrity, a completely restored personality, if he would but beg God's grace and make the few simple decisions that God's grace was asking of him. The appeal struck home, and a new man arose out of the moral ruins.

In the question period that followed at the forum, one of the interrogators was a non-Catholic, a former Communist, who had undergone a genuine and sincere conversion. "What so deeply moves me," he said, "in hearing of this occurrence, is the thought that I used, too, to try to offer a similar hope to the down-and-outs I met with as an active Communist. But my hands were empty. I could speak of ideals, but I could not give them love. That is what you, as a Catholic, are able to give your fellowman."

I mention this event merely to note the tremendous spiritual strength of the Christian who can successfully present his Christain faith where it is seen in direct relation to the most profound spiritual needs of his fellowman: where it appeals to the instinct of self-respect and the hope of really living as an image of God.

One-sided Evasions

3. An urgency to discover the full stature of Christian Humanism arises from the opposite end of the ideological spectrum. If we fail to present effectively the real Christian opposite to totalitarian humanism, our Catholic people will take refuge in a number of escapes and counterfeits. The most obvious of these is the passion

of extreme nationalism, with its dangerous brood: flight from the obligations of the international community; violent suspicions and reactions to people of other nations or national origins: exclusionist immigration policies, nationalistic myths, etc.

Nationalistic humanism gains impetus by selecting some of the more appealing elements in true Christian Humanism. The death of the brilliant French author, journalist, and political leader, Charles Maurras, recalls the skill with which he won a small army of followers through his violently French brand of nationalistic humanism. Avowedly agnostic in tendency, it paraded a noisy devotion to the Catholic Church as an element of law and order in a socially and politically disordered period.

A certain humanistic satisfaction lies in the mere combating of ideologies: and a clear and completely worthy goal, the fellowship of likeminded people interesting studies of human history and psychology, a sense of high adventure and even of power, as the work advances. When the original purpose grows dim, these attractions can become ends in themselves. What began as a defense of God and country may degenerate into another ideology, with its own special pitfall.

On several occasions our Holy Father, Pope Pius XII, has singled out for sharp condemnation a type of escape which is also a by-product of the neglect of a genuine humanism: a one-sided view of our task as Christians, in which we tend to one or the other of the two extremes of relying solely upon supernatural means or of neglecting them and so immersing ourselves in the material or the bureaucratic.

Under the pretense of saving the Church from the risk of being led astray in the "temporal" sphere, a slogan launched some ten years ago continues to gain acceptance: return to the purely "spiritual." And by that it is understood that the Church should confine her activities to a purely dogmatic teaching, to the offering of the Holy Sacrifice, the administration of the sacraments, and that all incursion into, or even the right of examination into, the domain of public life, all intervention in the civil or social order should be denied her. As if dogma did not have a bearing upon every aspect of human life, as if the mysteries of the faith with their supernatural wealth, were not to maintain and invigorate the lives of individuals and, as a logical consequence, to harmonize public life with the law of God, to impregnate it with the spirit of Christ! Such vivisection is nothing short of being anti-Catholic.

The slogan should be the very opposite: be present everywhere for the faith, for Christ, in every way and to the utmost possible limit, wherever vital interests are at stake, wherever laws bearing on the worship of God, marriage, the family, the school, the social order are proposed and discussed (Allocution of Pope Pius XII to the Congress of the International Union of Catholic Women's Leagues, Rome, September 11, 1947.)

If he possesses this character of love and respect toward the Divine order, the Catholic writer will know how to guard himself against mute servility as well as against uncontrolled criticism. With a firm clarity he will contribute toward the formation of a Catholic opinion within the Church, above all when, as is the case today, this opinion vacillates between an illusory and unreal spirituality and a defeatist and materialistic realism. Keeping itself far from these two extremes, the Catholic press must exert among the faithful its influence upon public opinion within the Church. It is only in this manner that it will be able to avoid all the ideas which are false by excess or defect regarding the role of the Church in the temporal order, and in our days particularly, with respect to the social question and the problem of peace. (Allocution of Pope Pius XII to the International Convention of the Catholic Press, February 18, 1950.)

Vitalizing of Social Action

4. Finally the very exigencies of Catholic social action demand a further exploration of the possibilities of Christian Humanism. We all rejoice at the marvelous growth of the Church in the world and especially in the United States; and we pray that this growth may continue. We are impressed with the sheer quantitative growth, as seen in the Catholic population, new dioceses, new missions, new territories won to Christ. We rejoice also at the Church's interior development: her multiple activities and her contacts with the world around us.

Yet in all this lies a certain danger. The vaster the Church, the heavier the weight of centralized administration, the more difficult is access to this administration by any part of the increased whole. Great is the temptation to develop a bureaucracy, and with it a loss in the sense of that cohesion that inherited from the days when the Church was but a struggling minority. Pick up the Catholic Directory for 1852, and you can read it through at one sitting, index and all. But who will undertake to read straight through Kennedy's mighty volume for 1952?

Social action can flourish for a time in unorganized fashion, yet organization of some sort is of its essence. Once it becomes, in the words of Pius XI, a *preventive* charity, which deals with the intricate and specialized causes of human disorders, from its nature it must set up an increasingly elaborate organization. But such organization is humanly deadening if it lacks the breath of spirituality which will convert the very human fact of organized work into a new and powerful means for leading a Christ-like life. This was the genius of St. Ignatius Loyola in spiritualizing the labors of the apostolate, as did St. Vincent de Paul for organized remedial charity, and Ozanam with the layman's participation in the work of St. Vincent. Much of the highest type of Catholic action today lies in the intensive development of a mature and responsible Catholic laity of both sexes. Such development, however, presupposes Christian Humanism as an ideal and as a way of life. It means the careful study of the relation of the ultimate and most sublime supernatural motives to the exigencies of the rounded, morally mature personality.

Restoration of Reason

Several elements seem vital to any such deepening and strengthening of lay responsibility so as to equip it for the task imposed by the Church's worldwide mission. One of these is the restoration of the integrity of ordinary human reason, a basic human value for which a large sector of the modern intellectual world has lost the key. This implies the *revaluation* of ideas and of language itself which have become devaluated in modern times. In the process of such revaluation we shall avoid the errors which in times past led to contrary errors: a largely nominal and abstract presentation of the doctrinal content of our Faith; a stubborn refusal to exemplify its full meaning in our daily lives. For if we, in our conduct as Catholics show that we devaluate our understanding of natural moral principles, the modern world and the youth of today will soon devaluate their thought. From this it is a natural step towards the devaluation of the language of revelation itself, of our Faith, towards a crass and deceptive "modernism."

The Layman's Mission

Crucial in the philosophy of Christian Humanism is the complete reconciliation of two apparently conflicting claims on the mind and heart of man. How are we to reconcile man's full status and obligations as a citizen of this world with his status and obligations as a citizen of the Kingdom of God? The difficulty of this reconciliation appears whenever there arises the question of the Church's espousal of basic natural rights. The Church, like the prophets of ancient Israel never ceases to proclaim and to defend these rights, and the violation of one of them—defrauding laborers of their wages—is stigmatized in traditional Christian teaching as a "sin which calls to Heaven for vengeance." Where the violations are simple and obvious the moral question raises little difficulty from a practical point of view. Where, however, the violations of natural rights are more complicated and unusual, a certain spiritual difficulty arises, as in the kindred field of highly developed preventive charity.

Where shall we find the genuine middle course and not be led into either of the two extremes which Pope Pius XII so sharply denounces: that of a mistaken escape into an exaggerated supernaturalism, or an equally mistaken lapse into a doctrinaire, materialistic humanitarianism? Yet work along these lines is eminently part of the Catholic layman's mission to the modern world.

It is for him to present in personal example, in teaching, and through his organizing and administrative ability, the synthesis of a transcendent, supernatural love and an unflinching insistence upon the complete gamut of natural rights and duties that attach to the persons and groups in the complex modern world. The unbelieving mind is quick to note a conflict or an inconsistency between the supreme role of the Catholic's allegiance and the scheme of activities in which he is immersed. By the same token it is deeply moved when, as in the simpler instance of the St. Vincent de Paul visitor, all his efforts evidently spring from one fundamental source, one basic faith and conviction.

It is not enough to send our laymen out into the domestic or the international world and bid them wrestle with the problem as they may. In the papal utterances on questions of the day they will find a remarkable harmony of natural and supernatural considerations, showing how absent is the aforesaid conflict from the mind of the Church itself. Yet to translate this harmony into practical life, and bring the full impact of the love and following of Christ into the sphere of long-distance, organized social activity is not solved by a few general considerations. We need an elaboration of Christian philosophy and asceticism, and the kerygmatic theology presented in our revised college religion curriculum. We need to interpret the problem in our retreats for the laity, men and women, and to devote much more intensive formation to small groups for the apostolate. Our goal is not the one-track zealot nor the shrewd opportunist, but the *formed* personality, who will combine mature judgment with an equally mature emotional and intellectual attitude when faced by the exciting and disturbing issues of peace and cold and hot war.

Such a Christ-centered and world oriented humanism demands a high degree of personal dedication, a love of Christ and of His Cross, with all that that means in personal self-denial, and the spiritual sustenance of the Holy Eucharist: Sacrifice and Sacrament.

In this brief discourse I have dwelt more upon the synthesis than upon the analysis of the concept of Christian Humanism. The heart of the question, from a practical point of view, lies in the exactitude and finish with which we speak *one* message of the *one* Jesus, with relation to all things, whether they be on earth or in heaven: wherever they touch in any way upon the Kingdom of God. The selected elements of that great whole can work harm as often as they work good, and the history of Christianity is littered with examples to this effect. We cannot combat monism—philosophical, anti-religious or political—by a pseudo-monism of our own, nor yet by a disjointed and imperfectly articulated dualism. Ours is the humanism and the dualism of the God-Man, who has made all things one, whether they be near or afar off, the inner mystery of the individual as well as the kingdom universal in space and time. It is this truth that we must "do in charity," and not let it be diminished or distorted. It is our only ultimately effective weapon against false humanisms. At the same time, it is open to welcome all that is genuine in the vast wealth of natural humanistic discoveries of our day. I see no reason why our Catholic thought cannot mature into this image.

The Church and Catherine Frances

(a letter to three grandnieces)

OCTOBER, 1953

Dear Trio

I am addressing you collectively since it would be quite a job
to write to you singly. I feel that some report might be due to you
as to what really went on last Saturday. All kinds of things happened, and from my point of view it began with Margaret, who
was there at the station ready to greet me when I arrived from New
York. Somewhere in the distance she pointed out her dad where-
upon we proceeded to Prospect Street to pick up Mummy and the
baby and Mrs. Woolsey and Barkie (Is that what you call her?—
a queer kind of a name). Incidentally, your grandma decided finally
that I am Uncle John, so that is now my official title. Margaret
thought it was all right to go ahead, as long as she would be
present. The weather could not have been better. It was 72 degrees
Fahrenheit at 10:30 a.m., humidity 40, wind from the SSE at 13½
miles an hour, barometer 30.40. Things were no worse in the
United Nations last Saturday than they had been any time during
the week, and President Eisenhower was said to be optimistic
about the agrarian situation in spite of the difficulties of Secretary
Benson.

When we arrived at Mount Carmel Church we found that
your two very courageous great-great aunts had beaten us to it,
Miss Edith and Miss Jane. Wasn't it wonderful their coming! And I
think they thoroughly enjoyed it. Then everybody turned up and
they all greeted Father Daly, pastor of Mount Carmel, who knows
the family from of old. Henry appeared, and Mary Lathrop and
two of their three, and then your Uncle Bancel was there and
Mr. Edgar Wilcock turned up to be godfather and Mrs. Wilcock
and their daughter Edith who took the place of godmother Sheila,

who was unable to attend. Father Daly welcomed us into the church and everyone sat down a little while in front of the lovely sanctuary that your great-Uncle Bancel and Uncle Tom had decorated, and the wonderful window of Our Lady of Mount Carmel.

I forgot to say the baby was there too, as of course she was essential, and before the ceremony took place we recorded her name in the parish register. So if you don't believe what I say, you can go there and look it up.

The baptistry is away down in the rear of the little church just where you enter, so Father Daly arranged to have the ceremony in three stages: first, outside the Communion rail as representing one outside the church asking to come in, then inside the Communion rail, and finally we all, including your two great-great aunts and everybody else, and Margaret too, walked down to the baptistry and there we all saw the baptism itself. This was quite a job, because the baptistry is a very small room. But Father Daly managed it by putting Ted and his sister on a table, and I forget where we put Margaret but she was fixed in somehow, and we nearly left Mummy out, but we got her in at the last moment so she could make sure it was being done right. We called her Catherine Frances, and Mummy can explain to you all about the name. If I had my own way entirely, I might have called her Therese, since it was the feast of St. Thérèse of Jesus. But possibly when Catherine Frances comes to be confirmed she can take Therese for a Confirmation name as she was baptized on her feast day, October 3.

But still you will be asking me just what did happen, so I'll try to explain. Catherine Frances began with an examination. As we stood before the Communion rail she was being held by Edith Wilcock and was very good and slept all the time; I mean Catherine Frances did. She was asked questions by the Church; not by just Mount Carmel or just a diocese or just one part of the Church, but she was asked questions by the whole Church, the Church throughout the world, the whole living Church, not only of today but of all time. She was asked these questions not just by the Church on earth but also by the Church in Heaven, the Church of all the blessed and saints and triumphant souls who were with us that day in spirit. The questions were very simple, the same questions that you ask when anybody comes to your house. If someone turns up and you go to the door at 625 Angell Street the first thing you ask them is what do you want? And so the Church asked Catherine Frances: What do you want? And immediately she answered, what I'm looking for is the answer to the question of my own destiny. What do I want? What does God tell me that I should want? What am I here for? What's it all about? I haven't that answer inside of me. I can look and look and search and search, but I have no answer with all my little human wits. I have to turn to God's voice and see what He says, and that answer is what we call faith. And so she said to the Church when the Church asked her what she wanted, she said "Faith." So then the Church spoke to Catherine Frances again and this time said to her, "What has God revealed and made known to men that He can give you as an answer to the question of your destiny?" And there again she made a very wonderful answer: "Life everlasting." She could not have made that answer out of her own brain. She was only able to make that answer because 2,000 years ago Jesus Christ, Who was invisibly baptizing her on this occasion, had told people that He would give people life everlasting. He would not just simply give them the promise of life everlasting, something in the future, but He would through His Church give them life everlasting now, just put it right in them, as the doctor puts physical life in you when he makes you well. You remember that the Samaritan woman stopped and talked to Him as He was resting at the wellside. He asked her if she would give Him a drink of cold water from the well, and then He told her that He could give her something more wonderful than any cold water, than anything on earth; He could give her an eternal freshness, a water which would spring up into eternal life.

Then Catherine Frances had a question to ask the Church, a very natural question which came right from the preceding ones. She did not need actually to say it, because it was immediately understood. The Church said to her: "If you want to enter into

everlasting life you must do certain things." For the unexpressed
question in her own mind was, if I have everlasting life what must
I do. And the Church said very simply, you must keep the
Commandments and you must love God above all things, and you
must love your neighbor as yourself. Christ our Lord has given
that life to the Church to pass on to you, but you must love God
and you must love your neighbor in order to keep it; otherwise
that gift will be taken away from you.

The Church then proceeded to instruct Catherine Frances and
though she was apparently asleep I am sure those words somehow went into her mind and soul. The Church reminded her
that it was going to be a struggle to keep this gift. Sometimes it
is a very terrible and bitter struggle. She would be battling with
pride, selfishness and all the things that drag us down, and there
was a spiritual enemy who would feel deep resentment because he
had felt that she was part of his kingdom and his possession, and
now he was driven out by the light and glorious power of the
Son of God, and he would be forever lurking to see if he could
regain the territory in her soul that he lost; and so strong, harsh
words were said by the Church against this enemy and he was
reminded that he no longer belonged here, that the cross of Christ
had banned him forever, that he was conquered and vanquished
and crushed, and that he must stay far away from this creature of
God.

Then she must be very steadfast, and she would need wisdom to
choose what was right, and so the Church put a bit of salt in her
mouth. But to make sure that she fully grasped it, once more she
was examined and pointedly the Church asked her, if she promised
to do what was right, did she promise not only not to do wicked
and criminal things, but did she promise not to be deceived by the
illusion of this world, all those curious things that operate in the
imagination, that come to us in the twilight between the mind and
the body, in that intermediate place of our being where reason
gives way to passion, and passion plays havoc with reason. She was
asked to renounce these illusions and to make certain promises
which she would repeat again all through her life at solemn mo-

ments even to the hour of death. And finally the Church said to her directly: Do you wish, Catherine Frances, to be baptized? She answered without any hesitation, "I will." Yet, exacting as was the lesson, wonderful and great were the promises the Church made, because the Church promised that she would have a claim on the grace of God, on His guidance day and night, even in hours of darkness, agony, confusion, dreariness and desolation. That grace was always there. The Church made her repeat the Creed so that her faith would remain unchanged. The Church invited everybody there and we all joined in, the great-aunts, the grandma, and Mummy and all the in-laws and uncles and aunts and cousins all joined in the wonderful prayer of the Our Father, in which we united ourselves with Catherine Frances in that prayer which she would be reciting every day of her life, always being heard, always gaining new riches and power and wisdom through its recitation. So it all ended on a note of victory, a victory symbolized by the candle and by the white garment which she would one day bear in glory before the judgment of God.

(I am not reporting on the actual baptism itself when I poured the water on her forehead and said: "Catherine Frances, I baptize thee in the name of the Father and of the Son and of the Holy Spirit," because everyone was there to see that it was done right, and Mr. Wilcock touched her with his hand to show that he was godfather.)

And of course it left with us, too, a query in our minds as to what would be God's plans for the future of Catherine Frances. That, of course, none of us would know, because those plans are mysterious. And yet we know that there is a different plan for each human being. There are different ways by which each of us works out our destiny on earth, and that is only learned by walking day by day with the grace of God. It will be unfolded to her in a continual tapestry of joy and of suffering, light and shade, day and night. If she will be quite faithful to that Divine grace moving into the inmost recesses of her heart and driving her on to a greater and greater love for God and for her fellowman, every now and then she will find God waiting for her, as it were, around the corner of her life and proposing to her some new venture of love, some expansion of her soul, some higher step to which she might climb, some wonder what He will have in store for her. She will learn the mysterious truth that His grace will not be just for her alone but will be for us all along with her, as it were, that none of us becomes more Christlike and closer to God just by ourselves, but that we are all united. So as we examined Catherine Frances that morning, we were all examining ourselves at the same time and repeating in our own minds the same questions and answers that had one day been addressed to us.

One question may have still remained in her mind as she thought of all that would be required of her in life: How can I be sure that I will really walk on the path that has been proclaimed for me? So she looked up at the window through which the bright autumn sun was beaming a few rays, and there may have come to her mind some intuition of the secret of Carmel, that sublime secret that so many miss, so few grasp, and yet those who do not miss it and those who do grasp it are so marvelously happy. That secret was the secret of the saint on whose day she was baptized, the secret of total simplicity, the humility of Christ. She was entering not only into the Kingdom of Christ but she was entering into the humility of Christ, which she symbolized herself in her humility as a little baby, and that humility of Christ would remain with her all through life if she wished to keep it. We see that humility and simplicity in the very little ones and the very aged, and I thought of it as I saw the two great-great aunts there both watching Catherine Frances as she was learning those great lessons. It seemed to remind me of the day when the Child Jesus was taken into the Temple and held there in the arms of the two ancients Simeon and Anna on the day of His Presentation.

There was no use making a prophecy, because none of us were prophets. The only prophet is the Holy Spirit. In three months' time Catherine Frances will begin to show the first flickers of her personality. She will begin to recognize other people; she will begin to recognize other things, that some things are her and some things are not her. And she will begin to use objects and she will begin to make a decision and reach a conclusion, and she will start that long process of thinking and reasoning that will continue, and none of us could tell at that moment what her personality would be. I talked to an East African student recently and asked him about the way children received their names in Uganda, and he said that each clan had its own set of names, some forty or fifty names which were passed down. The child was allotted one of those names, but he or she didn't receive the name until they had been about three months old, and then they were supposed to show their personality and a name was chosen which would resemble that of the person whose name was given to them. A boy, for instance, who belonged to the Lion Clan might receive the name "Mtali," which means a lion, or if it was a girl she would be called Natali, which means a lioness; and then they would be expected to be like a lion or a lioness, as the case might be. Nobody knows what Catherine Frances will have for a personality, but one thing we do know is that personality can only grow in and through the wonderful grace of God that was first given to her that morning at Mount Carmel Church.

Some day years from now, when some of us are gone and the rest of us are dispersed, Catherine Frances may return to that church and that Communion rail and she may once more look up at that glowing window of Our Lady of Mount Carmel. She will ask then, perhaps with very great feeling and perplexity, as to what God wants of her, what is the mystery of her life; and again she will receive the answer that Our Lady of Mount Carmel always gives, the answer of total simplicity, that of doing each day the will of God, each day walking the path that God has laid down for us and taking each day our cross very humbly, each day bearing the burden of our own weakness and taking on the burden of all other men and women and bearing their burdens along with our own and offering them up to God, and in so doing making a perpetual sacrifice of joy and of suffering for ourselves and for all the world.

If she asks that advice she will receive it; she will be told what God wants of her, and if she is wise she will do exactly what He wants and never swerve from it; or if she does swerve from it—because all of us are feeble and changeable—that she will come back once more and ask again.

When it was over we went up to "Acorn," and the Wilcocks sat under a tree and enjoyed a picnic lunch they had brought with them. I had to hurry back to New York and so say a quick good-bye.

Love to Mummy and Dad.

Uncle John

III.

The Church and the World

One might call this the prophetic section, in which an editor has allowed himself to say many things that might or might not please whole groups of readers. It was hardly his business, for instance, to prophesy what a Roman Pontiff would do. Yet summarizing the comprehensive program of our present Holy Father Pius XII, I find that my own prediction was not far off after all. This, of course, the reader can verify for himself. The Holy Father has stressed human unity; he has devoted immense attention to the problems and possibilities of all types of communications; he has initiated far-reaching liturgical reforms, the most recent of these, the new order for Holy Week, being the most extensive liturgical reconstruction since the days of Pope St. Pius V. He has written and spoken amply about questions of human liberty and the freedom of the Church in the modern world, both in the free world and behind the Iron Curtain.

In treating of religion and science as partners the prophet stands on fairly sure ground, though probably a good many would not agree with him. Partners in what? The answer to this question is in the very last line of the paper, namely, in facing problems created by pressure groups and threats of mass terror. Of course if this meant simply that scientists and religionists were both terrified at the impending catastrophes, their accord would not be much more worth than a shotgun wedding. It would have tremendous practical significance but would not go beyond that. But the prophet believes we are advancing beyond the mere all-in-the-same-boat situation. He is not content with simply seeking from science various proofs of an apologetic nature for the existence of God, finality of the Divine providence, spirituality of the soul, etc. Science today, or rather a considerable or respectable section of distinguished scientists both in this country and abroad is coming to respect the intel-

lectual integrity of those who have reached conclusions as to the universe based upon other than purely inductive methods of scientific verification. In the words of C. E. M. Joad, The Recovery of Belief *(Faber and Faber, 1951, pp. 134-135), "No analysis of the physical world in terms purely of sensory experience can ever be exhaustive, since sensory experience gives us information only about what seems and, as Plato insists, we cannot have* knowledge *of what seems; nor, indeed, if I am right, does science purport to give us such knowledge." In other words, "science does not exclude but rather demands the existence of other spheres of reality, known to us by different methods and evoking different kinds of experience, to explain the existence and the workings of the world which science itself studies. What, then, are the spheres of reality which elude the scientific method of approach?* Prima facie, *they are the spheres of ethics, aesthetics and religion."*

These are strong words from a quondam skeptic, but they are in line with other strong words increasingly uttered by men whose minds have been concentrated on profound scientific problems for the last decade or so. In other words, there is a progress of thought much in the line of the late Lecomte du Noüy's Human Destiny.

In this essay I skirt the margin of a pregnant topic which now preoccupies a painstaking area of social research, namely the application of scientific method to the problem of hate. In this sphere science and religion are each talking with little consideration of each other. So I venture the hypothesis that their talk must be coordinated if we are to grapple with this evasive but terribly actual problem in the human scene. Nuclear physics has handed to us and to our enemies the most powerful instrument of hate that the world has ever seen or probably ever will see. It is about time that religion and science should coordinate their efforts to control its use.

Advising Frenchmen as to the way they should feel about Americans or Americans about their proper attitude toward Frenchmen is an ancient and useless occupation. People continue to feel as did the Cockney who indignantly exclaimed " 'Ow can I respect a man who calls a 'at a shappo, and a bird a wazzo?" Or vice versa. I am personally allergic to discussions about national ways and national characteristics. They irritate me as I am alive to the exceptions rather than the rule. Yet in this case where I was asked specifically to address a Franco-American audience on this topic, it looked like the opportunity possibly to help clear up certain pretty serious misunderstandings.

The paper on the lay apostolate or Catholic elite deals with a topic now very widely discussed. In the near future it will probably be still more widely discussed in Catholic circles both here and abroad.

Somebody may warn me that I was belaboring the obvious when I went to such lengths, as I do in the paper on Thought Control, purporting to show how Catholics differ from one another in matters not pertaining to basic faith and morals. Well, that was my aim, to belabor the obvious. Just because it is so obvious I felt it ought to be said and said rather strongly. Nobody actually welcomes disagreement, when you feel you are right, and I find it hard to appreciate the heroic maxim attributed—erroneously I believe—to Voltaire, this idea about defending to the death something that you believe is absolutely untrue. Nevertheless, I deeply resent the notion that others are coerced to agree with me or that I have to agree with them in cases where we can legitimately differ and our beliefs are not prescribed by higher authority. So much is said about the scandal created by disputes among the faithful, about the need of presenting a united front in order to make a united impact on the world around us. If the differences take the form of wrangling, name calling and violent, bitter controversy, there is certainly a scandal. But an equal scandal and in many cases a much greater one is created, if the impression is generated that our respect and reverence for the great truths of faith and morals bind us to a rigid conformity in every detail of our thought and conduct. Our faith offers the answers to the ultimate questions but the answers to the proximate problems we must work out for ourselves.

The retrospect of America's 2,000 weeks speaks for itself. It will show, I think that America's editors have never been inclined to sidestep the issues of the day. It may also indicate what varied aspects those issues take with the advance of time.

The Holy Father's Problems

FEBRUARY, 1939

WHEN IN June, 1938, I received from a Vatican City mes-
senger the familiar white and yellow envelope summon-
ing to a private audience with Pope Pius XI, I experienced a sense of wonder which nothing else in this world could
give. The extraordinary circumstances surrounding his protracted
and painful illness in the first months of 1937 had, as it were, closed
that long life in one's imagination. Even the incredible issuance
from his sick bed of three dramatic appeals to the world on the
burning questions of the day, or his recovery which still kept him
living and reigning gloriously did not remove a latent impression
that Pius XI really belonged to the past.

This same mood remained as the auto bore me to Castel Gan-
dolfo and rounded for the second time in one week the olive grove
that casts its rich shade over a rustic drive skirting the hill just
before you enter the bustling little village and park your car
unceremoniously before the portals of the Papal Villa. It remained
with me during those long moments of anxious waiting in the audience chambers darkened against the summer blaze, and grew upon
me as I finally sat before a door over which was the matter-of-fact
inscription, PIUS XI PONTIFEX MAXIMUS, and saw the secretaries
frantically gliding over the polished floors to answer calls of an
invisible electric buzzer sounded (so I figured) by an invisible
pontifical hand. But it vanished when I saw the Holy Father in
person; when he bade me rise from the carpet as I knelt and sit
informally at his desk, occupying the chair in which a few weeks
later was seated the head of a near-by Government to hear from
the Pope some words of inquiry and advice concerning startling
and (to the Holy Father) deeply distressing pronouncements.

The august Personage who spoke to me first in German and

then in French—apparently rather enjoying my momentary per-plexity as to which language to select—and who invited me in the most simple and cordial manner to talk to him was of the present, not of the past. He who spoke was not young; he showed his four-score years; but there was a natural vigor which few who reach that age enjoy, and a supernatural vitality shone from his coun-tenance. His conversation was emphasized by vigorous gestures. On the table near the desk lay the familiar walking cane and his white skull-cap.

From that audience I learned how profoundly he grieved over the present divided state of the world; over the growth of Racism, condemned by reason, science and Faith; how he pondered over mankind's condition, torn by racial and national enmities, as he lay awake at night. He cited with smiling approval the expression "interracial justice," which I had endeavored to make more familiar to American Catholics, and was deeply interested over what was being written and done to further that principle in the United States. I learned, too, how intense, how unconquerable was his Faith. Yet no detail in the vast picture was too small for his attention.

No individual's personal sufferings have ever been followed at one time in all their intimacies by such multitudes nor with such universal sympathy as occurred in the illness of Pope Pius XI. Pope Pius witnessed by word, deed and suffering to the reality of the Church's indivisible unity and catholicity, that unity and catholic-ity which was the object of her Divine Founder as supreme prayer in His own last hours of agony. Through his words he exposed those devastating heresies—springing from a common root even though warring among themselves—which seek to destroy Christ through a devious perversion of the social order. Through his deeds he established the remedy for the disorders they created—the remedy of Catholic Action—and through his sufferings he offered a mystic pontifical sacrifice in expiation for the sins caused by the supreme denial of God in our age.

That he might offer that sacrifice, he was vested with a super-natural strength. Like "every high priest taken from among men," he was able to have "compassion on them that are ignorant and that err": because he himself also was "compassed with infirmity." But following his Divine Master he "learned obedience by the things which he suffered," and was given an unearthly joy in the midst of his physical crucifixion. This strength and joy came from the millions of prayers offered up for him all over the world, particularly, as he himself repeatedly emphasized, from the prayers of the little children.

Was he "heard for his reverence," like the Saviour with whom his supplications were united? Faith answers instantly and unhesitatingly yes. Hope seconds this reply, with the sublime confidence that through his unique action Pius XI dealt *the* great mortal blow to anti-Christ in our age. God's triumphs do not usually manifest themselves at once. But a blow was struck more mighty than any Excalibur ever smote, and its evidence will appear undoubtedly in the pontificate of his successor.

What problems will confront the new Pope? Let the reader imagine he himself has been elected to that high office. The crowd has dispersed, the greetings are over, and the Pope, being human, allows himself a bit of a rest. The rest over, he decides to take a little walk and survey the premises. The Vatican radio station is an attractive goal, perched as it is above the winding driveways among the garden plots about to waken of a March afternoon from their brief winter's sleep. The Pope enters, and summons for conversation the Spiritus of Radio, that angel who surveys the whole world and is visible to none but the Pontiff's eyes.

"Tell me," asks the Pontiff, "what do you see as you broadcast over this great universe?"

"Your Holiness," replies the Spiritus, "I see a divided world."

"Conscious of its division?" asks the Pope.

"Conscious," answers the Spiritus, "and agonizing over it. Its despairing efforts to achieve unity only create new divisions."

"Our Divine Lord has made me the custodian of unity," says the Holy Father, "for the Church *is* unity. It extends Christ's Presence and His Divine life through all time and all space inhabited by man. What peoples are furthest from that unity?"

"The mission countries," says the Spiritus, "where the visible Church is either unknown or imperfectly established. Many ask what will Your Holiness do about them."

"The policies laid down by my saintly predecessor will be continued," replies the Pope, "the policy of Saint Paul, followed by the Church in the conversion of Europe: that of making them self-subsistent by native clergy and native hierarchy. But mighty problems face this Pontificate. There is the question of mission support for those foundations which depended upon Germany and are now cut off. There is the active warfare against the very mission idea waged by Communists and the Nazis and by fanatics in India. There are regions closed to the missions like the entire Soviet Union, like Nepal, or Afghanistan."

"The mention of Russia," observes the Spiritus, "calls to mind those separated bodies in Russia and elsewhere who have kept their hierarchy and in large measure their Catholic Faith."

"Which means the problem of reunion," replies the Pontiff, "first, for those separated from Our See, the center of Christian unity, then for those who are scattered through the lands where the visible unity of the Church is established, yet whose ancestors fell away through heresy."

"As never before," replies the Spiritus, "never before in the world's history did such vast multitudes of men of good will separated from us by religious belief look so eagerly as they now do to Your Holiness for spiritual guidance.

"But let us look closer to home," continues the Pontiff, "and see how the fullness of unity must be developed and perfected among Catholics themselves, through the knowledge and practice of their religion. New possibilities exist through this radio and its future companion, television, through the press and the lecture platform, and through the pulpit where the Church speaks officially to the multitudes, for promoting some of these matters which the very program of this station has been describing. Bringing closer to the people the liturgy, as the official prayer of the Church and vital principle of her social action; stimulating retreats for the laity; studying social questions. You get reactions; tell me what people are inquiring about."

"They are wondering," replies the Spiritus, "how these broad outlines as laid down in the utterances of Pope Leo XIII and Pope Pius XI will be elaborated, in view of new and changing circumstances, such as the principle of the corporative economy. They are asking what practical administrative measures Your Holiness will take in order to bring pressure to bear upon the consciences of Catholics, especially those in influential positions, to *observe* these teachings. They are listening to know what direction will be given to the great spiritual forces latent in Catholic Action, and exemplified by the Jocist and allied movements. They are looking to see these principles pushed further and further into every ramification of modern life, urban, rural, professional, trades-union, etc. Now that the mask has been ripped off the insidious errors of Communism and state-centered or race-centered totalism, now that racial persecution has been condemned, the Holy See is faced by problems of the atheist and totalist state, that religious worship may not perish; by the paradoxes of the secular yet tolerant state; then, by the newly formed Catholic states, such as Portgual and nascent Spain.

"Your last remark," observes the Holy Father, "is particularly true. One of the most difficult and delicate tasks facing the Pope in our days is that of preserving the liberty of the Church in her relations with states which formally recognize Catholicism as their religion."

"From this post, too," adds the Spiritus, "I find that men of many nations look to the new Pontiff to hasten, even if the goal be distant, the first steps toward the formation of a world society. They ask what institutions, associations, courts of arbitration, cultural affiliations his high office can promote; whether he may lay foundations for a Christianly-inspired association of nations."

"To do that," replies the Pope gravely, "we must again insist that the Christian concept of the human person be restored in all its fullness and dignity, which means, among other things, still further sounding of the depths of the family and the Sacrament of Matrimony. Though the problem of Unity may well be the fundamental problem of my reign, that problem is none other than that of my predecessors, to 'restore all things in Christ.' "

2,000 Weeks of *America*

A MERICA'S cover this week announces that the issue of September 13, 1947 is our 2,000th. By the help of the most recently devised electronic calculator we figured out in the 16th-1000th part of a second that we have put down 54,000,000 words on paper during the 38 years of *America's* existence. The reader can attach to this interesting item whatever importance he wishes. It simply emphasizes the weakness of language as a gesture, as Sir Richard Paget, inventor of the improved sign-language system, would explain.

Our interest, however, is not in mere vocal gestures. If we turn back to the 1,000th number, we find it is dated November 24, 1928. (In point of fact that was really the 1,020th issue, owing to an omission in calculation made on June 28, 1918, which we did not detect until June 30, 1945.)

November 24, 1928, was a fateful date in more ways than one, for it registered the defeat of Al Smith. And that was the date of the issue in which there appeared "The Brown Derby," by Father Leonard Feeney, S.J., the most successful article that *America* ever published.

The word "issue" itself has a peculiar double meaning. According to the dictionary, the older meaning is that which "issues" from events. It is an end result, just as Al Smith's defeat was the end result of what bigotry did to the cause of a Catholic candidate. "Issue" also means something which is now up for decision. The transition from the older to the newer meaning was made in the law courts. After the plaintiff and the defendant had exhausted upon each other their respective arguments, the judge finally told the expectant jury what was left as a residue for discussion and *that*, he said, is the "issue" of the legal dispute. Thus the word gained the added meaning of something which must be decided about the future.

Today, with *America's* 2,000th number, we are experiencing the
issues in the older sense: the outcome of those things which were
the issues in the newer sense in 1928. *America's* 1,000th number
described what was going on in that Europe. That world had only
the vaguest possible inkling, if any at all, of the terrible catastrophe
that in less than twelve months' time was to engulf the whole of
our Western civilization in the icy claws of the depression, and all
the consequent disasters. On that date we heard that M. Poincaré
had formed a new Government in France; that in Germany President von Hindenburg gave full approval to the naval construction
program and demanded that Herr Müller should withhold his vote
in the Reichstag when the Socialists' motion to discontinue building
the $20-million armed cruiser came up for action. In Yugoslavia a
happy agreement had been reached between the Serbs and the
Croats; in Austria Pan-Germanists had seized the opportunity to
issue a manifesto showing the progress of the *Anschluss* movement
for union with Germany. And in Rumania the entire nation, with
the exception of the Bratianu Liberal party, was rejoicing over the
formation by Dr. Julius Maniu of a new Government party in control. The new Premier was the first Roman Catholic to head the
Greek Orthodox nation. He was elected on a platform of complete democracy. What a magnificent augury for the future! This
is the same Julius Maniu who is now awaiting trial for collaboration under the Rumanian puppet government, for whose life the
Communists are clamoring.

Our readers may be interested in refreshing their minds on the
points of Dr. Maniu's program. We quote it here from the issue of
November 24, 1928:

First, complete freedom of the press, "my best friend because it is
truthful."
Second, the slogan of equality between men and lawful procedure in
Government.
Third, work in the open, not in the dark.
Fourth, the free elections which will reveal the will of the people,
such elections being provided for by special decrees before the vote
is polled.

Fifth, the continuation of the loan negotiations for the stabilization of the currency.

Sixth, repeal of all unfair economic laws enacted in past years, to give again to foreign capital equal rights and privileges with domestic capital in Rumania.

Seventh, revision of the customs tariff downward.

Those issues of November 24, 1928, were fewer and, in general, simpler and easier to handle than those of the present day. And yet those of today are somehow blended into one great issue about which we were then already warning, but which since has shaped up with startling clarity. In the words of President Truman to the Pope, it is the "preservation and support of the principles of freedom, morality and justice"; the issue of the Christian concept of liberty, as opposed to totalitarianism. We see now that what then looked to us so trifling, so transitory, was pregnant with the unspeakable horrors of the future.

All this makes us very humble as we approach the issues of the present day. It makes us all the humbler because we realize now something that only partly, at the very best, could be realized in 1928—the terrific responsibility of the United States for the welfare of the world—and consequently the severe obligation that rests upon us of this country today, somehow to understand these issues and look into their inner and permanent meaning.

But when we undertake to gauge these issues there are certain cautions which we need to observe; and they are tied up with the effectiveness of our Catholic journalism.

The first caution is not to confuse the transitory with the permanent. A transitory event rouses us from our lethargy and is a challenge to our courage and intelligence. But the permanent issue remains as a subject for study and an ever greater clarification of objectives and methods. Taking an obvious example, the imprisonment and trial of Dr. Maniu is such an immediate challenge, as is the imprisonment of Archbishop Stepinac. But the permanent issues of human rights and human liberty remain, and we should not relax our efforts to see these permanent issues incorporated into treaties and political institutions.

Our second rule is that we should not confuse various levels at which the issue is posed. It is all too easy to shift from one level to another and try to make religion do the work of politics, or make politics do the work of religion: to make government undertake the job that falls upon society locally organized or to confuse the function of military defense and that of international peace organization.

It is in a sense true to say—and it cannot be too strongly emphasized—that the issue of totalitarianism *vs.* freedom can only be solved at the level of religion. But it must also be solved at the level of politics and political knowledge; at the level of international organization and at that of social reform and economic cooperation; of public morals and the cultural level. It requires conjoint action at every level. But to conceive of such joint action demands a certain concentration of thought which does not always make for the easiest kind of reading.

Mere analysis, however, will not do the work. As the scientist Lecomte du Noüy says in his *Human Destiny:* "The more deeply man analyzes, the farther away he gets from the principal problem which he meant to solve." The whole must not be lost through over-occupation with the parts; yet the parts must not be neglected through our absorption in the vision of the whole.

If I may say it once more, I think that one of the outstanding weaknesses of our religious thought—or at least of our religious handling of these issues—is precisely our difficulty in reconciling ourselves to the fact that there *are* so many different levels on which an identical problem can be treated. Those who speak one language—whether the language of the psychologist or the political scientist or of the moralist or the theologian or of the day-to-day journalist or of the labor analyst or whatever you wish—find it difficult and almost intolerable to have to listen to the language of those who speak a different tongue. Yet we should all be working together and we should all be intelligent and broadminded enough to appreciate the contributions to the same problem which are suggested by those who enjoy another approach, another background of experience.

Our third consideration is that if we are to influence the thought of those who make the policies of the times, we must speak to them in language that they themselves can accept; we must speak to them at the level of thought and argument which is their own and we must propose to them that which they can and do accept in order that they may in their turn also accept that reasoning which is ours.

Obviously, when we speak the language of divine faith and propound truths of revelation to an unbelieving world, we can and we must ask for a complete acceptance on the authority of God. We do not declare the truths of Christ's revelation on mere grounds of their inner reasonableness. These truths command the obeisance of our faith on the ground that they are witnessed to by the Son of God Himself, who can neither deceive nor be deceived.

But where we speak the language of unaided human reason, we have to propose those truths on grounds which can be accepted by those to whom we speak. In arguing on such matters as human rights and human freedom, we may be too inclined to rely upon the authoritarian language of faith instead of the persuasive language of reason.

If I ask, for instance, that human rights shall be observed in any one part of the world or in all parts of the world, I cannot take any chance on my consistency and risk my argument's being weakened by my unwillingness to accept their applications to some other region about which I do not feel the same intimate and personal concern. A neglect of this principle by Communists reveals the hypocrisy of their fulminations against violations of human rights in Western nations, when they themselves are the principal offenders. But we ourselves cannot afford to neglect the same principle if our exposition of Communist hypocrisy is to command a merited respect from the world.

As editors we are troubled by a certain dilemma. If we aspire to the role of minor prophets we are inclined to concentrate on what one of our subscribers calls "the high drama of the crisis of Western civilization." In view of the terror and the agony of that cosmic drama, we revolt at spending time on mere statistics, shiftings of politicians, changes of cabinets, details of conferences, etc. Yet, as working journalists, we cannot afford to avoid the details, the analytical treatment, for this drama is, as it were, made incarnate in modern society and politics. With its root fibres, it penetrates every phase of our civilization, and if we are to treat it adequately and effectively, we must dig into these homely matters of daily life and daily bread.

So we hope that *America's* readers will be patient with us. We are struggling with what we can see was the problem; we are struggling with what we know you think is the problem. We know that thousands of you penetrate into secrets which we ourselves with our own limited minds and souls have not fully fathomed. We know that you can help us with your thoughts, your ideas, your prayers, your suggestions. We depend on you. We ask of you comprehension, tolerance, initiative—all those things which we demand of ourselves.

If any world at all will survive, it will be the result of our collectively envisioning the "issue"—that is to say, the *consequence*, the *result*, the unfolding of those things which have now become the "issues of decision" in the year 1947.

Are Catholics Thought-controlled?

OCTOBER, 1951

THIS AUGUST past a million or so German youth marched the streets of the Russian sector of Berlin. Every mother's son and daughter from tots to adults was drilled to sing one same theme: to praise the great Stalin, to shout the same slogans of hate against Americans, to swallow the same Leninist-Marxian, made-to-order ideas. If any one dared to think or speak differently he or she was on the way to the cattle cars or to the concentration camps. And when a free mind falls into the clutches of the commissars behind the Iron Curtain bodies are tortured, brains are washed.

Every American is determined, cost what it may, never to permit that such a system be imposed on this country. The most telling accusation we can make against an American citizen is to suggest that he is in any way sympathetic to such procedures.

Yet against some twenty-five million American citizens just such an accusation is leveled. Along with the vast majority of their Protestant and Jewish brethren, who worship the Creator and honor the Ten Commandments, these twenty-five million American Catholics abhor the Stalinist-Marxian slavery as they abhor everything that destroys the very image of God in man. To anyone who has even a passing acquaintance with Catholics such an imputation seems absurd. To one who like myself is a Catholic it seems not only absurd but criminal.

Last winter a Catholic priest and professor, a profound student of social and economic problems in questions of population growth, attended the annual meeting of a national learned society at one of our major universities. One of the scientists who took part in the discussion used the opportunity to denounce the Catholic belief shared by countless non-Catholics that pre-marital intercourse was sinful. The professor had gone out of his way and out of his spe-

cialty to make this un-called-for attack. When the priest ventured
a quiet and reasoned reply the scientist shut off the discussion with
the remark that of course the Reverend Father had to talk that way
since he belonged to a Church that permitted no free thought or
free discussion among its members. Again, one of our most widely
advertised 1951 books on religious questions warned the American
public that Catholics are thought-controlled.

If I drop into a rear pew of St. Patrick's Cathedral Sunday morning and take a look at that congregation, I find it hard to figure out
they are of the thought-control type. Without being a mind-reader
or using a dowsing rod I can state two things confidently of all these
people who are quietly reading their book or saying their beads.
First, they all do accept and hold as more precious than life itself
that body of teaching which in their belief is given by the Creator
to mankind by His Scriptures, His prophets and most of all by His
own Son Jesus Christ. It has been passed on for near two thousand
years by the Church that Christ founded. Lots of their fellow citizens don't hold this belief. But the Catholics do hold it for reasons
that seem to them to be good and sound. They have no intention of
giving it up on anyone's say-so. In this they are like all other sincere religious believers. Some people assume that Catholics are the
type of people who are easily impressed, for instance, by claims of
absolute authority; that they are psychologically or temperamen-
tally different from other human beings. But do the facts bear
this out?

Nothing but their conscience forces Catholics to stay in the
Church. Priests and bishops make a very eloquent appeal to that
conscience but no priest or bishop or Pope can stop anyone in that
whole congregation—or all of them for that matter—from walking
out of the Church at any time that they felt like doing so. The final
reckoning for such conduct would be with God and not with man.
As I said, this is a free country and Catholics to a man are determined it shall remain so. If you *accept* that body of teaching you
accept it as a whole because it hangs together logically. If it didn't
hang together it wouldn't be worth the attention of a logical mind.
No alien is obliged to become a citizen of the United States, but if

he does take out his American citizenship papers he is expected to subscribe to our Constitution, our laws, our Government, our entire Federal system as a whole. He cannot pick and choose for the simple reason that he undertakes to be an American. So if you accept the Catholic teaching you accept the standards, the safeguards, the institutions which that teaching has set up. You deeply deplore any sins and the weaknesses of the Church's members, high and low, but if you believe in the Church you take the Church in its essentials. You do not, however, need to accept or approve of its accidental shortcomings.

The second item I would notice about these people in St. Patrick's to whom the usher is now passing the church collection basket is a simple matter of ordinary observation. Outside of that common bond of religious faith and belief in a relatively small number of doctrines, they are as disputatious as any body of people in the world. The idea that Catholics are thought-regimented, that they all think and talk alike—outside of trifling disputes—is so far from being the truth that it is laughable. My own experience is that Catholics by and large make up for their unity in the matter of essential religious belief by differing vigorously about everything else. Let us look at some of these differences in detail.

1. *The political scene.* In every national election for the past hundred years the political dopesters have tried to figure out the Catholic vote. Yet Catholics were fiercely divided about Franklin D. Roosevelt through every one of his four terms. Some of his most intense and persistent opponents before as well as after his death were found in Catholic ranks. So, too, among Catholics were found some of his staunchest friends and most ardent admirers. The same rule applies to the political situation today. Whoever may be the future candidates, however violently they may differ, Catholics will infallibly be on both sides of the political fence.

Yes, some prejudiced members of the Church, journalists or professional campaigners or just ordinary Joes may try to insinuate that the Pope has taken sides either with the Democrats or with the Republicans. Outside the Church there will always be people who speculate or accuse along the same line. They will be definitely and positively wrong. In order to clear up any misunderstandings on that line Pope Pius XII told the 1,300 delegates from seventy-four countries who attended the World Congress on the Lay Apostolate held in Rome October 7-15, 1951 that it was of course the duty of Catholics to assume political responsibility. As citizens of the State they should shoulder the citizens' burdens in the State. This means it is a matter of sound Catholic conscience for them to unite with all decent citizens in fighting abuses and advocating sound legislation. It does not mean they should as Catholics become "entangled in party politics." The Church wants its members to be politically responsible and politically active. It doesn't want them to be dodging elementary duties of the citizen of a democracy. It doesn't want them to write "count me out" on the walls as young people were doing in Germany shortly after the war. At the same time it doesn't want its own members or any of its friends or foes to be trying to use her authority on behalf of their own pet candidates.

2. *The atom bomb.* Among Catholics as among religious people of other beliefs there are wide differences of opinion as to our right to use so terrible an instrument of human destruction as the atom bomb. Should the A-bomb be used at all even in self-defense? Few Catholics at least in this country go so far in their thinking as to hold that it would not be necessary for us to use the A-bomb in defense were our country to be attacked by the same weapon. Yet some do hold even this radically pacificist view and they are Catholics in good standing who voice their views without let or hindrance from the Church. Some who would indignantly reject such an attitude seriously doubt whether it would be right to use the A-bomb even a moment in advance of others, even if they were reasonably sure the enemy was about to explode his deadly weapon. On the other hand, one of the country's most distinguished Catholic educators holds tenaciously to the view that we should be amply justified in using the A-bomb if we were reasonably certain that the bomb was immediately to be launched against us.

3. *American representation at the Vatican.* So loud and so

numerous have been the protests against President Truman's nomi-
nation of General Mark Clark as Ambassador to the State of
Vatican City that many might believe the Catholics are just as
thoroughly in favor of the idea as Protestants are opposed to it.
In point of fact, this is far from being the case. The majority of
Catholics in this country have never given ten minutes thought to
the idea of U.S. diplomatic representation to the Holy See. Among
those who have done a little thinking along this line I don't know
of any who object to the idea of diplomatic representation in
principle. I know Catholics who think the step would be unwise
and a mistake in view of all the commotion it seems to cause among
our non-Catholic brethren; others who believe that regardless how
people feel about the matter our country is losing a valuable contact with the great center of moral world leadership as long as
we have no way to deal with the Holy See directly. Personally, I
share this latter view and I think that in time a calmer attitude will
prevail among my fellow citizens. However, I am completely free
to judge differently. If and when the U.S. Senate debates the
matter, after reconvening in 1952, I shall expect the Catholic members of the Senate to debate the Mark Clark appointment simply
and solely from the standpoint of what is good for the country
here and now. Any other attitude would be untrue not only to
their duty as legislators but as Catholics themselves.

4. *Schools and education.* The proposal of the Federal Government of the United States to provide for national assistance to the
schools has met all along with varied reactions from Catholics.
Some feel it is only fair that Catholic schools and colleges built
and supported by American citizens should not be excluded from
any aid given to tax-supported schools by the Government. Others
would be unwilling to receive such help even if it were offered
since they fear it would lead to complete Government control of
non-tax-supported as well as public schools, and whatever benefits
the aid might confer would be bought at the price of educational
freedom. Today I do not know that Catholics oppose the idea as
such of Federal aid to the country's schools. The needs of the
country are too obvious, problems are too grave and too many

backward regions are handicapped. Catholics, however, do stand firm in their insistence that Catholics who attend free schools should not be stigmatized as second-class citizens. For this reason they consider they are entirely fair in asking for some form of *indirect* aid in case the Federal legislation is ever enacted.

5. *Literary criticism.*   The last thing you will find is a uniform judgment on current productions, even from a strictly religious or Catholic point of view. There is the greatest width of individual judgment. All Catholic critics without exception, like other decent Americans, are completely opposed to pornographic literature. They show, however, varying degrees of sensitiveness in putting up with degrees of realism. Some of our critics are impressed first and last by the amount of artistic humbug that is palmed off on the public under "realism's" hallowed title. They see clean and young minds being introduced by a spate of popular writers to plain smut in the guise of a factual presentation of life. Hence they feel fairly cool even to very famous Catholic authors such as Evelyn Waugh, François Mauriac, Georges Bernanos or Graham Greene who make free use of what to them is always a dangerous, sometimes a suspect medium. Others, however, hold Christian art itself is stultified by what seems to them to be a too fastidious attitude towards realism. They quote Shakespeare, Chaucer, the Bible itself as their justification. Such Catholic critics have naturally no respect for a writer who abuses his brilliant talents merely to tell of man's foulness, vileness with no clear moral principle behind the story. But they do see genuine merit in an author who sets down in print the grim story of man's weaknesses and sins not because he is sympathetic to sin but because he loathes it.

Every week brings new books, new plays which in one way or another try to wrestle with man's big spiritual problems. The biggest drama today, as it always has been, is that played between man's soul, his passions, his conscience and his God. The story that grips a Frenchman or German may confuse an American, and vice versa. None of us think alike in any particular instance, and so help us we never will.

Someone will ask: "How can a church that tolerates any differences still maintain an Index of Forbidden Books?" The Index is concerned with writings that clearly contradict certain of the Church's limited list of express teachings as to doctrine or as to morals, or else—in certain instances—encourage the reader to serious sin. I think that most people would agree that any responsible teacher who is aware that a certain book can do serious harm to his pupils would feel justified in keeping it out of their hands, especially where it is likely to be confusing and contains errors that are not apt to be detected by the ordinary reader. The existence of the Index is a witness to the Church's conviction that it is passing on to mankind, through its teaching, certain unchanging and necessary truths entrusted to it by its Founder, Jesus Christ. On the same principle, the Church forbids certain books as seductive and subversive of morals precisely because the Church, in a demoralized age, holds to the absolute validity of certain primary moral truths. The "Index" is an index of the Church's deep concern for the souls of its members; and most Catholics, I would say, consider that abiding by it is a very small item in the cost of belonging to the true Church.

In point of fact, the number of works designated by the Index is small, and most of these are of interest only to clergymen and theologians.

6. *Films.* In regard to realism in films Catholic critics of literary realism are more cautious and sensitive, for the motion pictures are mass media. Any group of children can drop into the motion picture theatre at any time and the stuff is handed to them in visual form. As to the worth of the individual screen plays, Catholic theatre-goers and critics differ very widely like everybody else.

7. *Modern art.* Catholics disagree and constructively disagree on the subject of "Modern Art." The Catholic Church is the home of beauty, the greatest of all patrons of the arts, painting, music, sculpture, architecture, the crafts, etc. I think most Catholics who think or talk about such things agree that art when placed at the service of the Church's worship should not be hidebound by too rigid an adherence to forms which derive from the past. We

don't always have to be building pseudo-Gothic churches; we don't always have to imitate the stained-glass windows of Chartres. There is ample difference as to what form and how far this adaptation in the modern spirit should take place. Many Catholics are disgusted with much that is palmed off as religious art in this country and abroad and sold as commercial venture by certain church-goods dealers. There is discussion in turn among Catholic artists and art lovers as to what form a genuine non-commercial religious art should take. How far should we use for our churches the techniques and trends developed by modern types of artistic workmen, the so-called "abstract" or non-objective art?

What place has modern music in the service of the Church? Do we train our congregations to learn and appreciate the ancient ritual chants of the Church, some three thousand in number, or should we develop modern religious church music which people can sing and like?

8. *Franco.* On no topic can you start more arguments in Catholic circles than on the rights and wrongs of Spain. The only point is that they are arguments. The Church has no prescription for Americans or anyone else on the matter of Franco or any other Government for that matter, except as of course when in the case of Russia and its satellites it is openly and avowedly atheistic and persecutory of all religion. There are thousands of practicing Catholics of the Basque Republic in exile. Yet they are bitter opponents of General Franco. Even among those who live in friendly relations with the government there is criticism. Spain's own Archbishop of Valencia did not hesitate recently to point out frankly certain patent faults of the regime. American Catholic views on Franco range over a wide sector. Some very articulate persons are one hundred percent admirers of Franco and all that he is or will be. Others admire him for his past achievements and believe he was supremely necessary when Spain had the grim alternative of going Communist or staging the Nationalist revolt, and yet they are dubious as to his continued value at the present time. Many Catholics feel intensely that whether we like Franco or not at any time the only practical

thing for the U.S. to do is to extend to his Government sincere co-operation in the face of the acute economic and strategic needs of Europe and the world today. There are dozens of anti- and pro-Franco opinions but there is no Catholic Franco party line.

9. *Attitude on Non-Catholics.* Catholics differ, too, as to how to deal with their friends and neighbors who are not members of the Catholic Church. There is no sense just crying narrow-minded-ness in this respect. No American likes to be considered a second-class citizen whether it be for his creed or his national descent or for his race and color. But there are plenty of places in this country where to be a Catholic means just that. In some country sections you are nobody if not an Odd Fellow or a Mason. In New England until very recent years there was a stigma attached to the fact that your progenitors had entered the country later than 1800. Catholics, rightly or wrongly, feel a good many sore griev-ances on the school question. All Catholics who know their Faith agree that religious differences are not to be watered down or submerged. But they are in continual disagreement as to the em-phasis that is to be placed upon these differences once we are outside the respective houses of worship. Some Catholics find it hard to put much credence in the good faith of Protestants and Jews. They are skeptical and suspicious of them even in ordinary affairs of daily living. Others, however, believe the soundest policy is to take good faith for granted wherever and whenever possible. They share the viewpoint of the Knights of Columbus of Plainfield, N.J. who every year get together with the Masons in the same town for a friendly social gathering, and work with them wholeheartedly throughout the rest of the year.

From coast to coast in 1943 Americans of all three major faiths, Protestants, Catholics and Jews, united in publicizing "The Pattern for Peace" issued by the Federal (now National) Council of Churches of Christ, the Synagogue Council of America, and the National Catholic Welfare Conference of Catholic Bishops. The effect of this document was stronger than perhaps any religious utterance that has been known in recent times in the history of this

country. It profoundly influenced the thinking of the founders of
the United Nations and of our Government officials. Since that
time the same course has been followed in numerous other instances in this country and abroad. Today an increasing number
of intelligent and educated Catholics believe in "the policy of
presence," that it is their duty *as Catholics* just as it is their duty
as American citizens to take their full share in the active organized
life of the community, to be "involved" in the cares and joys of
their fellowmen.

Roughly speaking, we can say that there are three main policies
among Catholics with regard to the relation of Catholics and non-
Catholics. One attitude is that of habitual criticism of the
non-Catholic which, however, I do not think is the prevailing view.
Secondly, simply to ignore those who are not of our Faith,
forget about them and devote ourselves to leading an integrally
Catholic life, carrying out our Faith in all its details. The third
point of view is the policy of "presence."

10. *Nationalists and internationalists.* At once the deepest and
the most surprising difference among U.S. Catholics has to do with
international organization. There is a sharp division between
nationalists and internationalists. In view of the centuries of official
teaching on the necessity of some sort of world organization, no
other example of dissent so clearly gives the lie to the charge that
Catholics are intellectually regimented.

For many seemingly compelling reasons, American Catholics
should be more international-minded than any of their fellow-
citizens. They belong to a universal Church, they worship in
Latin, a universal language, they send their sons and daughters as
missionaries to all parts of the world, they read in their diocesan
weeklies of the activities of the Church in every country on the
face of the globe. The greatest Catholic thinkers have taught that
the whole world must someday be organized into some sort of
political unit, as the smaller groups of society have been progressively organized. In our day, the Holy Father, Pope Pius XII has
taken for granted the need for an international organization, as did

the American Bishops in their annual Statement of 1944, when they said, "The international community already exists; now it is necessary to organize it." The Catholic Association for International Peace, affiliated with the Social Action Department of the National Catholic Welfare Conference, has for twenty-five years published pamphlets and held conferences on various phases of world organization.

Despite this weight of practice and theory, it must be admitted that some American Catholics are belligerently nationalist-isolationist. It is likely that most of this group would take the same stand even if Soviet Russia were not anomalously numbered among the "peace-loving" United Nations. A complete analysis of their attitude is not in place here. Suffice it to say that they seem to be trying to prove their "100 per cent Americanism" to those who they imagine question it. Having heard their loyalty to America so often questioned, they are led by a certain sense of inferiority to the opposite extreme of perfervent protestations of loyalty. In this frame of mind, they are easy victims of professional isolationist agitators, and are willing accomplices of reactionary groups in opposing anything that smacks of internationalism, down to and including liberalization of immigration quotas.

Even among Catholic internationalists, there is a wide variety of opinion on organization of the world for peace. The dominant part played by the Soviet Union in the United Nations is so repugnant to most Catholics, that they see little future for the organization unless the Soviet influence is reduced or removed. Others, equally detesting being linked in any way with the empire of politically organized atheism, are inclined to go along in every way humanly possible with the UN, in the hope of staving off the final and irrevocable cleavage of the world. And they wish that their co-religionists would not use Russia as an excuse for opposing such UN agencies as the dozen or so specialized agencies, in which the Soviets do not participate.

11. *Society and Government.* On the domestic scene Catholics show a startling variety of opinions as to the merits or demerits of the New Deal, the Fair Deal, the right of labor to organize and

campaign for organization, or the right of the individual working-man to refuse organization. At the time the New Deal came into being many outstanding Catholics hailed it as something profoundly Catholic in spirit if not in letter. One of the strongest supporters of the New Deal's social and economic principles was the late Monsignor John D. Ryan, a professor of moral theology at the Catholic University of America, Washington, D. C. Monsignor Ryan held that it was entirely a Catholic idea to hold that the Government should exercise certain controls over business and industry. A large and influential group of Catholic writers and teachers, and clergy and laymen think today along the same line. The Department of Social Action of the National Catholic Welfare Conference in Washington, D. C. is a center and clearing house for Catholic thought on social questions. It believes in a relentless battle of defense against Communism, since we are facing a vastly subtle and malicious conspiracy. But it also believes that a purely negative and defensive action gets us nowhere unless it is united with sharp constructive action and courageous social reform as well.

Many social-minded Catholics believe that the most effective way to get the Communists out of the unions is to encourage sound unionism from the inside, and they appeal to experience in support of their view. They take very literally the language of the great utterances that priests and popes have made on the subject of social and economic justice. They quote the encyclical "On the Condition of the Workingman," *Rerum Novarum*, of Pope Leo XIII issued in 1891 and "On the Reconstruction of the Social Order," *Quadragesimo Anno*, of Pope Pius XI issued in 1941, and the many discourses and pronouncements of Pope Pius XII and the American Bishops collectively and individually.

On the other hand, many Catholics are uneasy about anything that seems to them to savor even remotely of the New Deal or of the Fair Deal. They are disturbed at what they see as the growing power of unionism. The Hearst press, in general, is widely read and enjoyed among Catholics, and Westbrook Pegler can count on a fair body of Catholic adherents.

James Carey, militant secretary of the CIO and James Farley, conservative-minded head of the Coca Cola Corporation are pretty hard to list under one common denominator in their public life, yet Mr. Carey and Mr. Farley are both practicing Catholics. Different as are their social viewpoints, each of them is striving might and main to interpret the Church's teachings about the love of their fellowman according to what he judges is the most thoroughly Catholic course. Even persons so radically conflicting as Walter Trohan of the *Chicago Tribune* and Ed Marciniak, editor of the labor-minded monthly *Work*, are bound by a common basic faith.

12. *Free enterprise.* You do not need to search far to find a sharp cleavage of Catholic thought upon the subject of Free Enterprise, as you can suspect from what has just been said about social policies and the unions. On the one side you find those who place a practically unlimited faith in the American system of free enterprise. They look upon it as the salvation of the country and, through our nation's influence, as the economic salvation of the world. They have great confidence in the essential integrity of American business at all levels. They fear any restrictions placed upon it as tending to Socialism, and do not consider that their religion should have any part in such restrictions. Other Catholic teachers and publicists, however, are deeply concerned with what they consider to be dangerous tendencies in Big Business itself. They fear that without certain necessary governmental restrictions and without the careful development of a network of voluntary self-help and cooperative organizations to protect the individual, huge business monopolies will develop their own planned economy, and in that way pave the way for socialism to take over.

This cleavage in Catholic social thought was brought to a focus during 1951 by the publication of a book strongly favoring the Free Enterprise point of view, "Key to Peace," by Dr. Clarence E. Manion, Dean of Notre Dame University's Law School. Dr. Manion's book was sharply condemned and warmly praised by Catholic critics, and the controversy it created will doubtless continue. William F. Buckley's *God, Man and Yale*, which espoused a view on economic matters in many ways similar to that of Dr. Manion, has likewise met with a varied Catholic reception.

13. *Racial questions.* When Governor James F. Byrnes of South Carolina declared on January 24 and March 16, 1951, his undying opposition to any change in the South's segregated school system, plenty of Southern Catholics were ready to go along with him. They believe that the Church would have got nowhere in the South in the last fifty years if it had not conformed to the South's social structure. Furthermore, they believe that the Church's mission work for the Southern Negroes would have been hopelessly frustrated if the Negroes had not been cared for in separate churches and separate schools. Under existing circumstances, therefore, they are opposed to any move to change the segregation policy in public life or in the life of the Church.

However, a steadily growing body of Southern Catholics are taking a definitely different attitude. Whatever need there may have been for compulsory segregation in the past, they look upon it as a wasteful and unworkable policy if continued indefinitely in the future. They believe a start should be made now to prepare people's minds, by a carefully planned education of the public as to the Christian concept of human rights, for a change that is bound to come in the fairly near future. Catholics need to learn more of the teaching of their own religion as to sinfulness of racialism, the equality of all souls before God, and the world scope of the Redemption.

They are backed up in this position by the strong stand taken on racial justice by Southern church authorities in recent times, as well as by recognized Catholic organizations like the dynamic Catholic Committee of the South.

In other parts of the country, we find a somewhat similar cleavage among Catholics on the racial question. The vast migration in recent decades of Negroes from the South to the cities of the North and West has changed the population in countless Catholic parishes. Immigrants from the West Indies, from Puerto Rico and from Mexico have raised still further problems. In many a locality these newcomers have met with firm resistance on the part of the older Catholic parishioners: the parishioners have set up restrictive measures, such as neighborhood "improvement" associations born out of a very serious concern for real-estate values and the morale of the local community.

Yet a rising tide of Catholic opinion wants to deal with the alleged danger in quite a different way. They are afraid that the lid-sitting process will result in more and more race-conflict explosions such as have already occurred in some of our larger cities. So they have embarked on a policy of systematic enlightenment of the public on the main ideas of interracial justice. They are active in working out plans whereby the different racial and religious or national-origin groups in the community can learn to cooperate with one another.

Catholics not only differ in their views on racial matters, but they also find ways and means to discuss these differences. Among the most interesting experiences of my life have been the interracial forums which I have personally conducted at which the proponents of the opposing points of view talk the matter out in friendly fashion, but perfectly frankly. Catholics can argue and do argue with one another bluntly and plainly, because we have certain definitely agreed-upon premises to start from. We like clear definitions and well-defined question matter, and we like, too, to reach clear-cut and definite working conclusions. One of the most interesting of these experiences has been in the form of a courtroom scene, where the public itself is supposed to be on trial for prejudice and unfair racial discrimination. The "law" is declared by a competent theologian, who quotes the Church's teachings on human unity and social justice. The "public" is indicted by an official of one of the various Catholic Interracial Councils, and members of the minority group testify as to the factual truth of his indictments, while the opposing defense is made by questions from the floor. The "judges" hand down a decision and some practical resolutions or declarations are drawn up. In this way contested issues are clarified, and lasting policies are projected.

Why they differ. After all, there is nothing particularly surprising that Catholics differ. True, they all hold to a common faith.
These differences will crop up most readily when people who
hold the same basic belief take, as we have already seen, very varying views of its application to questions of social, political or international morality.

The Church, too, is a *universal church* in which no two peoples
feel alike. Missionaries have told me how their congregations in the
Arctic or in Tropical Africa learn and sing the ancient chants of
the Church with the greatest of ease and joy. Yet you will struggle
a long time before you will induce an educated congregation in
one of our big American cities to sing the same ancient music.
Young Americans squirm under the Church's strict teaching on
the obedience due to parents by the young, yet Oriental youth
would take these teachings for granted. People think that all
Catholic nuns are the same the world over. Yes, they are the same
in their consecration to a great ideal of love and service. They have
a like dress and like customs and rules with only slight variations.
Yet an American nun humorously confided to me how many good
old Anglo-Saxon prejudices she had to lay aside when living
with her genuinely loved and immensely respected native fellow
nuns in faraway China.

People with a common faith will also clash in their very attitude
toward life itself. In my boyhood I knew two old Irish ladies, by
name Miss Ann Hogan and Miss Ann Ward, who lived in the
same household for some fifty years. Ann Hogan believed that
the best way to prepare for the future life was to get the feel of
death while she was still in this world, so she ordered her coffin
ahead of time and kept it in her bedroom and lay in it each night
for a little meditation. Ann Ward, equally pious, was cheerfully
convinced that there was no use anticipating trouble and she was
not interested in her companion's penitential practices. Yet both
of these were good loving souls. To my young mind they stood
for two approaches to the one unshaken belief. The Church has had
her optimists and her pessimists, her stricter and her broader inter-
preters since the beginning. There will always be discussion as to

how much part is to be allotted to sorrow over evil and how much
to rejoicing in the good, how much is to be accomplished by the
use of our native reason and how much is to be trusted to the grace
of God. Someone may ask why the Church permits such differences
to exist. If she is so definite on some things, why not definite on
everything? The simple reason is that the Church sticks to her
God-given character and function. Her task is not to lay down a
party line but to preserve and transmit to all ages and countries a
certain body of teaching that was entrusted to her by the Divine
Founder, and she depends upon the Holy Spirit of God to keep this
body of teaching intact. She relies, moreover, on men's natural
wits and reason to study this teaching and to apply it to the thousand and one circumstances of our lives.

If someone asks me what this diversity of Catholics happens to
mean I give my own opinion in reply. Personally I feel that it is
a testimony to the vitality of the Christian Faith. If a man has no
settled convictions, if he claims to have a mind completely open
on everything, completely convinced of nothing, I consider him
simply as a neurasthenic. The healthy mind, as I see it, is one which
adheres to certain deep and settled convictions and is willing to
pay the price of holding them at personal inconvenience and
even great personal sacrifice. At the same time such a mind can
distinguish between basic unalterable belief and things that are
merely matters of speculation. Since the Catholic Church is a
living body offering a living message to a world of living men, its
members, if they are reasonably familiar with the Church's spirit,
have no difficulty in making such a distinction. They will differ
vigorously and merrily where the essentials of their Faith are not
concerned, but the very vigor of their differences serves to emphasize its unity.

As a body, the Catholics of the United States welcome discussion
—with their own, and with everybody else. If you want to convince yourself, drop in at the meeting—national, regional or local
—of any of the Catholic associations specializing in education,
sociology, economics, rural life problems, the press, race or labor
relations, international peace, juvenile guidance, family life,

Christian art, etc. Or take a look at any of the parish forums, such as the Barclay Street Institute run by old St. Peter's parish, in lower New York City, or the Social Action forums in Brooklyn or Chicago.

Catholics have no fear of reason nor of honest democratic frankness; they do fear the rule of prejudice and the suppression of reason in the name of democracy or for any other cause. They believe that God's cause flourishes in the full light of day, and they are convinced that all true Americans, whatever be their personal beliefs, are determined to keep that light shining.

Science and Religion as Partners

MAY, 1954

A CONGRESSMAN of my acquaintance has sent our editorial office some samples of the emotional pressure stuff that piles up daily upon his desk. I do not need to trouble anyone's peace of mind with quotations, and I certainly do not want to spread the infection any further, copious as it is. The disturbing thing about that mass of hate-literature is not so much that there are people who produce it, for they may be just normal rascals out to make a quick living. It is rather the increase of people who relish it: the existence of neurotic hate as a sort of independent phenomenon, regardless of the object toward which it may be directed.

A young Washington couple, a music critic and his wife, had some three years ago a curious experience of this sort. The critic undertook—rightly or wrongly—to find a bit substandard the singing of the daughter of a highly prominent person, who immediately sent the critic a letter of strong fatherly rebuke. The press, quite naturally, had its day with the event, and so did the young couple, though not to their liking. Mail speedily brought them 602 letters, 54 telegrams and 32 postcards, expressing vehement opinions from completely contradictory points of view. The affair was a dirty Republican scheme to smear the Democrats, a low Democratic plot, was pro-Negro, anti-Negro, anti-Semitic, a Jewish device, etc. Only an alien, wrote one correspondent, would stoop so low as to say that a good American girl doesn't sing on pitch. Another, with no explanation, sent an anti-Catholic pamphlet of the Pope-in-league-with-Moscow type. The young couple had long been interested in the question of prejudice. What had escaped them, as they later remarked, was the chilling realization that this preoccupation was powerful enough to work its way out of a subject so remote from questions of race and religion

134

as a music review; so close to the surface that it popped out at the drop of a hat.

Worst of all, the growth of this neurotic state of mind reflects in part a world phenomenon which is causing us much anxiety here at home. It is a daytime nightmare that today billions of dollars are being spent abroad as part of a shrewdly calculated policy in order to propagate hatred of Americans, hatred of us *as Americans*. When we are subjected to such pressure from outside, it is difficult for us to keep our own composure and mental balance, and not yield in some way or other to the universal contagion. Dealing directly with an emotional disturbance is the best way to become emotionally upset yourself; and in such a condition your expressions of feeling can take any direction.

Our concern today is not so much with the actions of the individual, however clever and perverse, as with the terror created by the mass mind. Such a terror is unfortunately bound up with the very forces which man's mind has liberated, yet which seem to work as readily for man's enslavement as for his freedom. And we are very deeply concerned with the factors and circumstances in which a potentially terrorist state of mind flourishes. We are equally concerned with the hidden depths of consciousness out of which it grows. This concern is greatly expressed by two very articulate elements in our midst: the religious organizations and the scientific intellectuals. Yet at times they seem to work at cross purposes. Is greater cooperation possible?

Contemporary social science has plenty of discourse on the causes and circumstances of hate and hate movements. Indeed, nobody but a specialist could hope to cover even the major part of its utterances. It has done, and is doing, a tremendous job in dragging the anti-social neuroses out of their lairs, and showing us how they begin and how they operate. Out of all the investigations and analyses with their warring opinions a certain body of conclusions seems to be emerging. We understand better each year how to avoid conflicts between cultural or religious groups in our crowded neighborhoods. We are better informed as to the effects of migration within our country, and ways to adjust the differences between rural and city dwellers. We know more about the images and associations that people unconsciously absorb from their environment, and even "prejudiced" people do not sling racial or group names and epithets around with anything like the freedom of a couple of generations ago, when nobody blinked an eye over the black-face minstrel or the stage Chinee. Differences may be still strange, or unpleasant for that matter, but are no longer just plain funny. The comic strip must find some other subject than the green-capped foreigner just landed at the Battery. As for social psychiatry itself, with its hallowed lore on personality development and personality structure, the layman does seem to spot a winnowing out of the more eccentric differences, and lessened strife among its leading lights. Social sciences have long been a happy hunting ground for the lunatic fringe, and to some extent will probably continue to be so. Nevertheless, the fringe can be restrained and so make the general public feel more kindly toward its findings.

The social analyst ascertains that people are more likely to lay aside their hates and prejudices when they labor together in some common task for the benefit of the community. But they observe also that it takes a spirit of self-sacrifice, a real love for your fellowman, to initiate such a joint undertaking. Time must be spared from busy lives, and apathy and opposition must be overcome. Yet difficult as it is to arouse oneself or others to active love, it is still possible if you consider that what you do for your neighbor is in fulfillment of a personal God's love for him as well; and that in cooperating with this divine plan you are helping to fulfill the ultimate perfection of your own personality: your own spiritual and moral maturity, your own *life* itself.

Here is where the religious organizations enter the wide discussion, whether on purely local matters, or whether on the world scene. The religious groups do not of themselves command, nor can they be expected to command, the special techniques for analyzing and classifying these social phenomena. But they have something infinitely more important: they can provide the positive motivation without which all analysis will fall short of its purpose. Such a positive affirmation is supremely necessary. Scientific analysis of a negation—for hate is largely negative—lacks any adequate meaning, if no notice is taken of a positive affirmation to take its place. Unless the religious group reminds us, hate's dynamism is apt to make us forget that love, as St. Thomas Aquinas said, is still a stronger force than hate, even though hate makes a more immediate and vivid appeal to the senses and the imagination. "Neither 'rational' nor 'character-conditioned' (emotional) hate can exist," says Gordon W. Allport (The Nature of Prejudice, p. 364), "unless something one values has been violated. Love is the precondition of hate." It is not so easy for the scientist to pinpoint hate's opposites, the positive motives for justice and love.

The worst aspect in a disordered society is not so much the existence of hate, which has been with us in one form or another ever since Cain's anti-parental complex induced him to slay Abel, but the loss of men's power to love. The most terrifying feature in St. Paul's description of the pagan world is the fact that they had lost their natural affections.

Only when that power to love has disappeared will we realize the part that love, in some form or other, plays in the adjustment of all human relations. Just as the presence of hate in the community spreads a baneful influence far beyond its explicit line of attack, so in still greater fashion the *presence* of completely disinterested love wields an influence that extends far out into quite unexpected regions. For love itself, given any kind of an even chance, is more powerful than hate. In point of fact, love seems to need hate in order to display its full intensity, as shown in the meditative work of the contemporary religious muralist, André Girard.

Believing as it does in the goodness of the Creator and the corresponding goodness of His final designs for mankind, the religious body is confident that love will win out over hate, provided it is given any kind of an equal chance. The tragedy of the growth of communism in the nineteenth century was that those who should have been preaching and practicing love to suffering people left the field open to the apostles of hate. They could have won hands down if they had not temporized through their own shortsightedness and timidity.

The presence, the mere *existence* of any great love in the community is bound to radiate an influence far beyond its immediate personal contacts. This is the principle upon which groups of men and groups of women are operating today in the footsteps of the late Father Charles de Foucauld, the martyr of the Sahara desert: the idea that you can profoundly influence even the most case-hardened and embittered people by living among them a life of total unselfish love. Every now and then I stop by the front porch of old St. Peter's Church in Barclay Street, across the way from Dun and Bradstreet's new building, and reflect upon two bronze tablets upon the portico's wall: one commemorating a great lady of old New York, the other honoring her contemporary, a humble West Indian slave. Each person in their own fashion left an imperishable mark upon the life of our city and of our country, through the influence of religiously motivated love. Yet these mighty souls are only a very distinguished sample of a great current of religiously motivated love that flows from generation to generation through the lifeblood of our huge, noisy city of New York, and of our whole country. It keeps a million projects moving. If you look for it, you will find it operating in every block and every countryside—diluted and timid here, fervent and heroic elsewhere. If the power to love were lost, our social life could only be held together by craft and violence. The difficulty from the standpoint of the intellectuals is that love does not readily submit to analysis. Love is best understood by lovers, and speaks in parables and symbols to those who have not experienced it. Psychologically dissected, it ceases to be love, and shrivels into mere enlightened self-interest. Love, according to a time-honored definition, is essentially a communication that a person makes, from his own abundance to another person. It is not conceivable without an element of gratuitous gift; of immediate "presence"—of the "thou" as opposed to the mere "it" or cold object.

"Ideas need hands and feet" said that skilled and indirect pedagogue, the late Father Jimmy Tompkins, of Antigonish. Love needs hands and feet for its expression, and they do not materialize out of the air; they fructify as the legitimate products of a university.

But the hands and feet need love in order to get going. It is difficult, therefore, for the scientist, if he is more than a mere reporter, to leave love out of the picture. Genuinely *human* relations stubbornly refuse to be manipulated. Today's social psychology prides itself on a scrupulous adherence to strictly scientific methods of analytical exploration and statistical verification, much of which can be done quite impersonally. Yet when tangible results are sought, the "interpersonal" element comes to the fore; and you cannot treat persons, as persons, as mere objects. Where any degree of loveableness, however slight, can be found in human beings, it is usually the best guide to some understanding of their motives.

Hence the scientist, even if he has carefully excluded front-door entrance to that love which the religious organization so sedulously preaches, finds it entering the back door, as a condition for the integrity of his own work. The success of his own processes depends upon his recognizing the dynamic force of love, and the possibility of a theologically motivated love. As Sir Geoffrey Vickers, chairman of the newly formed Mental Health Research Board, remarked at Toronto on August 15: "By far the most significant discovery of mental science is the power of love to protect and restore the mind. This alone, in my view, entitled mental science to be regarded not as a rival [of religion] but as a partner in the eternal effort to realize spiritual values in the daily life of men and women—even perhaps in the policies of governments."

Organized religion, on the other hand, is greatly dependent upon the social scientists in fulfilling its own message of love and justice. As a Christian and as a priest, I have no hesitation in declaring that man's ultimate goal is not bounded by the brief space of this life. I frankly insist to all and sundry that they are created for eternity, not for time, and that this life is a time of preparation: a seed-time, not a harvest. But I am equally emphatic in reminding people, according to the Gospel, that each man's destiny must be worked out under concrete conditions and associations: as a member of the family, of the community, indeed of the entire human race. Man is involved here in a network of dependencies and obligations. I want him to praise God—morning, noon and night—but how can he offer honest praise if, at the same time, he neglects his duty to find and keep a job for the support of his household, and to discover a way to live in peace with his ever-multiplying neighbors in a crowded world? If he can manage this all out of his own wisdom, well and good. The more externally independent a man's life appears—whether as a fisherman in Nova Scotia or the Gaspé Peninsula, or a fruit grower in the West Indies, the more he learns of his dependence upon the wisdom and know-how of those who have made a study not only of the mechanics of economic cooperation, but of the human and spiritual side as well. The teacher of religion finds that he needs the findings of science—of social welfare, social analysis, social psychology—in order for love to operate.

In a memorable conversation with Arthur H. Compton, Premier Nehru of India expressed a desire for a religion which should "help to do the things that you ought to be doing for people"; a help that he did not find in the purely contemplative religion of the East. In default of such a religion, he said, "we turn to science and industry."

If science and industry are expected to supply that ultimate motivation which only religion can provide, we are certainly doing them an ill turn. This Mr. Nehru himself seemed to see. A "closed" science—closed to the idea of any type of discourse save that which lies within the scope of its own methods of measurement, may appeal to professional self-satisfaction. It is a stimulus to ingenuity to try to fit the entire cosmos into your elaborated scheme; and the attempt appeals strongly to the modern mind. We are allured by the hope of reducing everything, material and spiritual, to some sort of a unified field theory. Yet we are quick to sense the unreason of the converse proposal. The theologian should not try to make revealed truth extend its own proper domain and perform the functions for which science, and science only is competent. It is sometimes difficult to persuade a skeptical contemporary that the ancient Doctors of the Church were not such fools, and in their own time and circumstances, were as clear about the prerogatives of science as people are today. As the same St. Thomas Aquinas remarked: "To make light of creatures is to depreciate divine power." And among God's creatures none is nobler than the human reason.

The notion of a completely "closed-circuit" science dies hard; but the idea of an "open" science, from all appearances, appears to be steadily gaining: one that acknowledges that at a certain point in its reasoning it must yield the platform to philosophy. Philosophy, in turn, cannot afford to close its ears to the possibility of a knowledge and a strength arising from outside the narrow circle of man's experience, and perfecting that experience through man's willing response.

Cooperation is a magic word here in the United States, and we are fond of preaching it to industry, to labor and to politicians abroad. Cooperation of organized religion and analytic science, each working in its own sphere and its own proper integrity, is completely possible, for it is in already fairly abundant operation. We should be in a much better position to face the problems created by pressure groups and the threats of mass terror, if we made it universal.

Thoughts on a Catholic Elite

MARCH, 1955

FOREIGN STATEMENTS about the Catholic Church in the United States usually follow one or the other line. They are merely descriptive, telling for the astonished European some of the marvels of American Catholicism or else they are rather sharply critical. Few have made an intelligent, general appraisal of what American Catholicism really means and its significance for the Catholics of other countries. For this reason it is refreshing to read the following opinion expressed in the Brussels monthly *Bulletin des Industriels:*

Catholics in America are outstanding not so much as a spiritual elite but rather as a coherent, disciplined and clearly defined mass. Thanks to their far reaching religious and social activities, American Catholics can rely upon one another's aid. American Catholicism is the first form of Catholicism in modern times to base itself on the masses and not on the elite . . . This is a matter of plain fact, and by its very existence it upsets theories elaborated in Europe which we are too inclined to look upon as of universal application . . . These masses extend their influence and they will help to abolish social atheism which is Western Europe's plague.

Reading this passage arouses a twofold reflection: first, it is valuable for us to recall the particular strength of the American church which the author points out; secondly, we need to inquire whether our deficiencies in the matter of an elite are an unmixed good.

If the European asks what elements in American Catholic history contributed to the mass character of American Catholicism, three can be mentioned. The first is the identification of the Church with the American Republic from its very beginning. Catholics took part in the exploration of the North American

Continent and Catholic martyrs watered its soil by their blood. Archbishop Carroll's policy in insisting upon a native clergy and the establishment of a Catholic hierarchy under American bishops sealed in striking fashion the Americanism (in the good sense) of the American Church. His apostolic zeal as well as his practical wisdom prevented us from continuing as a mere mission field for the old Catholic establishments of France, Belgium, and other European countries.

The second element that contributed to the mass character of American Catholicism was its immigrant character, especially as a result of the Irish emigration. For the Irish emigrant the priest was their "Soggarth Aroon," their champion, their friend, their companion in all sufferings. The intimate, popular character of emigrant Irish Catholicism set its stamp on the Church in the United States, and other emigrant elements which helped to build up the mighty body of the Church in this country followed in greater or less degree the same pattern.

The third element contributing to the popular and "mass" nature of American Catholicism was the Catholic school system of the United States. Our Catholic schools were supported by the masses of the people. Our schools traditionally are for everybody. The fact that our schools are not subsidized by the State has imposed severe burdens on our Catholic people. This burden has hindered certain developments but it has enabled us to maintain an independent, dynamic Catholic school system.

For this reason the main religious tensions that Catholics experience in this country are not so much between the devout and the anti-clerical or non-practicing elements in Catholicism itself, but rather between the Catholic and the frankly non-Catholic, either Protestant or non-Christian elements outside the Church.

Our statement of these great factors of strength and unity in American Catholicism do not blind us to some of its patent defects to which our non-American friends advert, such as a certain stress on outward efficiency, a predominant emphasis on the material—buildings, plant, furnishings, etc.—a tendency to judge by statistical quantity and minimum standards rather than by quality and integral

Catholic living; a readiness to look for comfort and convenience first in the ordering of our churches, etc.

There are also graver matters: such as the indisputable leakage from the Church, the increase in mixed marriages, Catholic complacency with birth control practice, or racist thinking in Catholic neighborhoods, as well as the basic religious ignorance noted with alarm by our chaplains in dealing with the armed troops. These and other such phenomena remind us that the Church cannot rely on mass strength alone and must turn to the laity for help.

The development of the Church brings with it the need of a body of laity who are more than ordinarily devoted to the lay apostolate and who possess more than ordinary competence. Two great areas of the Church's activity have led particularly to this realization. One is the social problem from which Catholics in the past largely held themselves aloof. As the Church has been concerned with the great problems of economic, racial and social justice in this country, the need has become more apparent for trained workers in the different social agencies, local, State and Federal, and for dedicated men and women who will devote themselves in their own areas to a sound program of social reform. The same need is evident in the field of apologetics and Catholic evidence, of organized charity, in industrial relations, and in the difficult area of race relations. Organizations like the St. Vincent de Paul Society, the Sodality of the Blessed Virgin, the Legion of Mary, the Young Christian Workers, the Confraternity of Christian Doctrine, and so on, have each been active in developing their particular type of elite.

The need of elite groups, great as it is, within the confines of the United States is still more evident as American Catholicism comes in contact with the problems of other lands. United States moral leadership cannot be confined to merely general principles. Unless Catholics in this country are trained to a more than ordinary degree of competence in problems of the spiritual as well as the technical order in dealing with the peoples of the so-called undeveloped countries, we shall find ourselves pushed aside and projects like Point Four entrusted to people devoid of spiritual philosophy or hostile to the Faith itself.

So evident is the need of an elite that there is no need of any further elaboration. A few reflections, however, are in order as to the concept of elite in general and some of the requirements for its formation.

1. In the first place, an elite today can no longer be achieved simply by a process of certain selection. The old idea of an elite was a group selected from those who were in better circumstances, economically or socially or spiritually, and became an elite in the apostolic sense because of their devotion to good works. They received a general direction and some specific aids, but they were an elite largely by their origin and background rather than by any deliberate process. Today an elite has to be formed, and the creation of an elite is one of the major works of Catholic education and pastoral theology. It is true they must be created from select material, and in that respect there is a correspondence between the newer and the older concept; but that material has to be given definite aims, definite spiritual and intellectual formation and launched on its task as a more or less finished product.

2. We have great need of priests and professors who will devote themselves to the laborious but fascinating task of working with small groups and developing them intensively over the years. The American priest is generously accessible to the laity. They are free to consult and ask his help on all possible occasions, and he has no hesitation, as a rule, to friendly intercourse, visiting their homes, interesting himself in their affairs. All of this is to the good provided it is conducted in a pastoral and Christlike fashion. On the other hand, we lack men who will take the trouble to work continuously with a small group, who feel that the priest is not only a kindly adviser and counselor when they are in need but a man who is willing to develop through them a systematic plan of lay apostolic education. If this type of work is neglected we shall see emerging groups of well-meaning laity who try to engage in one or other form of apostolic activity but who go off

on various tangents, are captivated by spiritual novelties and are embarrassed by incurring conflict with the Church authorities. An infinite amount needs to be accomplished of careful steering between the Scylla and Charybdis of initiative on the one hand and Church loyalty on the other. I speak with special conviction since I have learned the value of that type of formation as applied to the intricate and serious racial problem.

I sometimes ask myself if we have not come to rely too much on formal organization and the requirement that every group shall be specially ticketed. So much can be done by small informal groups with the minimum of organization but a maximum of planning and method, a group of ten or fifteen men who will meet with the priest, say at the rectory or in his college study once or twice a week over a period of time and delve into the heart of some great social, economic or educational problem, something in each case that intimately concerns the relation of the Church with the world. This might even be a mixed group of priests and laity, but nevertheless with a moderating head. Obviously some such groups, too, among the clergy are not out of place. A fine example of what is being done in that line is that provided by the popular social study movement promoted by Father Joseph Grémillion in Shreveport, La., described by Stephen P. Ryan in *America* for March 1, 1952. Only through such intensive work can one cultivate hidden individual potentialities. Leaders, I repeat, need to be formed. Of course, the fundamental formations are the lessons of the school; the high school or the college or university. But an *immediate* formation is also required, in that precise field of spiritual and intellectual competency which lies between the standard lessons of the institution and the immediate snap judgments that must be made in daily life. The Church, in older times, did not hesitate to set priests aside that they might devote themselves to spiritual direction for individuals: kings, princes and powerful statesmen. She always commended the work of directing individual souls. As I heard one great apostle remark: "It is worth while giving your whole life to be able to raise a soul one degree in sanctity." But small groups, too, are a challenge to the zeal and talent of the spiritual director. These need to be led to higher and higher levels of personal sanctity and of practical wisdom. The main requisite is that a relationship of confidence should be established between the group and the priest leader. Furthermore, he should be able to put at their disposal a great multitude of aids, literary and technical, etc., and provide for them interesting and stimulating contacts. Once such a group has been established outside advisers can be brought in, Catholic and non-Catholic alike, experts in different fields, who will be only too glad to convey to them some of their own particular type of riches and thereby afford interesting discussion for their future meetings.

3. Obviously the training of such a group presupposes a deep spiritual foundation, the heart of which is the retreat. Here we touch on a point that is ever recurring and yet has not been satisfactorily settled, the objective of our men's retreats. We do not wish to minimize the value of the week-end recollection dignified by the title of retreat, which begins on Friday night and closes Sunday evening; the current two-day exercise of our retreat houses. The value of these short recollections is evident: we admire the marvelous development of the men's retreat movement in the United States, and yet there is desparate need of something deeper and more satisfactory and there is more desire for it among our Catholic laity than is commonly supposed. Here again if our trained and recognized retreat masters do not see the possibility of providing such help owing to the crowded schedules from which they already suffer, this spiritual thirst may be satisfied in other ways, good in themselves but yet not measuring up to the possibilities of the retreat movement as such. Any elite apostolic work in the Church today demands a coordination not only with fundamental truths of the faith but with certain special elucidations of the apostolic idea and a more intimate study of the Gospels and the intentions of and desires of the Sacred Heart of Our Lord, and also a better and more far-reaching coordination with the Holy Eucharist both in its sacrificial and sacramental aspects. Certainly it is a magnificent sign of deepening spiritual life that many of our laymen are eager to share the atmosphere of

the great contemplative orders and seek in them an escape from the hurly-burly of our daily work. From such participation they draw inspiration and refreshment. Yet there is need also of an intensified apostolic retreat, something that will stand midway between the mere retreat of spiritual renewal, which we provide currently in our retreat houses, and the more mystical and contemplative type: a retreat of union with the apostolic Heart of Christ in its fullest sense and with a considerable penetration into the problems of the Christian zealously working in the world and consecrating himself to God.

4. Intimately connected with the foregoing is the need of a greater coordination between the spiritual life and the exercise of technical competence. At present lay elite groups find these two elements too far removed from one another, too much separated into two distinct compartments. The pay-off for neglecting such a study is the development of a well-meaning bureaucracy in the American's Catholic life. Its pay-off also is a certain false type of spirituality, the type of thought, unfortunately expressed not infrequently by Catholic writers and preachers, to the effect that the Church is not concerned with concrete problems of life, the objection that we as Catholics are purely spiritual and that prosaic matters of social organization and inter-group relation are something foreign to our inner world of devotion. These aberrations spring from a failure to coordinate and arrange in proper hierarchical order the technical applications of the law of charity and the dignity of the law of charity itself. If a strong supernatural motive of charity does not inform the various types of welfare activity these degenerate into bureaucracy or into mere good will performances. On the other hand, if charity is contented merely with general sentiments of good will it loses its own force. It must be implemented; it cannot be satisfied with a mere gesture of compassion for the wounded man on the road to Jericho but it takes care of his wounds and pays his bill.

In these few lines I have but touched on a great problem; I have not provided a complete solution. It will be sufficient reward if this brief consideration will at least start some more thinking as to how, in our day, we can do more to imitate concretely the action of Him who spent three long years of His precious earthly life and the forty days after His Resurrection in schooling a troublesome band of captious men in the secrets of the apostolate.

Franco-American Understanding

DECEMBER, 1954

E ACH DAY brings us further evidence of a curious paradox with regard to the relationship of France and the United States. The two nations need each other more and more. Each day they are more aware that each country in its own way is a key to the world's peace, and our statesmen and politicians are continually reassuring us on this point. Yet we seem to drift further apart and the less optimistic political prophets foretell an increase of tensions between the two nations during the coming months.

Nobody needs to elaborate the evidence for our mutual need. As for the ways in which we drift apart, we in this country are disconcerted with the French political confusion. It seems to us at the present time unconscionably annoying and we were dismayed at the failure to realize the European Defense Community. Irritation and fear on our side are increased by other factors old and new. Experience of two world wars and all the contacts they have produced have not enabled the average American GI to feel much more at home in France. On returning from his European service in that country he will cheerfully say that he had been far more at home in Germany than he ever was on French territory. "The German hausfrau will invite you into the kitchen for a supper with the kids but the French keep you at a distance." And the situation has not been helped by some of the recent religious developments in France. The affair of the worker-priests, despite the tact and care with which it was handled, produced, as we know, an unpleasant impression in this country; and it is not helped by the bitterness and vindictiveness of some of the highly conservative elements in France as well.

The French are alarmed at our own United States foreign policy. While neutralism is not as fashionable now as it was a year ago, there is still concern over what we are trying to do. Our words and professions seem to them more impressive than our deeds in a social sense. They are disturbed by what they call Americanization, an alarming increase, pervading the whole world, of American technical and organizational methods. Certain features of our American culture, such as our films and our television do not add to their comfort of mind. Our Catholic brethren in France are not always comforted by what they see of the Church in this country. They admire its marvelous growth, if they happen to know of it, but on direct contact our Catholicism does not seem to fit into the pattern to which they are accustomed, as we experience in our contacts with them. Visitors to this country not infrequently complain that American Catholicism seems to them remote and impersonal, although they are impressed by its splendid organization on a parish and school basis. On our part, we are disturbed by what seems to us the traditionalism and the institutionalized character of the Church in France coupled with unusual apostolic adventures.

To discuss any of these topics in an adequate way would mean not just a lecture but a book. Now my thought is only that a few simple observations may sometimes help to clear things up. The German philosopher Karl Jaspers said that the criticism of a social or political process is itself a part of the process. So a few random remarks on various ways and means of better understanding may help to further the understanding itself. These remarks are drawn largely from conversation with visitors to the United States, or attempts when traveling to interpret the United States to our friends abroad. They are mere suggestions but may help to reduce the tension at some or the other focal point, and no service we can render in that way is quite negligible.

I. *Psychology and Politics*

Writers and lecturers on national and international relations never lose their appetite for comparing national psychologies. Were I more capable I might join the procession of mutual commentators on the peculiar psychology of the French, the American point of view and the oddities of the Americans as seen by our Gallic brethren, even though we don't, like the British, surprise French tourists who cross the Channel by driving autos on the left hand side of the road. Such speculation is entertaining in its own way; yet it can be overdone. We can often reach an understanding better by recalling the historical background of other countries or groups in other countries. The more I have seen of any foreign people the less easy I find it to classify or categorize them under any particular formula. I see them in their differences and individualities more than in any generalized traits. The same would apply to other nationalities, and would naturally apply to my own as well. Professor Carl Friedrich of Harvard says we can so easily err by speculating on the psychology of the Germans. The Germans developed a violently nationalistic ruling class—who embarked on two world wars—not just because of some innate peculiarity in the Teutonic nature, which of itself is pretty much like other human natures, but a good deal because of traits which developed in the national character through the long torment and crisis of the Thirty Years' War in the 17th century, and then later by the emergence of Prussia with its boundaries open to all sides and its consequent drive to self-preservation and domination. In the same way, as the French remind us, we cannot understand their position today without taking into account those historical events which are so frightfully real to the French and to every French family and to every French village in the countryside but which remain remote to Americans and are easily forgotten even by those who took part in the wars abroad.

We would ask a similar indulgence for people of other lands who comment with asperity upon the racial situation in this country. We cannot explain these racial conflicts and attitudes by merely saying that Americans are made that way. We need to study history: to look at the persons, the institutions, the migrations of populace, changes of immediate and remote contacts and the conflicts that arise from them. Such an historical turning point as the recent decision of the Supreme Court declaring segregation in schools unconstitutional and the reactions that it produces are intelligible only against the background of the entire United States history, especially the story of slavery as an institution in this country and the gradual steps, stage by stage, by which it was first deprived of institutional existence and later on its effects or consequences expressed in social inequality were deprived of their legal standing. It is a long story and a fascinating one. The more we are acquainted with the entire record the less readily will we yield to easy generalizations.

In the field of political institutions, France's stability in civil service—despite the frequent changes in the parliamentary government—parallels the extraordinary stability of our own American government, that has remained unchanged now for 160 years. It is true our country began from a revolution, a revolution which in part was a predecessor and an inspiration for the French Revolution, yet the American Revolution differed profoundly in its nature from that of France, for our revolution was simply the separation of one nation from another, a nation from its parent metropolis, but politically we remained conservative. We jealously preserved the laws and in great part the institutions of the parent country, and in some ways surpassed Britain in the tenaciousness with which we clung and still continue to cling to many legal and political traditions. The government which we set up, our tripartite government, has elements of great fixity and strength but is often hampered by a certain cumbersome and self-impeding character in contrast to the flexible parliamentary system of the Old World. Frenchmen look with wonder upon the complications we face when the nation's executive power must operate, for better or worse, in conjunction with a legislature controlled by an opposite political party.

Bitter as was the recent political campaign, nevertheless it illustrated to the amazement of those of other nations the fact that we were able to keep our party system intact. The conflict's intensity did not prevent our keeping our two major parties intact without split or splinter.

II. *Economy*

If the keynote of American politics is faithfulness to certain ancient traditions, our industry is committed to an endless succession of startling changes. Yet our economy contains elements of great stability. In the long run our expanding and enterprising American production is more stable in character than a restrictive and cautious economic Malthusianism based on limitation of production and high prices that is still unfortunately prevalent in the European scene. In our trade union situation tensions exist, yet we cheerfully live with the tensions. We manage to cooperate and to carry on our characteristic American system of collective bargaining even though we find ourselves occasionally in critical situations of disagreement. Nevertheless those situations are not permanent, and occasional flareups like the experiences on the metropolitan waterfront around New York and New Jersey are only exceptions to the hundreds, indeed thousands, of satisfactory agreements reached between management and labor all over the United States both in large and in small enterprises. As yet we do not see the way to that complete harmony of labor and management which would be the ideal. Nevertheless there is a rapprochement and a marked progress from the bitter dog-eat-dog situation of the end of the 19th century to the spectacle recently of United States Steel and the United States Steelworkers touring the country to present jointly their situation to the nation. For trades-union relations between the two countries it is doubtless significant that in October of this year our own Congress of Industrial Organizations surprised M. Gaston Tessier, the veteran President of France's Confederation of Christian Trades Unions, by celebrating a dinner in his honor.

III. *Security*

This brings us to a point which I think needs particular elucidation at the present time, namely, the varying attitudes between the two nations on the question of security.

In this connection we need only recall the universal disturbance of the French mind over the case of the Rosenbergs, husband and wife, accused of delivering to the Russians the secret of the atomic bomb. In French minds, as in the minds of many other peoples in Europe, there was extreme dismay over what seemed to them a shocking miscarriage of justice. So great was the agitation that the highest leaders both in ecclesiastical and in civil life protested against what seemed to them like American hysteria or barbarism. Complaints were even sent to the Holy Father in Rome who acknowledged having received them, but did not express any approbation. On two points in particular they were disturbed: first, what seemed like a shocking treatment by the Supreme Court which had decided against the various appeals. The appeals had been, to use their own expression, shunted from court to court, keeping the unfortunate defendants in a state of alternate hope and despair. Secondly, they were disturbed by the refusal of President Eisenhower to exercise what seemed to them like an elementary act of clemency after such a long delay, even to grant a stay of punishment. The situation instanced how a complete misunderstanding can grow up between two nations and between two parts of the Catholic Church in regard to something over which either side holds a deep moral conviction, for undoubtedly the French objectors were deeply sincere and moved both by humanity and by a profound sense of justice. Yet to us in this country their action was disturbing and perplexing. The differences, then, must be ascribed to completely varying situations, such as differing concepts as to the nature and function of their highest tribunals and thus the courts themselves.

The president of the United States Supreme Court, as the French would call him, our Chief Justice, is not chosen even by the Court itself but by the President of the United States independently of the Congress, and the Court is empowered to judge the constitutionality even of our own congressional legislation. Moreover, Americans, for the greater part, entertain towards our justices a quite special spirit of reverence. Those very appeals which hustled the defendants from trial to trial, from court to court, in a manner shocking to our French neighbors, illustrated from our point of view the scrupulous care with which our American legal system acts in order to insure for the defendant a fair opportunity to prove his innocence and to obtain a review of his case if for such there is any foundation. The very fact that the appeals in this criminal case were so dramatic and attended by enormous publicity, emphasized the unwillingness of our American judicial system to railroad people to punishment through a rapid decision.

More basic even than the question of the courts is today's United States position in the matter of security itself, namely, as the last bastion, we might say, of freedom in the world; for if America were to yield and our strength of defense and our potentiality of justified retaliation were to be impaired the free world would have lost all hope of resistance against the steady onmarch of totalitarianism. Hence this country is obliged by the very nature of things to keep itself intact. Hence our extreme concern, a concern which unfortunately flowered too late for it to be fully protective against the sharing of atomic and hydrogen bomb secrets. France, of course, has her military secrets, secrets with regard to matériel and other elements of defense which are of supreme importance both to France and this country. But the secrets of the United States are the ultimate pledges of the physical defense of the world. Harsh as some of our security measures may seem, they are in the main part justified by the unique world position of the United States. The situation, I think, is becoming better understood abroad. Violent as was the reaction to the Rosenberg case, at the time, it has passed into history. The fact that so democratic and conciliatory a person as President Eisenhower was unwilling to exercise clemency in that case has made, I think, a certain impression on thoughtful people abroad. Europeans may also fail to consider that if from purely humanitarian reasons clemency had been exercised for what we considered a proved and supremely heinous crime, it would have provoked a wide democratic resentment in the United States among the small people, the man in the street, the humble proletariat. They would have deeply resented that persons who had put the country and the world in jeopardy should themselves be left scot free. The condemnation of the Rosenbergs—whether it was justified or unjustified—was not a racial or a religious or a class issue. It was an act motivated by a very real concern for the security not of the United States alone, but of the entire world, France included. And mutual understanding was not helped by M. Mauriac's bitter and quite unwarranted attack against Cardinal Spellman.

How far such considerations can be made intelligible to people of other countries is of course always problematical. Elements of hysteria in the United States can justly merit a reproach. On our part we need to understand that for the Frenchman communism does not always present the same threat to the integral loyalty of his country that it does to the American. The French are used to revolutionary movements, and the revolutionary aspect of Communism they regard rather as an annoyance, as something to be kept in abeyance, to be combatted, it is true, against which political and police measures must be taken and traitors must be punished. Countries which have suffered a succession of revolutions through the ages cannot feel the same perturbation as we do about groups which differ with the majority or even seek destruction of their government. As was recently remarked by a European observer, for us it is a new phenomenon that we should discover, so to speak, in our body politic a political virus against which we react with instant and legitimate allergy and which we must forthwith expel from the system. In the Communist virus we see a complete negation of our nation itself. What we still have to learn in this country is the danger of trying to harness the issue of domestic communism to the chariot of political expediency. As an outstanding American authority on this subject, the Rev. John F. Cronin, S.S., observes, the very complexity of the issue makes it imperative that it be kept out of politics once and for all and treated from a strictly nonpolitical, presently current standpoint, without useless recriminations over the past.

Lest, however, we yield to the temptation of smugness, we recall that though the French political attitude towards Communism differs from our own we still can learn of their forefront position in the intellectual struggle with Marxism. It is to the Europeans that we look for the profound analysis of Marxist fallacies and the ultimate probing of the nature of the Communist movement. The Marxist in this country of the Communist variety, outside of a few prominent fellow travelers, is a marginal creature with whom argument or controversy would be wasted. Few, if any, of our highly prominent figures in literature, art or science profess themselves unashamedly as Communists or challenge the Christian and the believer to debate.

IV. *Religion*

As Catholics concerned with the question of religious differences we cannot be content merely to register the fact that some parts of France are devout and others are relatively irreligious. We need to know the whole historical picture as well, as is stressed by such outstanding religious French sociologists as Professor Gabriel LeBraz and Canon Boulard. Facts, it is true, are not a substitute for Divine grace, for we cannot plan a system of individual or social redemption. But a careful study of the facts, contemporary and past, enables us to understand religious phenomena that otherwise only confuse and baffle us.

The facts of the religious situation in France fall, as we know, largely into three types coincident with certain geographic areas. In one part of the country the Church is in regular contact with the whole of the population; in another section it enjoys what you might call episodic contacts, i.e., for some of the basic functions of life: baptisms, marriages, funerals, etc. In the third part of the country contact is completely broken off with a notable part of the population; you have total alienation. These sections are, in the strictest sense, a mission territory. This does not signify, as the authors just mentioned carefully point out, any religious determinism but a sort of natural indication of human tendencies, an habitual drift which human forces can and should divert to the right direction. What certain persons have done others can do. For this reason, they maintain it is possible to separate the various elements in the picture that have been much too fatalistically looked upon as inevitably connected. For instance, technical progress is not necessarily linked to materialism.

Many popular assumptions do not hold up under analysis: the idea, for instance, that certain regions place on a human being such a profound stamp that his faith cannot be upset by a change of circumstances. On the contrary, much depends on the effect of the immediate environment. Remarks Canon Boulard: "If a Breton migrates from Brittany to Beauce I have no way of knowing whether he will or will not continue to practice his faith. He may belong to the practising minority. But if 200 Bretons taken at random are scattered over the Beauce area I can guess in advance that 150 to 160 will more or less rapidly give up all religious practice, at least unless we organize in a *quite special fashion* their spiritual care." It is true that we find in France or Spain or Belgium or Germany a considerable number of people whose faith is preserved by their being separated from disturbing elements. Their religious life is sheltered by the peace of their traditional social life. But we find others who are surprisingly strong in their Catholicism in spite of their contact with unbelieving and disturbing elements. As Canon Boulard notes, in the Caux area in the diocese of Rouen Christian life is still solid in spite of the proximity of the large towns of Havre and Rouen.

Again many of the regions we think of as being habitually Catholic owe their present-day flourishing Catholicism not to the weight of long centuries of steady, fervent practice, but to the simple fact that they were evangelized in fairly recent years by one or the other zealous missionary: by people like St. Francis de Sales, St. John Francis Regis, St. Louis Grignion de Montfort and others. Even holy Brittany which Blessed Julian de Maunoir visited in the 17th century was on the way to becoming a pagan country. It was his intelligent, tenacious, indefatigable zeal over a long period of time that established the faith in Brittany on the roots that we have it today. Henri de Queffélec's famous novel and film, "Un Recteur de l'Ile de Sein," purported to portray an event of the Napoleonic era early in the last century. But the real incident upon which the novel was based, occurred three centuries ago in the apostolate of Julian de Maunoir.

Those who have followed the events of the last year are thrilled at knowing now that the Mission de France is now reconstituted and set on a sound canonical and pastoral basis and can continue and amplify its magnificent work. I venture to predict vast fruitfulness for the same.

V. "France eternal"

Amidst all these differences of the East and the West, the North and the South, the Latin and the Anglo-Saxon there remains always the fundamental task of making Christianity present to the modern world. A tremendous spiritual struggle has taken place in the minds not only of the French but of all our European Catholic brethren. They have had to convince themselves that the Faith must finally be preserved not by a blind clinging to social and political institutions of the past, not by a reckless grasping of all the novelties of the present, but by an intelligent approach to the inevitably changing world in which we live. This does not and should not mean that we must resign ourselves to some form of economic or social determinism. The Church has the function of changing and moderating the flow of human institutions in those matters where they come under the moral law. The Church is militant, and militant in the social field as well as in the purely spiritual, as the whole history of the social movement both in France and the United States has shown and as our Roman Pontiffs have so gloriously proclaimed in their encyclicals and in their public and private discourses. This point was urged with particular cogency by our present Holy Father, Pope Pius XII, in his discourse to the Cardinals and members of the hierarchy assembled for the International Marian Congress in Rome on November 3, 1954.

The Church, on the other hand, fully recognizes the inevitable changes in the world: the march of human inventiveness and technology, the continual unfolding and integration of that noösphere so dear to the mind of my old friend and colleague Father Teilhard de Chardin. We cannot abolish the noösphere. Its complexity will increase, its possibilities, its anxieties and its inevitable pressure on the entire physical and psychological environment of man. Crime and mass terror are the pay-off for a noösphere left to its own ungodly devices. Nevertheless the noösphere can be incorporated in the Christosphere. There are no limits to the realm of divine grace, just as there are no limits to the goodness and the power of God. From France we Catholics in this country can learn, courage, initiative and inventiveness in meeting violent changes and in reconciling old and stubborn social antagonisms. From America the French can learn the art of adapting ourselves to the impetuous rhythm of an expanding, many-sided Catholic spiritual and cultural life independent of political vicissitudes.

From France, *audacieuse et patiente*, we in the United States need to learn two lessons of sovereign import in the midst of this environment of hustling, bustling change: total dedication and commitment to the rich exigencies of our Faith—in the chivalrous spirit of France's saints and martyrs—and the spirit of tranquil, humanist poise, cherishing even under great difficulties certain basic treasures of human existence: "the good bread, the good earth," the home and family ties; the amenities and enrichments of human discourse. France is the perpetual corrective for our tending to the mediocre and the one-sided; America can give courage and leadership to France in meeting the grim perplexities of a "brave, new world." Our needs are mutual; our Providence is one and the same.

Speaking of Liberals

DECEMBER, 1955

NEARLY 100 YEARS AGO, Orestes A. Brownson (1803-1876), social reformer, political thinker, literary critic and lay theologian, complained that he was being regarded as a bad Catholic because of his strong stand for political liberty:

> Just now, popular opinion among Catholics as among non-Catholics identifies Catholicity and despotism, and the controversialist who seeks to prove that the Catholic religion has no natural association with despotism but is favorable to liberty and the inherent rights of man runs the risk of being denounced on all hands as a bad Catholic.

He also complained that those who invaded the enemy's camp and tried to meet the rationalistic scientists on their own ground, using the current terminology and framework of thought, incurred suspicion of being intellectual liberals.

CHANGING VIEWS OF LIBERALISM

Most of the political causes that Brownson defended in his day would arouse in ours no notable suspicion. He was an ardent Abolitionist and advocate of universal human rights, regardless of race, creed or color: a position which is now generally accepted even in quite conservative circles. He was militantly pro-American, a tremendous admirer of the American system of government, and went so far as to say: "The system is no invention of man, no creation of the convention, but is given up by Providence in the living constitution of the American people."

Such sentiments today can pass muster. American Catholics go so far as to hang an American flag in the church sanctuary, a practice which deeply shocked a pious German priest who visited our office some time ago. He saw in the practice a display of "nationalism." But when Dr. Brownson, in his oration at an annual Fordham College commencement, expressed the notion that Catholics could and really ought to be proud of being good Americans, Archbishop Hughes of New York was so scandalized that he walked off the platform.

(It was in reparation for this humiliation, I believe, that Fordham University a few years ago arranged to have the impressive bronze bust of Brownson removed from Riverside Park at 103rd Street and transferred to the Fordham campus.)

At the end of his life, says Dr. Alvan S. Ryan in his very excellent *Brownson Reader* (Kenedy, 1955), Brownson became worried over the reproaches hurled at him and made a curious retraction of his previous stand. But his words remain and they are not without application to our own times.

The word liberal today is an anxious word: anxious because of its associations; but in itself is it anxious?

Highly respectable people defend liberal causes; that is to say, causes very similar to those which created so much anxiety for Orestes Brownson. Yet such defenses seem to occasion no comment. Thus, for instance, the Catholic hierarchy of the United States, in their recent statement on church-related schools, touch upon distinctively liberal issues. Replying to the charge that such schools are by their nature "divisive," the bishops remark:

Rather, is it not obvious that positive Christian training, with its emphasis on the sanctions of the divine law, of the natural law and of civil law, on the social nature of the virtues of justice and charity, on the moral obligations of patriotism and public service, provides the strongest cement that can possibly bind a nation together? Criticism of these schools at times seems to forget that we are a pluralistic society that postulates, not uniformity, but rather unity in variety.

Church-related schools reflect nothing so clearly as that American spirit which demands unity in the essentials of citizenship while defending to the death those things in which the citizen is guaranteed his freedom.

When I use the word liberal, I am not trying to add another definition of a much-discussed term. I am only conforming to a common type of popular usage which in fact calls anybody a liberal (whether in praise or in blame) who is very much concerned with precisely those things which the bishops assert are safeguarded by church-related schools; such things, that is to say, as problems of social justice and charity, the moral obligations of patriotism and public service, or the fact that today we are living and operating in a pluralistic society.

The word liberal acquired a definitely bad reputation in the mid-19th century from its association with Europe's intellectual liberals: anticlericals and militant secularists. It was in this sense that liberals and liberalism merited the condemnation of Pius IX in the Syllabus. We cannot forget that in our own country the very foundations of religion have been and still are under persistent attack from people who glory in the name of liberal. Yet in numberless instances such people espouse genuinely liberal causes of human rights and human welfare with a constancy and skill that sometimes put the rest of us to shame.

For the almost 47 years of its existence, *America* has vigorously combated the secularism and anticlericalism which the 19th-century liberals espoused and which their successors among the present-day intelligentsia—in dwindling proportion—continue to espouse. Yet *America* today is ticketed as a Catholic "liberal" publication by some friends and also by some foes of its ideas.

Should we disown the term? Yes, say those who believe that it is already hopelessly compromised, that it cannot be detached from its disreputable associations. No, say those who wish to preserve the term, and who recall a Vatican document issued under Pope St. Pius X which said that Catholics could legitimately apply it to themselves.

Which course should we choose? I am not enterprising enough to suggest any final decision. Our concern, after all, is not primarily with nomenclature but with reality: with maintaining an honest attitude in our comment on the manifold issues of the day.

PORTRAIT OF A LIBERAL

Call yourself what you will, I know of no title that will bring you praise from all casts of mind. The main job would seem to be to determine our attitude first and then let free choice and wise discretion determine how we are to entitle that attitude—that is, if we want *any* precise appellation in a day of slogans and catch-words.

If we wish to call a person a liberal (in the sense that we might call *America* a liberal-minded review) we could, I believe, characterize him as one who sees the complexity of the issues that confront our faith in passing judgment on the events of the contemporary world. Such a person is aware of the conflicts of rights and of the many circumstances that affect those conflicts. He is aware, too, of the need of striving, for country's sake and for conscience' sake, to vindicate such rights.

As a Catholic and a Christian such a person is particularly and deeply concerned where certain basic human rights, of the individual and the family, are violated. Being sincere and honest, he is not *selective* in his choice of vindications but is concerned for the entire gamut of human rights. He sees these as linked up with civic rights as well, rights under statute law and common law, rights under the fundamental law of our U. S. Constitution, rights arising from the mutual obligations of nations.

Hence he will stand for the freedom of education as against educational monism and state monopoly; for equal freedom of education for all citizens, regardless of race, color or creed. He will stand for social justice in economic relations and for the practical action necessary to achieve such justice. The Catholic liberal will be particularly conscious, in a genuinely Catholic sense, of the world-wide repercussions of American positions on these questions. He will be honest enough to realize that neither social justice nor human rights can be secured without the support and at times the intervention of authority, both temporal and spiritual.

WAY OF A CATHOLIC LIBERAL

It is at this point that a Catholic liberal runs into a hornets' nest of contrasting oppositions. He parts company here with the type of liberal who is passionately concerned with only one phenomenon, that of undue restraint on freedom of human utterance, whether in speech or written word. Yet he will also be mindful that few if any social reforms have been achieved without a certain degree of shock, a certain quota of aggressiveness, risk and intense preoccupation.

It took long, persistent and fiery actions on the part of the Jesuit Father Frederick von Spee to root out the frightful injustices of the persecution of witchcraft in 17th century Germany. His *Cautio Criminalis* against some of the judicial procedures of the time might conceivably be needed in our own day if political excitement and ambition allowed governmental investigations to get out of hand. Its strictures are totally applicable to what is going on in Communist China.

On the other hand, an otherwise legitimate preoccupation gets out of hand when it denies to Congress the right of investigating and exposing in a manner consonant with American tradition and equity possible acts of conspiracy against our nation.

I am optimist enough to believe that the contemporary American mind *can* rid itself of excessive and one-sided prepossessions without giving up any of the genuine elements of concern for human freedom. Such a mind can be reassured by the repeated instances where the authority of religion itself is outstanding in defense of human rights, even in sharp conflict with the massive pressure of public opinion and prejudiced social conformity.

Witness the firm attitude taken by the Catholic bishops of the Southern States with regard to implementing the nation's policy of racial integration in the schools or the rights of citizens to petition the Government. Witness, too, the stand taken by members of the hierarchy in the North in the matters of housing and neighborhood tensions, or the attitude of the bishops in the Southwestern

States toward Mexican migrants and other Spanish-speaking peoples. These are 100-per-cent liberal policies, even though the intervention of Church authority in their behalf is not exactly in accord with traditional liberal formulas.

The path of the Catholic liberal is, in a true sense, a *difficult* path. He steers his way between two extremes, never an easy thing to do. Furthermore, he is exposed to violent assault and misinterpretation by either extreme. The going will be particularly difficult during the coming election year.

SOUND AND FURY

The aim of each party or of contending candidates is to show that the others are wrong; and any issue—the threat of Communist infiltration, for instance—can be utilized for this end. Modern advertising methods, however legitimate in themselves, have developed in us the art of subtle one-sided presentation. Human nature, especially in the pulpit or at the Communion-breakfast table, is easily tempted to conceal paucity of knowledge about a complex issue by resorting to loud cries of alarm. The "all-embracing tentacles" and the "unknown, hidden force" are an easy means of creating a delusive appearance of homiletic strength in the midst of real weakness, and it is easy to escape carefully reasoned argument by imputing—directly or by implication—sinister motives to your adversary.

Liberals will be berated and liberals will be glorified, and with new implications and nuances as the fashion of the moment may suggest. Shall we continue to apply the term liberal to a painstaking Catholic criticism of the current scene? Once more, I attempt no decision. Names or no names, let us be mindful that the course of Catholic public comment upon the events of the day is by its nature a hard course, a stiff course, a course where we cannnot allow ourselves to be seduced by fanatics of any extreme or variety. People want, and will buy, exciting answers; and the politicians are ready to invent and diffuse such answers. But honest Catholic comment is not always exciting. To those who intensely love it, all truth is exciting; but not all people intensely love the truth.

In today's world the issue of freedom—and its correlative, the cause of legitimate authority—concerns, in one form or another, the majority of the human race. It is certainly a service to Christ our Lord to show with unfailing strength and consistency, at home and still more abroad, that the cause of freedom and the cause of God are one.

IV.

Social Action

Papers one and two are of the type that I mentioned in the Intro-
duction, of interest more as pioneer utterances once intensely real
to me but not a particularly original contribution to the present
scene. The editors included them since they represent a vital step in
the evolution of my own thought.

In my earlier years social action meant for me the effort to meet
and to solve some of the very tangible questions that troubled a
country pastor in an extremely isolated region. It was inspiring to
me, as it was to others in similar surroundings, to meet companion
minds looking for solutions of similar questions. The proceedings
of the National Catholic Rural Life Conference were therefore a
release for the heart as well as for the mind. All of this was recalled
with great vividness a few weeks ago when the surviving pioneers
of the National Rural Life Conference met in Lexington, Kentucky,
at the annual convention, enjoying the hospitality of Covington's
bishop, Most Rev. William T. Molloy.

Questions that were once extremely concrete became rather aca-
demic after I was transferred to the big city and the staff of America.
The immense changes that have occurred since the early days of
our rural life speculation have made new problems for the apostolate
and thus much that I wrote in those days seems now rather obsolete,
of interest more nostalgic than practical. But it is a nostalgia for
which I am both grateful and proud.

Readers may be puzzled and a bit annoyed by the title of the
third paper, the Authenticity of Temporal Action. By temporal
action is meant, of course, action for the good of our situation here
and now, action "for a better world," such as Pope Pius XII asked
us all to pray for during the month of December, 1955, the topic
preached with tremendous eloquence by Father Riccardo Lombardi,
S.J., in his worldwide crusade per un Mondo migliore.

Why then is there any question about authenticity? Curiously enough the question is raised from directly opposite angles. For one brand of social thinking it is intensely annoying that Christianity speaks on this topic at all. According to standard Communist propaganda the Christian social program is simply a blind invented by the capitalists, a pure fiction, a super-structure to divide and undermine the authentic movement of revolutionary struggle by the proletarian classes. In certain sections of Catholic or Christian thought, on the other hand, one encounters a sort of gnosticism, a falsely spiritual puritanism, which is deeply shocked if the Church, for instance, undertakes to speak on the problems of the marketplace or the more controversial aspects of human relations. The authenticity of temporal action is queried by the skeptical Voltairean and by the simon-pure spiritualist. The reader audience for whom this paper was written were more apt to be of the skeptical type, who resent such action because it is religiously motivated, than of the latter, or over-spiritualist type. As non-Catholics or non-religious people, they would be inclined to raise an eyebrow over what they would conceive as Christian or Catholic participation in temporal welfare activities. Hence the analysis and the insistence in the next to the last paragraph upon the incarnational character of Christian social philosophy: the intimate relationship in the plan of the Redemption between our concept of the God-man and of the human being as related to the God-man.

The fourth paper, on the Catholic elite, stresses a point that can be elucidated from many angles, the question of the spirit of the Church, its fundamental and habitual attitudes toward the problems of man's spiritual life. Only the Holy Spirit Himself can pronounce with authentic voice on what is the spirit of the Church. Yet every now and then it is important for us to recall that the Church's "spirit" is the spirit of Christ, the spirit of Jesus; that it reflects His approach, His attitude. That spirit, as Ignatius Loyola reminds us, is one and the same in the hierarchical Church as we see it existing in space and time, as well as in the Jesus of the Gospels. One and the same spirit unites His Church and unites those who are the men and women of the Church, those who interpret it and who try to live His life in the modern world.

Catholic Agrarians

R AIN WAS POURING when Father Estergaard and I drove into
Fargo from Big Stone City, S. D. Ten miles before we
reached Moorhead, across the river from Fargo, the gaso-
lene had given out, unexpectedly exhausted from constantly buf-
feting a northerly wind. Night fell, as did the thermometer. Were
it not for the kindly help of a passing farmer who bumped us over
a mathematically level road to the nearest service station (closed
for the night) at the hamlet of Rustad, we might have spent the
days of the fourteenth session of the National Catholic Rural Life
Conference freezing at the edge of a wheatfield. Rustad had a
pleasant Scandinavian sound to the ears of Father Estergaard,
whose heart goes out to his northern kinsmen, and he considered it
a good omen.

How North Dakota looks to the natives of North Dakota I find,
as an Easterner, difficult to visualize. Doubtless they see its huge
reaches in terms of little home neighborhoods, as people do everywhere: Uncle Joe's town, the place where Bill first met Mary, and
the farm where we went fishing as kids. But to the visitor from less
expansive regions, the prairie overwhelms the mind with the phenomenon of land. There is the same staggering inability to connect
in the imagination the small area that the eye takes in with the
infinite stretches of just the same sort of thing beyond and beyond
and beyond, that you experience when you first find yourself out
in the middle of the ocean. And the same queer mixture of the
friendly and threatening in nature.

A few minutes before, the sun as it sank caught broadside a sil-
vered grain elevator, blazoning it like an enchanted tower against
an inky sky. Acres of straw stubble gleamed sharp against black
soil and distant pale clumps of trees. Then the soil looked sweet.
Now it was bitter and gloomy. But sweet or bitter, rain-soaked or

dust-puffed into the clouds, we found during the following days that this land was intensely loved and those who had no wish to cling to it were negligible in number.

More than 5,000 persons gathered at the four-days' session in Fargo. It was held at the North Dakota State Agricultural College, on the outskirts of the city, through the kindness of President Shepherd and his faculty. The homelike and hospitable city was organized to welcome us through the genius of Father Vincent Ryan, that scholarly apostle who presides over St. Patrick's parish. A singular sight was presented in the main college auditorium, Festival Hall. Upstairs and downstairs galleries were a riot of displays: visual material for catechetics, children's books, catechetical exhibits from country parishes, exhibits of publishing and church-furnishing firms, various agencies and societies, most of which display has become in the last two or three years a recognized part of Catholic Action conventions. Some sixteen Bishops from the United States and Canada, and several Abbots attended the papers and discussions, while many more sent special messages. From city and country parishes in the Middle West and Northwest and scattering East and South came about 450 priests, while hundreds of teaching Sisters thronged the hall. Yet all were in a minority to the agricultural populace young and old who attended from start to finish.

Speaking with reference to the coming meeting at Fargo the Most Rev. John G. Murray, D.D., Archbishop of St. Paul observed:

The Conference renders invaluable service in drawing attention to the solicitude which the Church has always and everywhere exercised for the well-being of agriculture and those identified with it; in portraying the dignity of the agrarian occupation and its excellence as the surest source, normally, of material and spiritual security, in pleading for a practical recognition of the demands of Christian justice and charity within the ranks of agriculture itself, as also in the multiple situation where the interests of the industrialist and the farmer offer possibilities of conflict.

There are different ways in which the Church can operate to make life more feasible for those who dwell upon the land. In the first place, practice of religion can be made much more tolerable and easy than it usually is in the scattered rural regions of the United States. From its beginning, the Conference has devoted attention to the paramount question of religious instruction for rural children. Character training, visual education, the religious education of children in the home, the religious vacation school, the Confraternity of Christian Doctrine, religious correspondence schools, the work of the Sodality of the Blessed Virgin in rural parishes, are all part of its program, which were discussed by specialists.

But the facilitation of religious practice, the development of religious life, while it lays the foundation and secures the paramount good, is all vain, all its efforts are lost, unless the tiller of the soil can make his living from the soil. If he cannot keep his home, if he cannot educate his children, if he cannot make a livelihood, all the opportunities of religion are wasted upon empty pews. For he will bundle his belongings into the old Model T and make off to join the urban proletariat and so ultimately get upon the relief rolls.

Or he may start rolling West to Oregon or the Coulee Dam country in Washington. One lovely October day just past, some 230 families rolled into one Oregon town and they kept on rolling. If they cannot come in Fords they come on freight cars. The tune of the old Spiritual: "I'm a rollin' through an unfrien'ly worl'" might well be sung by them; for at many state lines in the West you now see neatly established "ports of entry," with no signs of welcome for such immigrants. Such a "port" meets you even as you enter Idaho from Washington.

Yet the optimism of the people in the drought-stricken regions is tremendous, and the Conference passed a special resolution commending it. You feel, rightly or wrongly, that such optimism cannot fail, that there is a power behind it which no force of mere nature can overcome.

But how can the Church get justice and charity applied to the land? One way is by advocating appropriate governmental legislation. Let us hope that with the task of getting re-elected laid upon the shelf, the present Administration will give thought to the fact that as yet little has been done to enable a young man to take up farming, even though he be competent and experienced. Nooks and corners of the more fertile and attractive regions of the country such as the Pacific Northwest, are dotted with makeshift cabins and garden patches that denote a despairing attempt to find access to the soil. But with the expenditure of billions upon public works, with all that is done to refinance home ownership, little appears to be done to finance those who wish to start when young.

The crucial question of rural taxation still remains unsolved. No method has yet been devised whereby the man who represents the backbone religiously and economically of the nation, the man who raises a family while actually living upon and operating the small tract of land that he owns shall not be penalized by the burden of land taxes. He bears a burden which should properly fall upon the absentee owners of large estates or upon agricultural corporations or upon the various agencies that obtain the smaller farmer's money.

Legislation however cannot substitute for voluntary effort, for what can be accomplished in the rural parishes by adult education and cooperative endeavor. Around this topic centered the most animated discussions of the Conference.

In the last couple of years interest in the United States has risen rapidly in the cooperative movement, both the finance cooperatives or credit unions and the consumers' cooperatives. Much of this interest was aroused by the success of the programs carried out for the people of Eastern Nova Scotia by the faculty of St. Francis Xavier University, Antigonish, and their associates. At the Fargo conference that work was described by the Rev. Michael Gillis, of St. Francis Xavier's. The Bishop of Fargo, the Most Rev. Aloysius J. Muench, D.D., recommended the establishment of the credit union in every parish of his diocese. At the conference he described the actual working of the credit union in the parishes.

While the vast possibilities for good of the cooperative movement were enthusiastically welcomed, it was not hailed as a panacea for all economic and social ills. In Canada the Church has drawn a sharp line between the socialistic application of cooperative methods to government advocated by the Woodsworth's Cooperative Commonwealth Federation and voluntary cooperative organiza-

tion encouraged and coordinated by the State, in the spirit of the
Encyclicals. At Fargo stress was laid upon the basic truth known
to all who have engaged in cooperative enterprises, that these are
not pledged to success unless those who take part in them, even as
mere beneficiaries, are previously thoroughly grounded in cooperative principles, not technical rules of the cooperative game alone,
but also in Christian virtues of justice and charity. The success of the
Antigonish experiment is attributable to its recognition of this truth.

That religion is the ground work of true American culture, that
the family is the unit of society and that its needs should determine
the size of the agricultural economic unit, that tenancy should be
restrained and distributed ownership of the land encouraged, that
the curricula of rural schools should consider the specific needs of
rural children, that the Four-H Club movement ably advocated by
the Rev. Felix Pitt, Superintendent of Schools of the diocese of
Louisville, is a prime extra-curricular means to this end, that Catholic children justly claim a share in vocational training, transportation and other extra-curricular benefits provided by the State at
the taxpayers' expense, and other matters embodied in the Conference resolutions, are becoming accepted by all thinking persons,
even non-Catholics, who are familiar with the rural situation.

The most difficult task of all still lies before the Catholic Rural
Life Conference: that of helping to formulate a truly organic social
and governmental policy for the nation from the standpoint of
Christian ethics, and of agriculture as man's most basic occupation.
Invitations from non-denominational groups have been received
for such an undertaking, which is expected to give plenty of work
for the Conference during the coming year.

The Catholic Agrarian movement displays less decorative foliage
than other more popular activities. The spectacular and the sentimental find little part in it. But its roots are deep in the physical
existence and basic moral problems of the Catholic people. Forgotten today, these cares of the humble will be the debate of the
mighty tomorrow. No other movement can more clearly demonstrate the creative power of religion.

Social Questions Are Many

O NE OF THE foremost Catholic analysts of Bolshevist history
and doctrine, Professor Waldemar Gurian, wrote in 1936:
"Bolshevism and National Socialism are not simply epi-
sodes in the internal politics of a particular state. They are the
expression of definite processes of social and intellectual disintegration." (*The Future of Bolshevism*, p. 109.)

The bearing of those words has been brought out to terrific
extent by the present war. The war has shown that the greatest
devastation is wrought not by the obliteration of national boundaries; not by the carnage and suffering inflicted on millions of
helpless people; but by the forward march of a social and political
philosophy which places humanity entirely at the mercy of a
power which knows no responsibility to God or man. This philosophy is the result of disintegration and is propagated by it.

Were we reasonably diligent and reasonably prepared, we could
surely defend this nation against any combination of armed forces
from a war-torn and already impoverished Europe. But we are in
the utmost plight when it comes to defending ourselves against the
forward march of world Socialism. Defeat and victory are alike
indifferent to it. To quote Gurian again: "Even a creed theoretically most inadequate will triumph over a world without faith
which takes its traditions and civilization seriously *only so long as
they are not actually shaken* and it is not asked to stake everything
in their defense."

Our traditions and civilization *have* been shaken to their roots.
Ours are a bourgeois tradition and a bourgeois civilization. This is
their strength. But it is also their weakness; for the middle classes
are stable as long as they are undisturbed. If, however, they lack a
firm religious foundation for their traditions; if these traditions
persist merely by force of habit, they are cast overboard like ballast
when middle-class stability is threatened.

For this reason, I wish to repeat again what I wrote on June 1: "We are still free, but we are not forming our Catholic social and political philosophy. We are taken up with immediate, not ultimate problems. But the ultimate will soon prove immediate. . . . For fear of coming world Socialism, let us build at once a sound and practical Catholic social program in the United States. Let us work while the day is still at hand."

The search for sound solutions is imperative because of the present situation. Questions of social and political order are not the supreme problems of man's existence. These remain the same at all times: to praise, reverence and serve God, and thereby to save his immortal soul. In itself, it is not of supreme importance for me to live in a thoroughly just social order nor a perfectly governed state. If it were, the vast majority of humankind would be doomed to the utmost disappointment; for most social orders and most governments are pretty wretched affairs by any absolute standards.

The importance of these matters arises from circumstances. We live in a time when men's souls as well as bodies are claimed in the name of the social and political order and this order itself is perverted and denaturalized in favor of a wholly atheistic or un-Christian point of view.

The social note, therefore, is sounded not because we are especially "social minded," though individual experience has made some of us more than others alert to social disorders. On the contrary, the fact is that, as Christians, we do *not* place man's be-all or end-all in the nation, the class, the race, or any other collectivity; because we stand above and beyond the temporal social order and view social problems in their just proportions.

All the imperativeness in the world, however, will get us nowhere unless we are willing to face two very stubborn and annoying conditions that, like watch-dogs, bar the path to any genuine and constructive solutions to social problems: the solutions are *complex*, not simple; they are *disagreeable*, not pleasant and amusing. In short, they are like war itself; and war, today, is neither simple nor pleasant.

People do not like complex answers to simple questions. They want a scheme, a plan which will do away with all their own or other people's troubles in a jiffy, Townsend plans or faith healing.

Many people fail to understand what a multitude of factors govern the most ordinary patterns of human relations. They imagine that instinct and passion suffice as a practical rule.

These answers are complex because broad principles, which any Communion-breakfast orator announces, take on a hundred phases when applied to actual life. It is easy to preach honesty in business; but a group of intelligent Catholic businessmen can spend a year of profitable evenings studying all the meanings of that assertion as it applies to their daily responsibilities: as salesmen, managers, financiers, owners, advertisers, etc. Labor and capital should collaborate, say the Encyclicals; but the when and the how of collaboration are a life study for either of the two principal parties.

Religious-minded people often try to dodge the watch-dog by exclaiming that all would be well if men loved God, or lived up to their duties as Catholics, or some other simple formula. "Let us bring God into public life" is splendid and resounding. But the relation of religion to material concerns is not always such a simple matter to formulate; and if incorrectly formulated can lead to devastating errors. Hitler made his own formula when he demanded "positive Christianity," a Christianity of deeds, not sentiments. But he soon showed that under that apparently innocent phraseology, as under his equally innocent expression *Gottgläubig* "believing in God"—lay an onslaught on the foundations of Christianity.

The student who has tried to unravel these complexities is faced with a nasty alternative. No matter how he tries to simplify matters, if he speaks or writes for the general public, he is sure to arouse a certain amount of weariness and disgust; which means that his message, after all his labors, is lost. On the other hand, if he yields to temptation, and offers a spellbinder's platform, he is bound to be challenged by those who are shrewd enough to see the lack of qualifications in his sweeping assertions. Or else he will be given a dig in the ribs for "talking generalities."

There is only one remedy for this discouraging state of affairs. Those who do *not* engage themselves as specialists with social prob-

lems should respect the difficulties of those who do, and be patient
enough to afford to their distinctions and their details the same
attention that they would, for instance, to a military man when he
talks of the intricacies of army tactics; or to a physicist when he
explains the elements of induction or atomic weight. In short: let
them realize that a complex disease means a complex remedy; and
the diseases of modern society—though simple enough in their ultimate cause, which is the abandonment of God and His moral law
—are most intricate in their daily manifestations.

There are no easy, pleasant solutions for any genuine social
questions. Humble, enlightened and practical men—rich or poor,
employers or workers—find their way to solutions with little difficulty. These men are an honor to our country and an example to
all the world. But the vast majority find these examples distasteful
and repugnant to an extreme. They remain entrenched in selfishness and prejudice. Nothing but appalling calamity—if even that—
or a miracle of grace can dislodge them from their positions. With
a world crashing around their ears they remain as pigheaded as
Lord Craigavon remains with de Valera.

Two years ago this writing, to a day, I walked at an early hour
through the quiet streets of Rheims with a French colleague—a
priest, patriot and World War hero. On that day France was celebrating at Rheims the restoration of the great Cathedral. Public
buildings and humbler dwellings were flaunting the Tricolor; but
scarce a flag was displayed upon the tight-shuttered homes of the
well-to-do. *Voilà nos bourgeois!* exclaimed my friend with some
bitterness. "They live for themselves and forget their country.
During the World War they threw the burden on others; and they
will suffer, in the future, for their folly of today."

In appalling fashion Father Doncoeur's prophecy has come true;
and his generous heart must be wrung with sorrow. The fundamental weakness of France was not her Soviet-ridden proletariat.
Communism weakened France frightfully. To the outbreak of the
present war it was an active agent in crippling and paralyzing the
nation's defense. Nevertheless, from 1934 on, forces lived and
moved in the nation which were steadily pushing communism off

the scene. These forces were religious and patriotic; primarily religious. They were lifting the nation's workers and peasants back to sanity. A terrific obstacle to their progress, however, were the religiously indifferent elements in the upper French bourgeoisie. Selfishly complacent, they played with radical elements abroad while at home they frowned upon every attempt to put Christian justice and charity into practice.

In recent years, the opinion generally expressed by the French hierarchy was that the country must be regenerated from below rather than from above: by that moral regeneration of the masses advocated by Pius XI in the *Quadragesimo Anno*. The greatest obstacle to such regeneration was the apathy of these bourgeois elements, on the one hand; on the other, the blind confidence placed by Catholic ultra-conservatives in the restoration of Christianity by governmental fiat.

Shall such a sharp lesson be needed in order to teach our vast and self-satisfied American middle-class that the privileged position they now enjoy in a famine-threatened world may be maintained only by severe personal sacrifices for the good of the social order: painful, laborious, personal sacrifices? The lesson should not be needed, for there is yet time. But the time is short. We face now the unpleasant fact that the sores of our present conditions, with their millions of unemployed, can be healed only by a complex, bitter medicine, administered in the clinic of the Divine Physician Himself. The least we can do is to be patient with those who help to prescribe it.

Religious Temporal Action

DECEMBER, 1954

I N THE PICTURE from an Amsterdam weekly that lies before me, two women numbered 54831 and 64631, are squatting on the floor with their backs to the photographer. The figures are marked in white on their prison garb, along with Chinese characters which are said to denote "South District." The picture shows little of their faces; long, stringy hair covers the backs of their partly turned heads, robbed now of their nun's bonnet and guimpe. These two women are "criminals" in China's People's Democracy. Their guilt—they were practicing an "active" religion: followers of the Eternal, but caring systematically for the temporal needs of orphans, or the aged, or the sick in hospitals.

How far will the modern world sympathize with these saintly "criminals?" What is our position as to the religious authenticity of such an "active" religion? The question is one of the modern age. As long as religion stayed within the bounds of the so-called "corporal works of mercy," nobody felt inclined to raise much difficulty. For the Christian to clothe the naked, harbor the harborless, bury the dead was a fairly simple and self-explanatory performance, to which none would object, unless the merciful largesse conflicted with some vested interests of pocket or power. So today, it is regarded as entirely in keeping, by people of every shade of belief and unbelief, that the Abbé Pierre should have emptied the wardrobes and larders of bourgeois Paris in a blitz-relief for the sufferers, the *clochards* and beleaguered families, during the bitter winter of 1953-54. Even the People's Government would abstain from unfavorable comment. It is quite a different affair when we ask how far religion should enter the field of "preventive" welfare: work scientifically organized, systematic work employing technical methods and, in some cases, disturbing the scheme of social relations or conflicting with established political patterns.

Will religion one of these days be accused of having overstepped its bounds, of poaching upon welfare territory supposedly reserved for the all-providing state, or more properly entrusted to the highly competent benevolencies of far-seeing private corporations? The answer to this question is, of course, a point of fact. My only query is in the field of religion itself: how does religion from its own nature justify such action, so that when you bring *force majeure* to bear upon Numbers 54831 and 64631—otherwise known as Mother Alphonsa and Mother Germana—the inference would be that you are not just discouraging the useless efforts of a couple of fascist busybodies; you are striking at the heart of religion itself, destroying one of its proper and authentic acts. From the history of the Bolshevik movement I find it difficult to avoid concluding that the basic reason for its persistent attacks upon all forms of religiously motivated charitable and social action is the sense that such activities *are* in fact religiously authentic; that the source of such particular virulence is something more truly ideological (and hence inversely religious) than a mere assertion of blind violence or political power-lust. A certain curious dynamism seeks to lurk in the quasi-romantic notion of combating the Divinity itself.

I

One may, of course, discreetly sidestep the whole question, taking refuge in a purely sublimated and extramundane religion. In this hypothesis, the truly spiritual man is in no manner concerned about the vicissitudes of this world. Religion would minister exclusively to the soul of man in such manner as if that soul were not incorporated in a material body but shared the freedom of the angels themselves. It is easy to point to the blatant and gross errors of a materialistic humanitarianism, the aberrations of a so-called "social Gospel," which had its day, and its subsequent night, in nineteenth-century Europe. From the strictly eschatological point of view, I know that my earthly life will end and I can't take it with me, and the heavens and the earth will pass away by fire. Hence I might infer that there is no use trying to create a better and more decent world in which to live and raise children; and the H-bomb at our doors utters a loud Amen. Moreover, it is clear that we cannot accurately picture Jesus of Nazareth as primarily a social reformer, although He did inveigh against a multitude of social disorders, such as public and private dishonesty, neglect of parents, exploitations of the poor, etc. Strong as was His language against the hypocrites, robbers and oppressors, He steadfastly refused to picture human life as a possible paradise. To sharpen the lesson, He chose to experience life in its most uncompromisingly rugged aspects, and reminded us that all the marketable grain stored in the most scientifically built barns was useless and worthless when God, at the moment of death, should require an account of the rich man's own soul. (I regret that I have to differ from Hannah Arendt who finds Luke 16, 23-31, the only passage in the teaching of Jesus that deals explicitly with hell, or that "it required several centuries after Jesus' death to assert itself at all." Surprising rather is the emphasis that He placed on the idea; an emphasis forgotten in the popular "social-reformer" picture of the Saviour, but vigorously followed up by the earliest preachers of Christianity.)

It is easy, in other words, to erect an impressive straw man out of these harsher aspects of Jesus' teaching, and with due vigor to knock it resoundingly down. But it is not the complete picture, nor does such an interpretation help to bridge the gap between the spiritual and the temporal. It fails to consider man as he is: born, living and dying as a member of a family, of a neighborhood, of a national and world community linked by ever-increasing intimacy and interdependence. Simple as is the "action" program of the Gospel, there is no reason for oversimplifying. It contains the germs of technically equipped and effectively organized social action. The Good Samaritan is not satisfied with staunching the wounds of the Jew who lies robbed and beaten by the wayside. He provides him with conveyance, and devises a little plan by which incidental expenses may be covered in case of need. The five thousand in the wilderness are organized in convenient rows before being miraculously fed, and proper persons are appointed to care for the operations. Critical hearers are reminded that the fiery prophet, in the ancient days, used the water of the River Jordan as part of his apparatus for healing the leper Naaman. Of the thirty-three years of His life on earth, the Saviour devoted thirty to exemplifying His philosophy of the family as the basic unit of society, and His "beginning of miracles" at Cana of Galilee was performed expressly in order to honor the institution of marriage.

The question of the spiritual authenticity of systematic religious action on behalf of temporal needs is not confined to a splitting of theological hairs. The question is bound to affect, to an ever-increasing degree, the position of religion and of religious bodies in the modern world. (Systematic, that is to say, as contrasted with mere spontaneous reactions to an immediate emotional appeal.) This authenticity is questioned by the omnicompetent welfare state, and sharply contested by the omnipotent totalitarian regime, whose answer to any of its manifestations is to accuse its agents of plotting against the state and put them in jail.

II

When we turn to examples of concrete action the question of authenticity raises the question of tests, for which I offer my own frank opinion. I believe that the basic test for any such type of operation is that it should be *genuine*, that is to say, it should deal with real human needs in a real way; a requirement easier to state than to fulfill. A genuinely religious person is sensitive to truly human needs from the very fact that he habitually considers people not as mere objects, statistical units of social construction or experimentation, but as subjects, associated with himself in the common lot of labor, service, suffering and joy. The religious person who sees these needs places himself in the situation of others whose condition is remote from his own personal experience: the *total* situation, of greatness as well as littleness, of talents, capacities and successes quite as well as of limitations and failures. Pity and mercy are divine virtues: seeing the multitude hungering in the desert, Jesus "had pity on them." Justice without pity or mercy is cruelty, says

St. Thomas Aquinas, but mercy without justice goes out into waste. Both justice and mercy demand intelligence, and the sharpest test of the genuine religious experience is its intelligence, its penetrating understanding glance at what the fellow human being really needs, which may be not at all what we here and now emotionally feel inclined to bestow upon him. In a genuinely religious spirit I would suggest to a group of poor fishermen or farm laborers that instead of looking for an immediate handout for themselves or their families, they should get busy, study hard, and find ways and means to solve their economic problems by tried methods of cooperation. In like manner, I would remind the victims of race prejudice that the surest way to escape from their social bondage is not to confine themselves solely to protests and complaints. They will make better progress if they also strive to better their own condition despite their handicaps, while at the same time seeking grounds for common action with their more fortunate neighbors in the general public interest; common labor for God and country.

The genuineness, the authenticity of my action on behalf of others' welfare, will not be determined quantitatively by the amount of beneficent machinery that I have set in motion—clubhouses or clinics or committees—or by the amount of time and energy that I manage to invest in it. It will be gauged by my understanding of the *entire* human person, in all his complexity and infinite possibilities toward himself, toward God and man.

Those of us who have tried to benefit any depressed group—racially or economically—know how easy it is to state these qualifications; how hard to make them generally accepted.

For the churchman, clergyman or layman, various snares and difficulties lie in wait, once he has embarked on the less strictly obvious forms of social action. He is exposed to the obvious lure of bureaucratic methods, to the seduction of an organization pursuing its own self-centered ends. Sharp problems of self-discipline beset the adventurer in this particular field. It is never easy to keep the even course of courage, strength and wisdom when exposed to the frustrating alternatives of timidity and overcaution, honored as prudence, and of rash exhibitionism, masking as moral courage. In his total dedication to the pressing spiritual and physical needs of the humblest of God's poor, the sheer force of purely remedial toil may discourage him from taking effective action of a more far-reaching, socially constructive nature. Such, for instance, was the predicament of the great Spanish "Apostle of the Negroes," Saint Pedro Claver, S.J., the three-hundredth anniversary of whose death at Cartagena, Colombia, was celebrated on September 9th of this year. Claver lived and died as the "slave of the slaves," ministering for a lifetime to the wretched victims of the African slave-trade, but he left to others the task of eventually securing its abolition. On the other hand, problems can arise like those of the Priest Workers in France, where militant ideologies borrow the glory of religious charity. It is not always easy to keep the lines of motive and spirit clear and not let a very genuine devotion to the human person become subtly appropriated as an instrument for the plans of a political party.

III

It would be easy to multiply these difficulties and illustrate them from the record of noble, but disappointed ambitions. The heart of the problem, apart from questions of personal integrity, courage and ordinary prudence, lies in assigning to religion its proper role, the sphere in which it operates as genuinely religious action. While religion supplies inspiration, lofty perspective, spiritual strength and guidance and contacts with the sources of divine grace, there is a point where inevitably other than strictly religious agencies must take over and work in their proper sphere. The history of Christianity is the history of initiatives; of beginnings in untried areas of human welfare and human rights. Voluntary and religion-promoted action has set in motion numberless remedial and preventive agencies that later developed into the laws and institutions of human society. So, too, the very institutions of the strictly religious society became in time models and inspiration for the institutions of the secular society as well. Thus much in our Anglo-Saxon common law and its associated freedoms originated in the chancery proceedings of the medieval church.

It is not always easy, therefore, for religio-temporal action to fulfill in all integrity its necessarily twofold direction: as action toward God and as action toward man. Both of these directions, in the Christian concept, operate in strict relationship to the person of the God-Man Himself, in whom they are perfectly fused. It is not always easy; but it is always possible, for the record of successful effort is steadily growing, and forms an enormously significant chapter in history. At any rate, in this field lies a major battleground for God-centered religion in our times; possibly the major battleground. Certainly religion will be judged by its accomplishments in this field, but at the same time appreciated, as the spiritual depths of such "units of experience" become more manifest. It is precisely here, for better or worse, that religion comes into face-to-face conflict with atheistic humanism and the ideologies of political violence that such humanism has engendered.

For religious institutions, the highly migratory, mobile and incredibly articulate technological age provides new and unheard of problems of adaptation and of sheer human contact. But the mightier the challenge the greater the opportunity. The recent waterfront situation in New York City was an example of such a challenge. It was met directly by a religious initiative in the person of a "waterfront priest," Father John Corridan, S.J. His initiative, in turn, set on foot those secular remedial forces needed to complete the job of securing peace and order for hard-pressed workers and a long-suffering public. The machinery of law, political organization, economic agencies, education and science are now working and moving steadily toward remedying the acute racial situation in this country, and eliminating at least a major part of its recurrent tensions. Yet religious initiative in great measure set these wheels in motion, and it is religious initiative, acting in its own proper sphere, that in many instances keeps them from grinding to a halt.

I have been able to offer only a few quite obvious remarks about a complex question. May I add further an observation, which in a way is the key to all the preceding. Utterly distasteful—to the modern mind and to all decent instincts—is a purely formal type of action, which treats men as mere objects, and results only in a display of social machinery and statistics. The action we expect of religion, and have the right to expect, is creative by nature: creative not only of better living conditions or more normal relations between human beings, but also creative of the life of God's Spirit as manifested in the affairs of men. But the condition for such creative action is the simplicity and humility of those who engage in it: the wisdom to seek help from God where He alone can aid and to use His methods, prayer, patience and suffering, where human resources are incompetent; the like wisdom to use our own resources of knowledge, investigation, scientific method, where these are entirely competent. Thus it will strive to make both spheres of activity harmonize and cooperate in the joint task of giving man, his family and his community, a home in this life that will best prepare him for the complete fulfillment of his being in the next.

That, I take it, was the basic philosophy of Mother Germana and Mother Alphonsa. It is an idea extremely distasteful to those who would like to make human welfare the mere agency of human power and greed; but it is a very ancient idea and, I think, will persist long after the prison-keepers are dead and forgotten.

The Catholic Intellectual
and Social Movements

MAY, 1955

I N RECENT TIMES, there has developed within the Church a gratifying interest in social movements. The term social movement does not excite the alarm and disquiet which it did a generation ago. We understand better the danger of neglecting problems raised by dislocation and misery; we are better informed as to the history of social movements, and especially of the Catholic social movement during the past hundred years. In this respect the utterances of the Holy Father are keeping us uncomfortably prodded.

Still, as we know, there remains a long distance for us to go. There is the unpleasant fact that in many cases the faithful attend our churches from one end of the year to the other and yet hear from the pulpit no expression that will suggest further study of their neighbor's problems. Obviously the pulpit is no place for discussing problems technically or in detail, but there still remains the great opportunity to create what one might call a social attitude as part of even the elementary gospel of our faith.

We are encouraged also by an increase in social action itself, and a steady growth in the concept of preventive charity as opposed to or contrasted with a merely remedial charity, to use the pregnant expression of Pius XI in his *Quadragesimo Anno*. We see this development in the better understanding of the moral obligation, as well as the political wisdom, of technical assistance to disadvantaged regions and countries. We note a corresponding evolution in the mission field. The value of systematic and preventive organization has become more apparent to our charitable and beneficent organizations. Such developments as the family life movement, the Catholic Rural Life Conference, the interracial movement in its various manifestations, and so on, have brought this closely to our attention.

Have Much to Show Others

I received a rather angry letter the other day from a fellow clergyman objecting to the coming of various prominent foreigners to our shores. What can they teach us about charitable work, he said, we have plenty to show of our own. My reaction was, first of all, that we can always learn something from anybody in such a wide field, and secondly, even if they had nothing to tell us, we might have a few things to tell them. We in this country have no occasion for an inferiority complex. We have developed certain techniques, overcome certain difficulties, especially in the field of community organization and the adjustment of racial difficulties, as well as in many phases of trade-union organization. We can show much to people of other countries.

But with all this a stock-taking is necessary, in view of formidable enemies. The field of social movements is to a considerable extent engineered in this country, especially in certain areas of thought, by people who are hostile to the Catholic Church or to religion itself. We can, of course, cope with a phenomenon like the Planned Parenthood movement on the basis strictly of ethics and of moral theology. But how far are we able to cope with such a movement on the basis of social science itself? How far is the Catholic intellectual equipped to expose the social fallacies that underlie a contraceptive solution of the immense and complex problem of world population, local or global?

Catholic intellectuals are making steadily great advances in the social sciences. Yet we have not yet achieved that firm position with which we can cope within the area itself, using its own techniques, its own language, its own concepts, whether they be in the field of anthropology, of community organization, of analysis of social structure, of social psychology, or other kindred branches of the human sciences.

There is a certain anomaly in the fact that the Catholic scholar in the present time has won his laurels more in the physical sciences than in the social or humane or human sciences. We who possess the key to that delicate complex of body and soul, of existence and development which we call the human being; we who rejoice in a coordinated philosophy of the spirit and its relation to the physical order; we who follow a consistent interpretation of history: why should we hesitate to enter precisely the field where we grapple with the problems of the human being as such? The Catholic scholar should be the first to pronounce with ease upon the laws of the spirit as they affect the structure of the social organism. With nearly 2,000 years of spiritual analysis and practice behind us, we should be the first to give a clue to the psychological problems involved in human relations.

Areas of Social Research

At a recent discussion by a group of Catholic intellectuals, certain dominant approaches were presented in crucial areas of social research. They were briefly, first, the problem-approach, which looks upon social science as a kind of fire-fighting apparatus which is to be employed whenever a crisis arises in society, the Church is threatened or morals are in danger of being impaired. The second is the economic approach, which gives the impression that economics constitutes either the only or the most important social science. Third, there is the moral approach, which involves the whole area of social values, and assumes that research in social science must be primarily concerned with what ought and ought not to be. All these are capital fields; as well as another field which was strongly emphasized at this discussion, which is the need of greater scientific knowledge as to the social and cultural system of American Catholicism itself, the study of the suburban parish, recruitment of new members, assimilation with the surrounding world, etc., the field of religious sociology which has recently been emphasized in Europe.

On all of these one can easily dilate, but I wish rather to indicate a particular phase of this matter which appeals to me as being particularly timely. Does our Catholic social action or the social action of Catholics—I have both in mind—receive the recognition it deserves, namely, *as Catholic*? Is it understood as Catholic? Is it seen as a declaration of our Faith?

Someone may reply: actions speak for themselves. This is a familiar slogan. Like other familiar slogans, it is only true in a certain sense. Actions do speak for themselves, yet they do not of themselves immediately declare the motive that lies behind them. Certainly everybody welcomes, for instance, Catholic relief work, Catholic hospitals, Catholic work for delinquents, and so on. It is all very excellent. But how far does the sight of such works as we perform lead to an inner knowledge of the high supernatural motive that lies behind them. Even if that knowledge is conceived speculatively, is it experienced, does it penetrate hearts? People are touched by the devotion of the nuns, but do they sense the supernatural faith that impels the nuns' devotion? In other words, why do Catholic thought and action not make a greater impact on the world?

This is not an idle question, particularly when in our present situation we consider the power of the totalitarian ideologies. Marxism may not gravely threaten us in this country, though its influence often extends far beyond its actual profession. But we experience it in dealing with the world at large, and Marxism's baffling characteristic, its terrific power lies precisely in its unity of thought and action. Marxism does not despise pure thought; on the contrary, it grew out of purely theoretical research. Nor does it despise pure action. It can utilize any form of action available. Yet it succeeds to an astonishing degree in fusing both thought and action into a new and formidable unity.

A simple testimony to that is the effect of the brainwashing technique. Unfortunates who are subjected to that treatment are not affected solely by arguments, nor are they browbeaten simply by physical torture. The fusing of the two into one dynamic whole is what does the work.

At the present moment in East Germany, Catholics and religious people in general are alarmed and appalled by the terrible efficiency of the East German Communist youth movement, the FDJ, with its quasi-sacramental system that requires from immature children a profession of faith similar to Confirmation. That experienced and authoritative person, Dr. Adolf Kindermann, recter of Koenigstein Seminary, now visiting this country, says that it is impossible for the younger generation of East German youth to resist this treatment indefinitely.

An Inverted Christianity

Yet the union of thought and action is precisely that of Christianity itself, for Marxism is an inverted Christianity that has profited by the divorce of thought and action lying at the root of modern unbelief. Hence the profound difference between the Marxist or Communist movement and the purely rationalistic movements that preceded it. These laid the groundwork for Marxism by creating that vacuum, that frightful cleft in human existence which simply had to be bridged.

The separation between thought and action, between matter and spirit, which came as a result of the dissolution of religious belief in the 17th and 18th centuries was by its very nature intolerable for the human spirit and had to be bridged in some way or other. Since the Christian solution was rejected, the Marxist was able to take hold. And it was the genius of Lenin to unite the two with incredible efficiency into one formidable movement.

For this reason, the Catholic intellectual may need to direct his attention to some extent in this particular direction. If we cannot solve this problem of the union of thought and action, particularly the supernatural thought of faith and of action under grace in the Christian community; if we cannot create and perfect this union on a philosophically, theologically and practically solid basis, we may expect a continued series of dangerous substitutes. An immense amount has been preached and written by Catholic scholars on the mistakes of John Dewey and his associates. Yet Dewey and Kilpatrick and others in the field of pragmatism or progressive education represent a *per se* laudable attempt to fill this gap and to answer this very natural craving in the human mind for such a dynamic union. The unfortunate thing is that they achieve it only by sacrificing the rich integrity of the diverse members which they strive to unite.

This divorce between thought and action has not only worked its devasting effect in the community in the world at large, it has its effect on the Church itself. Social apostles bitterly complain that there is fine preaching and theory about social matters, and on the other hand a lot of unrelated activity. Social movements, even Catholic social movements, can develop into a clattering bureaucracy.

I assume we all agree that it is extremely important at the present day to present the true spirit of the Church. What is the fundamental attitude of the Church, that basic position to which all its further actions and developments are referred? In the minds of a vast number of our fellow citizens, this attitude is either completely unknown or else it is misrepresented as being an attitude hostile to the ultimate good of humanity; an attitude of power seeking. The Church, in their view, is a tremendous organism, venerable, worthy of great respect, of enormous interest historically, with a career studded with bright luminaries of knowledge, holiness, and so on. But yet they conceive it as being in itself basically self-seeking. Nothing but a special divine grace can expel from certain minds such a false notion.

Spirit of the Church

Hence it is opportune that we do all in our power to present the true spirit of the Church to the present generation. We can of course, and should, display that spirit through theological and historical learning, explaining to people our true position, appealing to the documents of our Faith, to its official pronouncements, to textbooks, to catechetical teaching. Again we can attack misconceptions by pointing to our own acts and the past beneficence of the Church; thus offering an adequate refutation of such suspicion.

Yet there still remains something to be done. Even with all argument and demonstration there still remains a need to present the very *spirit of the Church*, that spirit which people sense immediately, the intimate connection between our Faith and its manifestations in human action, and the connection between that sacramental life of grace which is the life of the Church and her concern about the humble problems of daily living.

Good example, of course, accomplishes much. Yet good example as such is not the complete answer. People who have no perceptible religious faith often give admirable example. Certainly Albert Einstein has set an example of many Christian or Judeo-Christian virtues. He was of humble demeanor, he was modest and helpful, he was humanitarian and peace-loving and had a kindly sense of humor. He was in many ways an admirable person, and yet, from what we ascertain, religiously he was most vague. The complete answer does not lie with good deeds or theory alone, but in the evident combination of the two, the infusion in such a manner that they are seen and experienced as one in the interior of the human person.

To point up what I have just said: it could be one of the fine works of the Catholic intellectual today to work out ways and means in the light of our Faith, and in the light of social science as such, as to how this fusion can effectively be perfected within the human person itself. Wherever this occurs, it makes a profound effect. People experience, as it were, an insight into the spirit of the Church, a feeling that they can, as it were, touch it by perceiving this fusion of faith and action. And of course to grasp the true spirit of the Church, or the true attitude of the Church, is to sense the presence of the Holy Spirit Himself, who as the soul of the Church makes Himself known through her outward vesture and her outward acts. So, to sum up even more precisely, it is the work of the Catholic intellectual today to work toward the manifestation of the Holy Spirit in the world through the manifestation of His presence in the Church itself.

Faith and Action

One may say this is rather a mystical approach; nevertheless it is a specifically practical matter and is, I am convinced, capable of scientific investigation. We know that the Jociste movement under Canon Cardijn has done much to illuminate some of the more difficult angles of this idea. That movement was specifically concentrated on illuminating the kind of people remote from Christianity, completely severed from all Christian influence, through an immediate contact, as it were, between faith and action. This idea is the inspiration of a certain number of important religious ventures in the present day, of religious and of the laity.

I would go still further. I feel that this manifestation of faith and action should be made apparent not just in active individual kindness and immediate approach between Christians and non-Christians, or believers and unbelievers, but should become apparent in a much wider field. It should be seen even in the field of organized charity, of organized social movements. Our very manner of organization, our approach to the matter-of-fact duties of organization, of the human relations therein involved, should manifest this union of faith and works. Furthermore, it should appear in the participation of Catholics with social movements on the wider scale of the general public. In other words, where the Catholic is seen as taking part in social movements for the welfare of the state or the city or on an international basis, he should not only be on the defense against pernicious and immoral social doctrines, thereby vindicating his Faith and morals, but there should be a direct sense of the true spirit of Christianity in the very nature of his participation: in other words, a productive insight.

"The fund of truth contained in Western philosophy is largely a fund of 'insights,'" says perceptive Josef Pieper. "It is gained by an *intelligere* grounded upon a *credere*. After this *credere* had commenced to wither away, however, it was possible at first for men to continue their acceptance of these 'insights,' even without the perennial re-laying of the foundation of the *credere*. It seemed for centuries as though these were 'purely' philosophical cognitions. For a long time, however, this seeing has been recognized as illusory, and where it was impossible to derive these supposedly 'purely' philosophical insights from a coordinate source in a new faith, there remained and remains hardly any other course than, with progressively critical consciousness in philosophizing, to eliminate from the body of philosophical concepts such insights as have come into being on the basis of a *credere* that is no longer implemented." (*The End of Time*, Pantheon Press, New York, pp. 54-55.)

With a withering of the insights into the great basic metaphysical concepts such as truth, unity, goodness, holiness, moral duty, comes a corresponding decay of insight into the intimate human relationships based upon these concepts; and we suffer a loss of the spirit of Christianity itself.

May I make my point possibly still clearer? It is not enough to enunciate the Christian position as a proposition, however cogently defended. Nor again is it enough to exemplify our position by sheer force of example. The fusion of thought and action is a more arduous and subtle task than either of these two proposals. It is a work of many steps; a gradual gaining of ground, taking the occasions as God's Providence presents them: the traveling of a long and laborious road.

Today minds are more and more open to a sense that nothing is gained by an attempted escape from reality; that human life and the human situation can and ought to be viewed as a whole without falling into either extreme: existential pessimism or fatuous, Norman-V.-Pealish "positive" optimism. The very general favorable response to Paul Hutchinson's recent article in *Look* Magazine on the "Religion of Reassurance" seems like an indication of this healthy trend. If you ask for some points of contact that a program of thought-in-action makes readily with the contemporary mind, one might enumerate something as follows:

Spiritual Authority

Prompt and joyful obedience to spiritual authority shows our confidence in the essential truth and the essential goodness of the Creator; hence our action is a living vindication of the idea of authority itself. To say that we obey the Church out of a spirit of love makes little impression as a bald proposition. But the example of the apostolic man of wisdom, the true Catholic intellectual, who manifests that confidence and love even in the rude tasks of obedience, cannot fail to leave its impression.

In our dealing with the problems of human weakness and recovery, we can illustrate our dependence upon divine grace, as well as the power of a will that is wholly unified by an overwhelming master-love of God and man. The sense of such a unified will cannot be conveyed by mere talk, it must be seen to be appreciated. Similar considerations apply to many other manifestations of our Christian concept of man's conduct in the great dialog between God and man. Those who, as the spiritual writers say, are familiar with God can by their approach to concrete daily problems help save men from that sense of utter strangeness which the modern man experiences at the thought of the divinity. In this same way we can convey to a disordered world a truly theological point of view, the idea that there may be a meaning to a revelation from beyond the visible and tangible scene: the supremacy of love, the Christian notion of the ultimate meaning of history.

The Apocalypse may be for the modern man a closed book, a jumble of outmoded Oriental symbols and myths, but he cannot but feel the spiritual pressure of those who do understand some of its lessons, and who view the tragic and portentous developments of our time in the light of its somber revelations.

Let us study more closely the influence of persons in our times whose approach to the modern world shows some of the characteristics I have described; such men as Canon Cardijn, Jacques Maritain, Don Luigi Sturzo, Riccardo Lombardi and others from whose numbers it would be invidious to select: men and women who personally exemplify a policy of insight.

Fifty years from now, or in less time, our successors will recall the situation of our great cities with their migrant masses, and our suburbs with their shifting population, and will wonder that we did not seize the opportunity to bring men to Christ integrally before it was too late. The Catholic intellectual of today bears much of the burden of representing Christ to a Christless but ever-searching world. Yet intellectual leadership is little understood or cared for by the religious masses of the people. (The situation is not aided by the distance that seems to lie between the meticulous academic productions of our Catholic scholars and the somewhat anti-intellectual tone of much of our popular Catholic mass press or literature.) A really adequate understanding of preventive social charity's profound human-relations technique should by its very nature give us clues to relieving more effectively the world's spiritual misery. Further study of the situation may help us to bridge some of the prevailing gaps.

V

Russia and Communists

The following three items are a rather random selection from articles of my own on communism. Here again, so much has been written and so competently once the American public became really aroused on this subject that most of my own past utterances have now chiefly the interest of pioneer ventures.

I have never held that we can "cure" communism merely by social reform. Communism is a disease, a spiritual infection that can poison minds in any condition of life, the wealthy and privileged as well as the proletarian poor. Experience of those exposed to communist indoctrination forcibly and over long periods seems to suggest that there comes a moment in that process when a fateful decision must be made: Will the victim finally decide to swallow the potent drug and yield his mind to the deadly current, against which there is no natural reaction. Social reform—genuine reform of genuine abuses—is imperative if we hope to block the poison's entrance and offset communism's insidious appeal to discontented masses embittered by an oppressive colonialism, by racism and economic exploitation. But social reform is not genuine if it is adopted as a mere cautionary measure. The threat of communism arouses us to its need, warns us of duties neglected, but the motive of true social reform is the love of God and man, communism or no communism. Its sources are found in the Christian concept of man himself.

There is nothing profoundly original in my philosophy of the absolute prerequisites for meeting the challenge of communism. It was derived from long study of the standard sources of information and from concepts developed in the papal encyclicals and the many utterances of our present Holy Father, of our American bishops and of the leaders especially of free labor in the United States. Its postulates are evident enough. What puzzles me is that it has taken so long for so many people in this country, lay and clerical, Catholic

205

and non-Catholic, ultra-conservative or ultra-liberal to recognize it. My own views have remained substantially the same throughout and for the time still allotted me I see no reason why they should alter. Their most succinct expression is in the encyclical of our late Holy Father, Pius XI, "On Atheistic Communism" (Divini Redemptoris).

The three papers in this section deal with certain specific and live topics in our present struggle with naked power and Communist ideology. The question of the "United Front" (later the "Popular Front") or organized cooperation with Communists for worthy and ostensibly innocent projects, caused great perplexity and confusion in non-Communist circles when it was first proposed. My own article, entitled "Can We Cooperate With Communists?" was written to point out for American readers the basic equivocation in such proposals. "The Race Baiters" was written during the close of the period before the second World War. It dealt with some of the countless examples where extremes meet, a phenomenon to which my own experience has made me rather particularly alive. I believe that some of its lessons may be a warning to those who believe that racial prejudice is something you can enjoy with impunity. In the autumn of 1938, on my return from six months in Europe, I expressed the view to an American audience that Hitler and Stalin would eventually join hands. In point of fact they did—to the confusion of all their respective friends—and the lesson of "The Race Baiters" was once more exemplified.

"War Aid to Russia" was written in reply to a question that troubled the minds and hearts of God-fearing people in the United States. By an odd coincidence—or was it a coincidence—a rather militant Catholic diocesan weekly answered the question in quite similar fashion a couple of weeks after the appearance of my article. They quoted Roman authority in behalf of their ideas.

Can We Cooperate with Communists?

AUGUST, 1935

THE DECLARATIONS and resolutions at the seventh congress of the Communist International, held in Moscow during the first part of August of this year, raise an immediate question. The press professed surprise at the "indiscretion" of these statements of policy. Why we need be surprised, I do not see, since the plainness of the declarations is their best means of disarming hostile criticism. The Communist can say that his cards are now on the table, so there is no longer reason for investigating him any further. When his final purpose is made manifest, why accuse him of ulterior purpose? So why refuse to cooperate with him in his immediate projects?

The plan proposed at Moscow is the well-known one of the "united front," only made more explicit and far-reaching. The resolution of August 2 calls on the League of Youth in all Communist countries to join all

bourgeois democratic, reformist and Fascist parties, as well as religious bodies and united mass organizations of toiling youth and to carry on within them a systematic struggle to influence the broad masses of youth and mobilize them to oppose militarization and forced labor camps.

According to this plan Communist youth should join with an organization like the newly formed Catholic Youth Organization (C. Y. O.), with the purpose of drawing them into joint activity for ends which would presumably be acceptable to both Catholic and Communist young men. So definite is this proposal that on August 8 F. Walter, German Communist delegate, recommended to the Congress that Catholics and Communists should unite in Germany for the common aim of overthrowing Fascism. The idea is likewise proposed that a united governmental front should be formed, according to which Communists should take active part with moderate elements in sharing the responsibilities of government, in opposition to "Fascism and reaction."

The answer to these proposals is obviously contained in the proposals themselves. As this writer has for years maintained, not one jot or tittle is abated of the ultimate purpose of the Third International, which is likewise the purpose of the Soviet Government. This was made abundantly plain by the various speakers at the congress, as given by the press of the United States, and will doubtless be plainer as the fuller accounts of the Congress are available. Said the Bulgarian Georgi Dimitrov, made famous by his connection with the Reichstag fire trial, "Communists will support wholeheartedly" a united-front government. He added, however:

But we tell the masses frankly: Such a government cannot save you completely. . . . Therefore it is necessary to arm for the Socialist revolution. Only Soviet power can save you. . . .

We must draw increasing numbers into the revolutionary class struggle and lead them to a proletarian revolution.

Such statements can be multiplied indefinitely. They show that all the talk of cooperation is on the proviso that such cooperation shall be merely a stepping stone to "revolutionary leadership." This has been evidenced repeatedly wherever Communists have taken part in common activities with more "moderate" elements, whether these be Socialists or various humanitarian and philanthropic organizations. In itself this should be sufficient reason for regarding with distrust any proposal, no matter how plausibly put, for entering with Communists into any plan of common action. It is not a mere supposition, but the avowed purpose of the Communists to guide the participants into a framework of action in which the whole will be directed to the inevitable Communist goal, the overthrow of all existing forms of government, of all institutions based upon Christian principles, and of religion itself. Why then discuss the matter any further?

The ground for further discussion is the psychological fact that in an emergency cold reasoning is apt to yield to the exigencies of the moment. Where the emergency is extreme, and the type of action needed purely external and momentary, one can hardly refuse the assistance of one's avowed enemies. Boy Scouts and Young Pioneers, for instance, traveling by chance upon the same train, could with difficulty refuse to work together in extracting disabled passengers from under a train wreck. A missionary in the Arctic might welcome being rescued from starvation by a Soviet propaganda plane. The problem arises, however, when the principle that was applied to momentary external action for a transient emergency is now applied to organized cooperation, where principles and policy are brought into play.

In order to make this clear, let us imagine an "ideal" case—from the standpoint of cooperation. The immediate aims, with which we are asked to cooperate, are entirely valid, such as any Catholic may reasonably embrace, such as, for instance, measures to be advocated for social security; interracial justice against known instances of racial discrimination; the promotion of international peace; protection of our institutions against the threat of a dictatorship, etc.

Furthermore, there is a profession of complete sincerity as to any attempt to capture the leadership. Any scheme, open or covert, to ensnare Catholics into an ultimately revolutionary movement is strenuously denied. "You will be left entire freedom," is the reply to our anxious questionings. "We frankly acknowledge, as Communists, that we should like to see everyone of you enrolled in the Third International, and have you fight shoulder to shoulder with us at the barricades: just as you would like to see us converted to the Catholic religion. We would make you Communists if we could. But we pledge you our word of honor that in this instance we have no such intention. We are honestly, deeply concerned about this immediate threat to liberty, peace, security, or our other human rights. Non-Catholics of every description, Protestants, Jews, believers of every shade are joining with us in this fight for justice. You alone hang back, because you doubt our sincerity and believe you are being trapped into violence. Yet at this very moment those agencies, like the Nazis in Germany, who once pretended to befriend you by attacking Communism in their own country, have now turned upon you and are cruelly persecuting Catholics. Are you better than the Founder of your own religion, who so gravely warned against the sin of rash judgment?"

If we assume that such an argument is presented to those who are vaguely informed as to World Communism but painfully alive to the actual evils from which they suffer, evils which cry out for united effort, it is clear that cold reasoning has but a slim chance against the force of an appeal clothed in the emotional robes of moral dignity. While good sense demands that the patently insincere be branded as insincere, and that we be men enough to do so, yet it is anything but comforting to be *obliged* to cry insincerity in order to prove the logic of one's position. And the case is doubly complicated when those who are accused of fostering an insincere policy happen to be themselves, personally, innocent victims of clever propagandists. It is harder to tell an innocent man that he is duped, than it is to denounce a rascal.

At present there are a considerable number of genuinely idealistic persons enrolled under the banner of Communism. Their number will doubtless increase, in the form of sympathizers, as this program of accommodation and conciliation gains momentum. The problem of such persons is not to be lightly dismissed, for a policy confined exclusively to denunciation is apt to produce an effect contrary to that intended, to create a more deep-rooted distrust of the motives of the denouncer and to furnish more fuel to the flame. It is appropriate to ask, then: Is there not a still more fundamental reason for non-cooperation than that of the aim of the organized Communist movement as such? May we not find such a motive in the nature of action itself?

Much of the confusion that exists in this field comes from our unwarranted habit of considering *action*, in the field of human relations, as divorced from religion and the basic philosophy of life. In the guise of materialism and anti-religion, these latter are considered as forming one whole with action, in the Marxian scheme. Communism is super-dogmatic on this point.

If such a unity is true of Marxianism, it is infinitely more true of Catholicism. Catholicism is not a religion of mere speculation, it is a religion of action, and its action is part of its inner self. The Church, in her reply to the aberrations of Luther, made forever clear that faith and works are inseparable. Where the concepts drawn from our faith are ineffective, it is because we are still in some fashion affected by the Reformation divorce between faith and works, between religious philosophy and action.

The philosophy of action, in the Catholic sense, is developed as Catholics are called to meet newer and newer crises in the light of their ancient faith. Such development demands tremendous application and energy; hence there is nothing surprising in the fact that human nature, which seeks the line of least resistance, should be slow to tackle so formidable a job. Living in the midst of a non-Catholic civilization, it is easy for us to adopt methods and techniques created by those who are unfamiliar with Catholic ethical and religious principles, and persuade ourselves that we have thereby solved the problem of a Catholic plan of action for social reconstruction. It is easy to confuse the science of method with the philosophy of action. But the penalty for such confusion is to place us at the mercy of those who can produce the same methods, but whose idea of action is totally different from our own.

Where Catholicism is successful in coping with the problems of the age, it is always because it has remained true to its utterly distinctive, unique character of action. One of the most effective movements of our time is that of the J. O. C. (*Jeunesse Ouvrière Chrétienne*, "Christian Workers' Youth"), that has taken that stubborn fortress, industrial Belgium, by storm. But the strategy of the J. O. C. is Catholic strategy. It "raises Cain," but it is a Catholic Cain-raising, full of unction and the grace of God. The arsenal of Catholic militancy, or warfare, or strategy, or action-program, is full of a thousand weapons that deal death to sin, egotism, tyranny, greed, and corruption, but they are allowed to rest unused in our arsenals. Only when the enemy is actually thundering at our walls do we think of fitting to them our trembling and unaccustomed hands: such powerful action-weapons as the interior spirit, personal service, reliance in the midst of battle upon Divine Providence, cooperation and charity, filial obedience, the fire and light of grace, the nurture of the Sacraments, the crashing dynamism of the Passion of Christ, the courage of the Resurrection, the communal prayer of the liturgy.

Returning then to the supposedly *sincere* Communist or Communist sympathizer, may we not ask such a person point-blank: "Where principles are involved, that affect action, how *can* we manage to cooperate?" If Catholics act *as* Catholics, and Communists act *as Communists*, they can no more act *together* than an incendiary can cooperate with the fire department, even though they are both out for the same immediate end. If the Communist is sincere, it is not fair to propose such a plan to him, since in order to work with Catholics he is obliged, as a Communist wolf, to don Catholic sheep's clothing: a working attire that will speedily cramp his style. How then can he expect such a line of conduct from the Catholic?

In point of fact, the only actuality of this question arises from the fact that Catholics have been slow in extending the application of the Church's philosophy of action to the complex problems of the present day. The world has moved fast, impelled by steam, electricity, and high finance, and we have not caught up. When we catch up, and we are nearer the goal every day, we shall marvel that such a question should ever have been asked. The "social titanism" of communism, to use Berdyaev's expression, may be laid aside for the nonce. But not as a consistent policy, even in particulars. Let us be honest with the Communists as with ourselves, and devote our energies busily to working out, on the basis of authoritative doctrine, our own Catholic action-philosophy and action-methodology to cope with the evils of the age. If we dawdle any further, we face a serious dilemma.

War Aid to Russia

H IS DRAFT NUMBER had been called, and he put the question directly to his spiritual adviser.

"Tell me Father," he insisted, "tell me plainly what is my duty at the present moment. Is it permissible for me, as a Catholic, as a moral human being, to put myself at the disposal of our Government if this Government is engaged in a transaction which is *intrinsically wrong*? If I allow myself to enter the armed forces of our nation, am I not thereby cooperating with communism, something that my conscience cannot possibly sanction?"

Asked for further explanation of his difficulty, the draftee continued:

"For our Government to extend aid to Soviet Russia is clearly to 'make a covenant with Hell.' No elaborate reasoning is needed on this matter. Sufficient for me, as it must be sufficient for every Catholic—and for every right-minded person—is the word of our late Holy Father, Pope Pius XI, in his Encyclical on Atheistic Communism, *Divini Redemptoris*." Pulling the Encyclical out of his pocket, he read:

Communism is intrinsically wrong, and no one who would save Christian civilization may collaborate with it in any undertaking whatsoever. Those who permit themselves to be deceived into lending their aid toward the triumph of communism in their own country, will be the first to fall victims of their error.

" 'In any undertaking whatsover.' We cannot save Christian civilization by collaborating with such an undertaking. But if such collaboration is intrinsically wrong, if it *is* a 'covenant with Hell,' then there is no other course open to the individual than to make sure he has no part or parcel in such collaboration." Hence, concluded the interrogator, there is only one course open to Catholic young men in this country, once our Government decides to extend such aid: and that is for every single one of them, without exception, to register himself as a conscientious objector to any form of military service whatsoever.

"This is an extreme consequence," he frankly admitted. "It is so extreme, no one can see the vastness of its implications. But if a thing is wrong in itself, it is simply wrong, and no considerations of prudence or expediency can make it right."

Reader, what answer will *you* give to any person who puts to you a similar question—or to yourself, if you are in a similar situation? Yet answer we must; we may not toy with "covenants with Hell."

It will be a serious matter if America's twenty million Catholics—not to speak of many others outside the Catholic Church—consider themselves obliged to declare a complete and radical non-cooperation with our country's program of defense. Such an answer invites debate.

It seems to me that the discussion, complex as it is, will be considerably simplified if we separate its threads into two main components, two aspects upon which an authoritative decision is needed.

1. Does Pope Pius' prohibition of any collaboration with communism necessarily brand, as intrinsically wrong—and thereby something which no Catholic can engage in—the extending of any form of aid, under any circumstances, to the USSR?

2. If this extreme position is untenable, and we are not thereby driven into the corresponding extreme of universal conscientious objection—what position may be taken which does full justice to the menace of Communist collaboration, yet does justice likewise to the dread realities of the war?

I. Even speculatively no distinction can be entertained between the Soviet regime and the Third Communist International. The Stalin regime must unequivocally disavow the International Communist Party. The USSR is essentially committed to subversive policies, even though some of its activities may be held temporarily in abeyance; and it is primarily dedicated to the extirpation of religion. We cannot ignore these things and speak lightly of "any help in an emergency."

Nevertheless, it is not possible to maintain that it is necessarily, universally and intrinsically wrong for a decent government to collaborate in any shape or fashion with any government which is iniquitous and persecutory. The Holy See long since gave up, as hopeless, the idea of maintaining any diplomatic relations with the Soviets. But in the early days of the Bolshevist revolution, the Holy See, with the utmost caution, for purely humanitarian reasons, negotiated with the Soviet Government, through the Papal Mission, for the relief of Russia's starving children. Basic to such collaboration was the principle that it in no way involved even the remotest recognition of communism. Yet the Bolshevist regime was aided by this relief.

Long before our Government undertook to afford diplomatic recognition to Soviet Russia, it consented to sign a series of multilateral treaties or conventions to which the Soviet Government was a party, beginning with the international Sanitary Convention of 1926. These were non-political, non-controversial, but they were, none the less, a mild species of collaboration which, however, involved no approval of communism's principles or activities.

The *Divini Redemptoris* took the occasion of the insidious "outstretched hand," *la main tendue*, of Dimitrov's Popular Front, to make abundantly plain that in no conceivable way can Catholics or Christians allow themselves to further the interests of communism, as such. But does this prohibition apply to any assistance given to Communists in obtaining a worthy military objective in which, for reasons of their own, they are likewise interested? I do not answer this question. I merely raise it.

If any form, however guarded, of military assistance to Soviet Russia in the war against Hitler implies necessarily, immediately and *per se* a "covenant with Hell," if it necessarily implies that collaboration with communism—in any shape or fashion—which Pope Pius so clearly condemns, we may well ask why no reminder to that effect has so far come from our present Holy Father?

Yet, though nothing has mitigated the rigor of the present Holy Father's condemnation and abhorrence of communism, he has not yet warned us of an impending dilemma of conscience. All ears were attuned to his message of June 26, uttered to Catholics in the United States faced with this particular difficulty. Some hoped that the Pope would declare a "holy war" on Soviet Russia. Others were eager to depict him as a "Fascist." But his words contained no such declaration. He spoke, rather, of the "current of black paganism" which was threatening to engulf the world. This paganism Hitler knows how to spread quite as adroitly as do any of Stalin's finest.

From this we need not rashly infer the Pope was indifferent to the extreme gravity that the Russian war problem presents to the conscience of American Catholics. But we may suspect that he relies upon us to use our own wisdom and prudence.

II. Anyone who tries to chart for himself a clear course in this matter is bound to be vexed by a variety of quite contradictory circumstances.

Even a few months' experience has shown what a release the mere mention of aid to Russia affords to pent-up Communist political enthusiasms. Already the newsstands blossom out with pictures, in various types of ecclesiastical garb and pose, of the fatuously pro-Soviet Very Rev. Dr. Hewlett Johnson, Dean of Canterbury. The old "Little Lenin Library" is now being succeeded by the usual illustrated handbooks telling of joyful children on the collective farms and the exploits of Red Army fliers. An atmosphere, too, is created highly congenial to certain types of educators and Government officials, perennially attracted by the Soviet "experiment." And a crushing Russian victory would undoubtedly boost world communism.

On the other hand, Russia's battle against Hitler is being fought not by means of "communism"—a reasonless and impractical ideology—but with the ordinary means of warfare: men, war equipment and war organization. The strength that the Russian people have displayed up to the present in this battle is derived from the spirit of traditional Russian nationalism, now whipped up to fever heat, quite as much as from the propositions of Karl Marx. If the Soviet armies in this battle *necessarily* represent the cause of Marxism, so the German armies necessarily represent the cause of National Socialism, which the same Pope Pius XI characterized as "the obstinacy and provocations of those who deny, despise and hate God"; as "an aggressive paganism."

If, therefore, a serious question of conscience is thought to be created by even an indirect aid to a government that professes Communism, it is plain that another question of conscience arises when any substantial aid is refused to those, unworthy as they are, who are giving material assistance in the task of defending our civilization against the Christ-hating domination of Hitler. As so often occurs in these matters, one extreme position leads readily to an apparent opposite which is in reality its twin.

If the announcement of aid to Russia releases a state of CP enthusiasm in this country, Nazi propaganda is by no means slow to take advantage of an anti-Communist panic over its possibility. Both types of ideologies use the same techniques in order to befuddle the public mind; both can assume the same lofty tones and appeal to similar ingratiating slogans. And both find their happiest fishing ground in the fears of good persons who forget that the Devil may adroitly come around by the back door after resounding expulsion from the front.

The gravity of any sweeping decision in the matter is increased by a further circumstance. An undiscriminating identification of the Russian people and all that concerns them, with the very soul of Communism, plays into the corresponding error of identifying the German people with Nazism.

The Church has not countenanced making a religious issue in this country out of our preparations against the possibility of a Hitler invasion, despite the religious implications of Nazism and of Hitler's policies abroad. It is treated simply and directly as a matter of patriotic and prudent defense. In like manner, the Church as yet has raised no specifically religious issue out of the problem of collaboration with the USSR.

But in a matter of political prudence the interests of God, of Christ and His Church cannot be ignored. Where supreme prudence is to be exercised, supreme effort must be made to avoid evil consequences that would outweigh, even from a purely political standpoint, any good such a collaboration might achieve.

Enlightened public opinion, aroused conscience of all religious bodies, coupled with strict Governmental and local safeguards, should vigorously discourage all attempts of Soviet propagandists to capitalize upon this aid for their own evil purposes.

Last but not least, no stone should be left unturned by our Department of State to keep insisting that whatever aid is granted carries with it an understanding that full and unequivocal guarantees of religious freedom shall be given by the Soviets.

Race Baiters Embrace God Haters

FEBRUARY, 1938

T ODAY I RECEIVED in the mail what at first sight I took to be a belated New Year's greeting. It showed a smiling young Jeanne, Liberty cap and all. Bowing and dancing up to her from one side were a diminutive John Bull and a willowy Uncle Sam, with the weird leer these venerable figures take on when Latin artists manipulate them. To the left stood a huge, vague figure, wrapped in a military coat with a five-pointed star on his peaked cap. The Spanish text below explained that these were the good friends of struggling Loyalist Spain: Soviet Russia, France, Great Britain and the United States.

Uncle Sam's presence on the postcard would have been more convincing if there had been lined up behind him countenances of sixty members of Congress who sent a message of congratulation to the Spanish Cortes on January 30. Msgr. Ready, of the National Catholic Welfare Conference, and the New York Chapter of the National Catholic Alumni Federation, not to speak of *America*, have already expressed an opinion as to the conduct of the gentlemen, whose apparent aim is to involve the United States in a world war. Enough has been said to have elicited a speedy repudiation of the whole affair by at least six of the sixty, who now request that their names be stricken from the document. A study, however, of those who signed and who have not to date repudiated doing so reveals an interesting fact.

Sixteen or more fat issues of the *Congressional Record* are filled with current filibuster against the Wagner-Van Nuys Anti-Lynching Bill, in which event Senators Connally, Ellender and Pepper took a prominent part, along with the Hon. Theodore G. Bilbo and a squad of other professional vindicators of pure white supremacy.

According to Mr. Bilbo, "the presence of the Negro race has

been the greatest curse that has ever been visited upon the South. The shadow of the Ethiopian that has been cast across the white fields of Dixie, has been darker and more ominous than the fatal night that passed over Egypt. He has caused privation, suffering and shame beyond the power of omnipotence to measure." The Ethiopian, complained Mr. Bilbo, "is the one obstacle that has stood in the way of the industrial development of the South."

The Hon. Allen E. Ellender, of Terrebonne Parish, Louisiana, who was Bilbo's runner-up in the marathon of talking, also received a postcard:

I have in my pocket a picture as evidence to show the respect and the admiration the South as a whole has for the law-abiding Negro. I received a postcard this morning sent from a town in Natchitoches Parish, La. On the postcard appears the picture of a monument to an old Negro, who stands on a granite pedestal respectfully bowing his head, and on that granite pedestal is inscribed a tribute by the Southern people to the colored race:

"Erected by the city of Natchitoches, La., in grateful recognition of the arduous and faithful service of the good darkies (*sic*) of Louisiana."

Just how this agrees with Mr. Bilbo's dictum that the Negro is the greatest curse ever visited upon the South is not so clear, or what it has to do with the Anti-Lynching Bill. But perfectly clear, illumined by hours of oratory, is what Mr. Ellender means by a "good darky." He is an individual who recognizes, and shows in every possible fashion of subservience that he is essentially a sub-human creature, created by God and born for one purpose alone, to assist the white man in acquiring and enjoying material wealth and comfort. If he fulfils that purpose he is tolerated and may even get a statue in Natchitoches Parish; if he fails to understand that such is his sole destiny in life, and "develops impertinence," he is a human fiend and the sooner got rid of the better.

Mr. Ellender is not content with mere assertion. Exigencies of the filibuster as well as senatorial dignity require a scientific foundation for the doctrine of the essential inferiority of the Negro. This is at hand in the learned work, *Race or Mongrel*, by Schultz, "the book from which I read yesterday with reference to the Egyptians." Chapter X of this treatise, entitled *The Hindus*, begins thus, in the Senator's quotation:

The Hindus were one of the Aryan races. That is, they belong to the people who called themselves "Aryans" (the noble, the honorable). When they came to India, they found a mass of yellow-black-white mongrels, and recognized that the absorption of this mass was impossible. They also recognized that crossing with these people would destroy the Hindus quickly. . . .

The Hindus recognized that, unless they took vigorous precautions, the Aryans would soon be lost in the mongrel herd. To protect themselves they invented the caste system, one of the greatest inventions of the human mind.

But the downfall came. The pure Aryans were mixed with the sub-humans.

The Hindus were a great race. Their death was a loss to the world, a loss that it is impossible to estimate. Men who call themselves Hindus still exist, Sanscrit derivatives are still spoken, the Hindu spirit, however, is dead; the noble blood has been lost in the Indian quagmire, in the yellow-black-white swamp.

The history of the Hindus, like that of the Jews, proves that race is more important than home, country, flag and everything else put together.

Great was the Hindu; worthless is the mongrel.

Read *Indian Wisdom* by Monier Williams; *The Inequality of the Human Races*, by A. Comte de Gobineau; *Volkstum und Weltmacht in der Geschichte*, by Albrecht Wirth.

To which we may add: read *Mein Kampf*, by Adolf Hitler, and *The Myth of the Twentieth Century*, by Rosenberg (the latter with permission of the Ordinary, if you are a Catholic), and you will be equipped with a complete Nazi doctrine of essential race superiority, "more important than home, country, flag and everything else put together," including such trifles as religion, Christianity and the natural law, as "everything else."

That the Senator was not being misled, but was quoting the genuine doctrine of essential "Aryan" supremacy, is pledged by the erudite Schultz' source of information, Count Joseph Arthur de Gobineau, a Frenchman who shares with an Englishman, Houston

Stewart Chamberlain, the honor of being the ideological inspiration for that Nordic Aryan, Germany's Commander-in-Chief and *Führer*.

Considerable confusion came when some of the filibusterers appealed to the doctrine of States' rights against the application of the Fourteenth Amendment under proposed Federal legislation, for they happened to be individuals who were also ardent advocates of the wages-and-hours bill, attacked by Senator Tydings of Maryland on the ground of States' rights. Hasty retreat was beaten to the early Egyptians and the Hindu Kshatryas. After all, as Senator Ellender observed, we are no longer living in "the old horse-and-buggy days"; "we are now living in a new environment, under extremely new conditions in comparison to those conditions that prevailed when our forefathers drafted our basic law."

Here is where I must pinch myself to make sure I am not dreaming—these glorifiers of the aged servitor with hat in hand, these ardent converts to the approved doctrine of racial and Aryan supremacy, these disciples of Monier Williams and the Count de Gobineau, are none the less "liberals," glorying in a "changing world." They are not hauling down old tomes and looking up Babylonian history when it comes to Federal legislation that will enable them better to compete with other employers of human labor. They are so liberal that they can clasp hands with the Reds, and given the opportunity, stick to the Communist Party line.

Let us get the picture. Senator Ellender, of Louisiana, fills the hall of the Senate for days with pagan appeals to racial prejudice and racial discrimination and shreds and tatters of "Aryan" lore, of that "idolatrous cult of race" which Pope Pius XI has stigmatized as totally abhorrent to Christian teaching, that cult which is now being used as a powerful engine against the Catholic Church. The principles that he advocates would wreck all the mission work of the Catholic Church in the United States, were they carried to their full conclusion.

Senator Tom Connally, of Texas, aids patiently in the filibuster, prompting the orators by a leading question when their fervor ap-

pears to flag. Senator Claude Pepper, of Florida, appeals to the
Constitution and States' rights.

Yet these same men, Messrs. Connally, Ellender and Pepper send
over their own signatures a fervent message of congratulation to
the Reds of Spain, to the forces allied with and directed by Soviet
Russia, to the Communists and anarchists responsible for the cold-
blooded murder of thousands of priests and the murder and worse
than murder of thousands of nuns, the wreckers of culture and
civilization in Spain and the would-be destroyers of peace throughout the world. "Your struggle," say Connally, Ellender and Pepper,
"sets a stirring example to all democratic peoples. As members of
one democratically elected Parliament to another, we salute you."

Extremes meet, in the racial field as in all other fields of human
doctrine and policy. Those who pose as ultra-conservatives are nine
times out of ten the first to be won to ultra-radical causes. Unable
to distinguish between passion and moral principle, they are cap-
tured by anti-social schemers with a bait of material gain or appeals
to patronage and prestige. The racialist radical, ready to exploit
his "subhuman" fellowman for his own material ends, salutes the
Red radical, who exploits men for the benefit of the omnipotent
state. We may wonder how the same person who hails the Hindu
caste system as "one of the greatest inventions of the human mind"
can also say that he "cherishes freedom and democracy above all
else." But if you reflect that the type of democracy he favors is
the type exemplified in the ruined churches and schools of Spain,
the correspondence is not quite so difficult to understand. He would
doubtless feel equally at home under the caste system that is now
the mode in Russia. As Mr. Tydings has said, the Senator's "consistency makes him inconsistently consistent."

There are some who say that it is a calamity that such an ex-
hibition should have taken place in our Senate. It was a disgrace.
Of that there is no doubt. But it may not have been a calamity. It
is well that there should have been shown to the American people
once and for all the hollowness of the term "liberal" so eagerly
claimed by these men, who are avid for "advanced" social legisla-

tion when it suits their own interests. It is well that people know that God-hatred and race-hatred are but two branches from the same tree. And the future will soon show, I believe, that there are many thousands of *truly* "liberal" men and women in Louisiana and other parts of the South who are fully aware of these facts, and whose innate sense of justice and charity will provide an unpleasant awakening for the filibusterers who sent a love-message to the Reds.

VI.
Human Relations

As I indicated in the preceding section ("The Race Baiters") hate in whatever form is indivisible. It is bound to extend itself far beyond the group that has been selected as its specific object. People who hate others will wind up by hating themselves as well. Life is too complicated, our civilization too interdependent for us to indulge much in that type of luxury. Moreover, the teachings of our holy faith, as well as the ideals of our native country, forbid it.

The best way to overcome hate is along the line indicated in a couple of these aritcles, which is that we work together without self-consciousness on a common task for the common good. We don't overcome hate just by talking about it any more than we can create love and good will by telling other people how fond we are of them. Much of this process when carried on leads to the contrary effect.

However, group hate is a phenomenon, and this phenomenon is not exorcised by burying it in total silence. There are times and occasions when it needs to be soberly examined precisely for what it is, analyzed under the dry light of faith and morals. There are philosophical and psychological elements to be coped with. It is best to do this job in the daylight when things are still calm and not wait for the dreadful moment of desperation to seek a sudden remedy in a storm.

James Baldwin, Negro essayist, and keen, sensitive—some might say ultra-sensitive—analyst of the troubles of his own race in a white world concludes his latest volume Notes of a Native Son *(The Beacon Press, 1955) with these striking words: "The history of the American Negro problem is not merely shameful; it is also something of an achievement, for even when the worst has been said it must also be added that the perpetual challenge posed by this problem was always somehow perpetually met. It is precisely this black-white experience which may prove of indispensable value to us in the world we face today. This world is white no longer and it will never be white again." I believe in the indispensable value of this experience, and that belief has grown upon me through all stages of my observation. I have tried to indicate that belief in some of these papers, for it has profound religious as well as sociological depths. One of these days it will strike us with hammer force.*

I would ask those who read the final chapter in the series: "Christianity and the Negro," to meditate at some length on what is said there briefly about the colored person's depressing experience of being always identified with his own race, as well as the converse exhilarating experience, that of being identified with the whole human race, especially as that human race is seen in the light of the dignity God's grace has conferred upon it. Only when this issue is squarely met, on the basis of the universal message of our Redemption, and fully applied to all the concrete circumstances of our daily lives, will we be in a position to cope universally and convincingly with the dynamism of communism's universalist appeal. I would ask the reader, too, as another part of that meditation, to weigh in his or her heart the honor due to that noble army of forgotten souls—of either or any race—priests, religious, lay people—who have been and still are laboring right on the "battlefront" for the spiritual welfare and human rights and dignity of these "identified" and "identifiable" people.

Hate and Anti-Hate

NOVEMBER, 1943

ALONG WITH a few hundred thousand other citizens, I received recently a request to sign a pledge, entitled "Declaration of War on Hatemongers." The idea, as professed, is to give "cohesion and movement and direction and a fighting aim to the counterfront so needed to fight the angry Fascist storm of hate."

The pledge is to be filled in and sent "to your priest, your clergyman, your rabbi or a responsible public official." Wording of the pledge is such that any person will naturally subscribe to it who is opposed to racial intolerance or religious bigotry.

From the standpoint of pure method it is a question whether this procedure will not simply confirm the antagonisms which it professes to combat. It might work to give "cohesion and movement" to a counter-counterfront and so strengthen the "angry storm of hate."

However, there is a much more important consideration.

Communists, Nazis, Fascists and their various types of fellow travelers all make use in one form or another of the anti-hate motif as a way of popularizing their respective ideologies. It is an encouraging symptom in itself that the warfare against hate does carry such a popular appeal, even though the appeal may permit itself to be misused.

An appeal to dread of hate strikes a vibrant, powerful chord, whether that appeal originates from the depth of love or from the counsels of malice. The mass of normal people, for the most part, are fearful of hate. The war's development has revealed to the whole world hate's potentialities for evil and destruction. We are in terror not so much of the bombs and bombing planes as we are of the hate of those who control them. Again, the consciousness of what it means to be surrounded by a universe of hate and to be threatened by the retribution which such a universe of hate engenders, is a nightmare already oppressing midnight hours of the Axis aggressors. We ourselves will become uneasy if we discover that, through our own racial or national policies abroad, we are building up enemies where we imagined we had friends.

Another circumstance adds validity to the anti-hate propaganda. We not only fear hate, but we fear to wear the reputation of hate. None of the ideologies today, at least for purposes of wide-spread popular propaganda, wishes to be stigmatized as advocating hate, however its acts may belie the profession. Professor Sorokin may appear and explain to us that this is part of the cycle by which revolutions ultimately liquidate themselves: they end up by advocating the very things which they originally set out to destroy. But I venture to say this phenomenon means more than even that. It is not wholly wild to conjecture that this general fear of even the reputation of hatefulness may be the remote beginning of a worldwide recognition that love is the only adequate motivation for justice. It is a backhanded tribute to the power of love. Ultimately love is destined to reveal itself as the most dynamic element on earth. Such a development is not a mere swing to full circle in the revolutionary trend. It is part of the direction which God gives to human affairs. And in His Providence the first beginnings of great changes are apt to be terrifying.

But we are practically concerned with the question of how we can combat hate so as not to create more hate. How can we distinguish a genuine battle against hate from the counterfeit which the ideologies utilize?

There are many answers to this question, for there are many ways of creating counterfeits. One simple test, however, will suffice for most purposes—at least until Screwtape, the Abysmal Uncle, has added a few more quirks to his devious tactics. Let us simply ask, when approached on this matter whether the campaign against hate is universal or is limited to only certain peoples or minorities. That is an easy question to propound, but it is difficult to answer in full sincerely, since only a heart conformed to the Sacred Heart of the Redeemer is likely to be completely all-embracing in its sympathies. It is so easy to distinguish, to equivocate and to avoid conclusions that demand personal sacrifice and the overcoming of deep-lying personal prejudices and repugnances. It is so easy to be general, so painful to be specific. Yet the answer must be given, and now is the time for it, while emergencies are approaching, but we are not yet in their grip.

We are rightly shocked when we hear racism or anti-Semitism denounced by certain groups who are indifferent to insults against our most sacred convictions, doctrinal and moral, as Catholics. We agree instantly with the preaching of an anti-hate campaign on behalf of Catholics. It is well we should; otherwise we should be disloyal and untrue to our faith. But if we mean our anti-hate, if we mean to conquer hate and hate propaganda in all and in any form, we must grieve over and must protest against the beating of Jewish boys in urban Catholic neighborhoods. We cannot expect to blow hot for one and cold for another. Since these beatings are reported, with details of persons and circumstances, it would seem to be an elementary duty to inquire into the actual facts.

The demon that such manifestations of group hatred release in our midst respects no race, color or religion; and he is ready to serve any master who will feed his insatiable appetite.

It is easy enough to say "I am ready to love all men," in a vague, general way. But the test of our love's universality comes when we are willing to make the same allowances for all men, and treat each according to his individual merits and as a human being, judging him for better or worse, as he may act.

It is these qualifications and allowances that create most of the trouble. We make them easily for our own personal selves. As Saint Bernard remarked, we absolve ourselves all day long. We have little difficulty in making them for those we naturally love and understand, with whom we are kin by blood, association or training.

I find it easy, for instance, to see how a fine American boy, under certain terrible provocations, can go practically berserk and commit cruelties he would not think of under normal conditions, and yet remain fundamentally a fine American boy. I can make this allowance because I can put myself imaginatively in his place, and

I know how things would strike him and how they would doubtless arouse me to anger if I experienced them. But it is not easy to make these same allowances, to distinguish between the sinner and the sin, to extend the same essential love with complete impartiality to the murderer and his victim, in the case of persons whose experiences and background are entirely different from my own, whose emotions are not my emotions, whose fears are not my fears. It is not easy to follow this course while maintaining an absolute, complete condemnation of the sin and the crime, even while making reasonable allowance for the factors in training and environment which have encouraged these criminal tendencies. Yet this is precisely what we have to do if our own condemnation of hate is of genuine gold, and not just an alloy of egotism, timidity and group selfishness.

We can blame ourselves if we are gullible and let ourselves be taken in by fictitious Popular-Front anti-hate campaigns, whose only aim seems to be to stir up worse conflict than that which they profess to remedy. And it is similar folly to treat lightly the genuine fears, the deep-seated anxieties that beset our fellow citizens, of whatever racial or national origin. It is folly to refrain from genuine, bona fide campaigns against all hatred, racial, religious or national, simply because certain abuses are carried on under this pretext. And many who commit themselves to unreasonable, fantastic plans of action, do so because of genuine fears.

As God-fearing Christian people, we hold it entirely in our power to establish criteria for a genuine anti-hate policy. Reason and faith alike provide us with that positive philosophy of human rights which enables us to look below the surface and see man as God has created him. Furthermore, the universal outlook of our Catholic faith establishes those standards of all-embracing love which prevent our anti-hate policies from becoming a mere expression of enmity to one group under the guise of friendship for another.

Such a policy cannot be worked out in detail without careful study, labor and prayer. Let us take our own position. We shall incur plenty of dislike from certain left-wing groups by doing so.

We are not looking for favors, but for the truth. Such a policy can be worked out just the same. It is labor well expended. Let us engage in it now, while the sun is still shining, before the night come in which no man worketh.

Prejudice and Anti-Semitism

JANUARY, 1944

IT IS NOT surprising that a concomitant of the war should be a revival of disturbance with regard to anti-Semitism. Strains of any wartime lend themselves readily to rumors and propaganda; and since our Axis adversaries never cease to agitate the racist issue, it is bound to come to the fore in the progress of the present conflict.

Any issue which deeply stirs emotions and resentments is a happy hunting ground for persons who capitalize on just that sort of thing. Mass meetings and monster petitions contrived to combat anti-Semitism provide a convenient outlet for Communist "political education." Noisy demonstrations of "anti-anti-Semitism" stir up a hornet's nest of opposing indignation and result in a further strengthening of anti-Semitism itself. Wild accusations of "being anti-Semite" merely arouse resentment among the accused. The question whether the charges are factually true or not is soon forgotten in a welter of counter-recriminations.

Putting all other considerations aside, one necessity seems paramount, if a vicious circle is not to be ever more tightly drawn, and the false is to be separated from the true. Anti-Semitism should be recognized for what it is, and not confounded with things that are frequently called anti-Semitic, but are not such in the strict sense of the word. And this is one of those instances where a strict, rather than a loose use of words, is helpful to all parties concerned.

If anti-Semitism is clearly recognized, those who toy with it can be readily warned, if they are fairly innocent; can be stigmatized, if they are conscienceless and guilty. Thus a clear, rather than a loose, concept of anti-Semitism is helpful to anti-Semitism's own victims. On the other hand, clarity in language will keep those who are not accomplices of anti-Semitism from being charged with this particular vice. And this brings us to the point at issue, which is that anti-Jewish prejudice is one thing, but anti-Semitism is another.

Anti-Jewish prejudice is a word that can cover a multitude of ideas and feelings, manifested in an equally great variety of acts, customs or even institutions. It refers to practically anything which can be termed an unreasonable or unfounded dislike of Jews or antagonism to them. Certain Jews or types of Jews may be disliked as immigrants, as strangers, as economic competitors, as religious antagonists, or for other reasons. If these reasons are invalid, or if generalizations are made from the few to the many—from the known "these" to the vague "they"—the result is a sin of prejudice. In many instances the question as to what is really prejudice, and what is a reasonable or natural dislike, is a highly subjective affair. From opposing points of view, there will be widely differing interpretations as to what is or is not "prejudice." As said before, it is a wide, loose term covering a broad field of subjective interpretations.

Anti-Semitism, however, is a very definite and easily identifiable thing. It is a movement, not a mere emotion, that is sedulously and systematically propagated, usually by certain well-known and well-tried techniques. Like communism, it has its centers of propaganda and its distributing agencies; and is a *power movement*. It is not a mere doctrinal abstraction, but is used by unscrupulous leaders in order to achieve political or revolutionary ends. Like communism, too, it is recognizable by its formulae, its techniques of vilification, its extreme fanaticism and rigid adherence to a "party line." Hitler gave further impetus to the anti-Semitic movement with the peculiar ideology of Germanic racism. But essential to anti-Semitism is the doctrine that the Jews are to blame for practically all the evils of the world, as a sort of contemporary Original Sin, a universal scapegoat upon whose back may be laden everything that we fear, dislike or hate, from wars and pestilence to the conditions in the Second Ward.

Prejudice is the ready instrument of anti-Semitism, just as anti-Catholic prejudice lends itself readily to the propagation of organized anti-Catholic movements.

A young Catholic business man of our acquaintance was accosted a few days ago by a seventeen-year-old public-high-school boy in a section of the city where accusations and counter-accusations relative to anti-Semitism have been rife. Expressing his antipathy to Jews, the boy handed the man a carbon of a little poem, cleverly worded and set to a favorite tune, the burden of which was that the Christians were being sent to fight the Japs while the Jews stayed safely at home. A boy handing a bit of doggerel to a grown man was committing no act of violence. But the boy had obtained the literature, he acknowledged, from a distributing center, and it was being broadcast to the boys and girls at school. And none, even an adult, could read it, much less hum it, without receiving an indelible impression.

A child distributing such literature might or might not have been prejudiced against the Jews; though a dose of prejudice would have helped the anti-Semitic seed to gain root. The point is simply that here was a tangible instance, even though relatively trifling in its mechanism, of a world-wide movement which has as its ultimate aim the destruction of Christianity quite as much as that of Judaism. Drum-beating about "incidents" is a useless procedure. But when a social canker is thus recognized and "isolated," we can warn and educate against it, without the danger of either suffering or creating needless and harmful misunderstandings. Upon us as Catholics it is clearly incumbent to do just that; as it is likewise the duty of both Jews and Christians to combat all forms of prejudice, be it anti-Jewish, anti-Christian or anti-Catholic.

Peaceful Neighborhoods

JANUARY, 1942

WHAT HAPPENED to Rochester after his 1942 New Year's party I have not yet learned. I understand it was to be money back to the guest who did not have to be carried out at the conclusion of the proceedings. But the mention of his and Jack Benny's festivities makes me feel I should like to have a little New Year's party of my own. I should like to talk to my guests about a certain matter that we have all heard considerably about in the closing days of 1941, and that will come up still more in 1942. The guests would talk, too; pretty emphatically, in many instances. I have no objection to that. I know how they feel; I have heard it all and much more besides; and I know how their thoughts run. But they would not need to lift me onto a stretcher after the orchestra had played "Home, Sweet Home." I believe that when decent people get together and discuss frankly, but honestly, questions that touch very strongly on prejudices and emotions, there is still a place for reason and good sense. And this applies to the question of Negro migrants into our Northern cities quite as much as to other matters.

Every now and then feelings are aroused and thoughts are brought to a focus by some event that touches on the relations of white people and colored people in a city community. There were the Chicago Race Riots in 1919; in 1935 there was the so-called Harlem Riot in New York City, which was a sort of reckless protest by certain irresponsible elements against local employment conditions.

Recent press revelations concerning crime conditions in Harlem, conditions that bring crimes of violence into nearby white neighborhoods, have again focused public attention upon the situation of the colored people in the great cities. To these sensational press reports a popular magazine now adds a couple of highly spiced articles, embellished with still more spicy pictures. Since my name appears in these articles, adorned not with a picture but attached to some misplaced quotation marks, I feel moved to invite the general public to attend my New Year's party.

After the lemonade has been passed around, my proposal is not to deliver a lecture but to invite answers to a few, I think rather obvious, questions.

First of all, I should ask: why be surprised at the presence of crime and disorder in a neighborhood when all the factors are present that encourage crime and disorder in any group of people, of any race or nationality? Why such astonishment, such an explosion of emotion?

The surprising feature in the entire affair is not that so much wickedness exists, but that there is not a vastly greater amount of it. Food rather for surprise are the hundreds of Negro boys and girls who, after a long day's work crowd into nightschools to prepare themselves, against all conceivable odds, to be useful citizens of the nation. Or, that any young people at all can grow up into a measure of self-respect, when the only parents they have ever known are habitually unemployed parents, living flaccidly on a monthly relief check.

Since we are in the questioning mood, we can ask ourselves what breed of noble citizens would you or I have developed into if our own youth had been passed under similar circumstances?

There is no need to enumerate these factors here in detail. They are familiar to any one who has spent a few hours at a session of the Domestic Relations Court, or has engaged in a moderate amount of parish visiting. We have had our ghettos, our East Sides, our beyond-the-tracks, our San Juan hills, Tenderloins, Little Italy's, Polish Corridors and everything else in every city in the country. But there is this difference. The white lad or the white maiden can "graduate" from these ghettos. When they have made their little nest-egg and have invested in a suburban cottage, none but a few cousins and aunts know their origin. But the colored family bears a return ticket on its countenance which cannot be effaced. What incentive is there to *become* law-abiding, to become social and neighborly and orderly and altogether clean, quiet and nice, when the majority world has already established its stereotype of what you are and must, irrevocably and by Divine decree, ever remain?

The Negroes, particularly those who follow the great and glorious American quit-the-farm tradition and migrate by the millions into our immense cities, are rapidly becoming the nation's Number One proletariat. The question I should like to put to all those who refuse to give employment or training opportunity to intelligent and qualified Negro youth—future heads of families—is: do you wish them to remain a proletariat? If you do, how can you expect anything but social conflict and disorder as a result? If you do not so wish, then what steps are you taking to remove what is a much more gravely anti-social attitude in the minds of those who thus close the gates of opportunity?

Having consumed the lemonade, let us now broach the Pepsi-Cola and address a question or two to various secular agencies which are endeavoring to help the Negro's lot even under these adverse circumstances. The question is not put invidiously, but rather with the assumption that they themselves of late have not infrequently raised it, and are disposed to give it a serious answer.

Your work, in general, follows well tried methods. It has assimilated and put into practice the best lessons of modern social science and philanthropy. It has offered and continues to offer the only hope to great numbers of helpless people for opportunity, for social or civic, even physical security. But do you believe that what you expect the Negro to be and to accomplish, under your guidance, for his own benefit—in order to do his part in overcoming his own disabilities—can be fulfilled with the type of religion that the majority of the Negro masses now possess? Or that they will maintain even that much religion? No amount of *doing for* the Negro will help, unless home and community are built up spiritually from within.

In view of this simple consideration, does it not seem strange that in all the flock of utterances that have appeared of late in the public press, concerning, let us say, the situation in Harlem, little if anything is said about the work of the Catholic Church for the religious welfare of the Negro? Of the groups of priests and nuns who are devoting themselves to this particular task?

Tributes are paid in private; but some more tributes paid in public would be very much to the point. Even Richard Wright could add a postscript, to this effect, on his scroll of grievances.

Having queried the general public—periodically disturbed at finding that Negroes act much as other races act when under similar conditions—and having questioned the enlightened non-Catholic agencies, let us serve sherbet and greet some of our leading Catholic laity.

Some of these inform me, before I have time to speak further, that they are animated by sentiments of the utmost friendliness for members of the Negro race. So pronounced are these sentiments that they have attended Mass on Sunday at churches chiefly frequented by colored people. They assure me, moreover, that they were not impelled to this by mere fancy, but wished to give concrete evidence of their faith that all men, all races, are equal before God's altar and that the Catholic Church knows no racial distinctions.

For this I can only commend them, and all the party is impressed by these splendid sentiments. But since I am still master of ceremonies, I reserve the right to put an additional, even if seemingly ungracious question to these sincere and pious people. It happens to have been addressed to me by a colored Catholic man who used to be night-watchman in the Spelvin Building, but was fired when Mr. Spelvin cut his help by one third. "You have to draw the line somewhere," said Spelvin. I meet this little colored man occasionally on his way home from Church.

"Good news, Father," he said, when I last saw him. "My two boys have just succeeded in landing jobs with the Banner Corporation; one as a welder, the other as a concrete finisher's apprentice, Wages are not high, but enough to keep our little family together —enough, with the grace of the good Lord and the prayers of Our Lady in Heaven. We have laid a good deal of a burden upon her of late.

"The boys worked hard to get those jobs," he continued. "They joined Mr. Parker's job-hunting group, took his training—seventy-five per cent character and attitude, he told them, as well as knowing what you really want to fit yourself for. They worked hard, they helped the other boys and the other boys helped them. They sat up nights studying their manuals. But there was one thing I could never quite understand. Why was it that not one of these good Catholic men who have been coming to our church did anything to help them? I have heard those men talk on occasions. I have heard them even speak about the Popes' Encyclicals. Three of them are among the biggest employers in our town. A couple of them are personnel managers and at least five are prominent in union circles. They are religious men, they are pious men, and there's not one of them who wouldn't pass you a five-dollar bill if you were starving, or pay your rent if you told him you would be evicted.

"Yet when the boys spoke to some of them and said they were planning to put to use some of the training Dr. Pond gave them at the vocational high school, these men said that times were difficult, and that it would be better if colored people trained themselves to become good porters and such. Mr. Waddington, who I think is a straight honest Catholic man, was indignant, when Bob mentioned it, and said it was against social justice, which he speaks about in public. But when Bob asked him why he didn't tell that to his friends, he seemed a bit bewildered. Now my question is: Is there something the matter with these men's religion? Or is there something in our Faith they have missed?"

What *have* they missed? If we find the response to that question, we have an important answer to our queries concerning Negro neighborhood conflicts and local crime areas. Let us conclude by putting two questions the reader himself can settle.

The first question is: How can our religion be truly supernatural, how can we claim to possess or practise the fullness of Christian charity, when we are not concerned with the social and with the frankly economic conditions in which individual families are compelled to work out their salvation?

The second question is: How can we by any stretch of the imagination hope to find an adequate solution for these neighborhood problems until our Catholic faith and practice does concern itself— from supernatural, yea, from Eucharistic, motives—with these same problems: for *all* families in the community, since the family institution is for all?

The following truths seem obvious enough—they are frequently mentioned, in one or the other form, in the Papal Encyclicals—yet they are frequently forgotten.

Under normal circumstances, souls work out their eternal destiny not as scattered individuals but as members of families. Even youthful duties relate to future family responsibilities.

A continued apostolate of family life, therefore, is urgently needed in our time. The Rev. Dr. Thomas F. Coakley, pastor of Sacred Heart Church, Pittsburgh, speaks of it as a "supreme need of the hour" in his penetrating article on "Catholic Leakage" in the January, 1942 *Catholic World*. Parents need to be taught to impart religious instruction to their children. Family prayers and family consecration or corporate Holy Communion; natural virtues of thrift, helpfulness; family recreations, need to be encouraged. Family economic life cannot be neglected. The Christian family apostolate is not solely a parish work, but one for the entire community as well: a community project, in which non-Catholics as well as Catholics may profitably be enlisted. Catholic participation in youth guidance is an effective means of maintaining in the community spiritual standards of family life.

This is particularly true in the case of Negro neighborhoods, for the lives of Negro families are in great measure determined by the complexion of the large non-Catholic community.

Family life, even purely spiritual family life, however, is in great measure conditioned by the family's economic circumstances. This does not mean that families will be good and pious when comfortably placed and warmly housed. But it does mean that economic injustice strikes a deadly blow against the life of the family, against its integrity, its very existence as a permanent human institution. As Pope Pius XI says in his *Quadragesimo Anno*: "It may be said with all truth that nowadays the conditions of social and economic life are such that vast multitudes of men can only with great difficulty pay attention to that one thing necessary, namely, their eternal salvation."

If this is true for "great multitudes," it is in a superlative degree true for the Negro. For him, family economic conditions are determined to an amazing extent by the racial attitudes of the great national community. Families do not function in a social vacuum, they depend for their healthy existence upon civic and social opportunity. Physical hardships that result from denial of opportunity may be alleviated by relief; but no governmental or private relief program can heal wounds to youth's personality inflicted by idleness, frustration and racial despair.

If, therefore, our Catholic charity sincerely desires to aid the actual salvation of concrete and actual individual persons, let me ask, in conclusion, how can it be indifferent to the pattern of interracial justice? Can it be unconcerned with false attitudes, false concepts and pictures unthinkingly accepted by a large body of our well meaning Northern citizens about the Negro worker, as similar misconceptions about Catholics are accepted by other large groups of equally well meaning but misinformed citizens? A truly Christlike charity cannot be blind to the daily problems of countless fellow-citizens and fellow-Christians, to whom God's Providence has entrusted the care of their own present or future homes and families.

To the salvation of Negro souls, therefore, the apostolate of interracial justice would seem to be essential; just as the parish and community family apostolate is essential.

Unless, indeed, the pattern of interracial justice be made to stand out as clear as the pattern of prejudice, to be as tangible, as zealously and consistently sponsored, our talk is largely in vain. Here is a job for our leading Catholic laymen. It is worthy of those who, in Confirmation, received the Seal of the Spirit and the Bishop's blow upon the cheek.

True Face of Our Country

JUNE, 1954

I N ADDRESSING so distinguished and scholastic a gathering, I feel
that you will appreciate my interest in learning that the people
of York, Pennsylvania, have committed themselves munici-
pally to the study of the French language. They are responding to
the equally heroic resolve of the people of Arles in France to
undertake a mass study of English. This is the second such twin-
cities enterprise undertaken under the auspices of an international
project, entitled *Le Monde Bilingue,* or the bilingual world. Its
projectors hope that ultimately people everywhere will learn a
second great language, and so enable us all to talk to one another
and thus create better international understanding. I am captivated
by the idea that the people of Arles will pick up some of the time-
honored phrases of this grand old historic section of Pennsylvania.

I

Certainly we in this country are always glad to inform other
peoples of our progress and accomplishments, even if we are a
little puzzled at times as to just what items we should send over
the Voice of America or relay through the more intimate channels
of exchange visitors and students. At the present moment we wish
to communicate to the entire world the news of our recent great
liberating achievement: the unanimous decision of the Supreme
Court of the United States on May 17th, outlawing the principle
of racial segregation in the nation's public schools. We distributed
the news at once by shortwave broadcast in thirty-four languages,
and we want to continue telling of this event, because we believe
it removes a painful blemish from the true face of our country.
This decisive step refutes the gross caricatures spread wide by Communist propaganda; it corrects unduly pessimistic ideas as to the

racial situation in the United States which are currently accepted even in friendly nations abroad. It is quite characteristic that the Soviet press has abstained from mentioning it at all.

We want to do more than merely notify the globe of the event. There is a story in this business, the story of how a right principle does finally win out in a democracy, even though it may take a half-century to gain its point. For our friends we would like to trace the way in which each great political principle contains, as it were, the seeds of its successor and ultimate development. The framers of the Constitution compromised on slavery. But rooted as it were in our institutions, slavery could not resist the gradual, inevitable impact of our primary postulate that "all men are created equal." Similarly, when we adopted the Fourteenth Amendment in 1868 we embraced a right principle, "the equal protection of the laws," which in time would wipe out the last vestiges of slavery in the form of racial discrimination.

Such a development is an instance of what Cabot Lodge recently referred to as the "irresistible onward march of the human race in the direction of increase of human rights and increased belief in the dignity of the individual." But the human race does not march forward by some blind impulse. It moves ahead because people will and choose for it to move ahead.

It is not enough for us to inform our bilingual friends about the fact of this forward march; we want also to give them some idea of how it came about. The Emancipation Proclamation that in 1865 destroyed slavery as a legalized institution, though technically the act of one great man, was in point of fact the collective deed of the American people. So, too, when on May 17th of this year the Court erased all legal respectability from the last vestiges of slavery, it was also the people of the United States speaking. A fair account of the events that led up to that decision would have to recite the bitter lessons we learned as to the price required for the continuation of racial disunity: the toll it has taken in social and political division, retarding the progress of our nation. We would speak of all that our people have learned through new contacts, new opportunities, as well as new threats to civic peace resulting from our enormous internal migrations from country to city, from South to North. And we would need to take ample reckoning of what war experiences have meant for our young people, as well as for our armed forces as such; for the recent decision was made against the background of complete racial integration in all three branches of the armed forces, completed only a couple of weeks before May 17th.

But the story I should like most to stress for our foreign friends and visitors is that of the great army of the forgotten or even unknown: dedicated people, who worked in obscurity for the education and the inner development of the racial minorities, particularly in the South: Negro educators who overcame extreme personal handicaps of poverty and timidity, who braved the pessimism of their own kith and kin and struggled to build something out of nothing. White men and women faced violent disapproval, social ostracism, or even personal danger. We should have to include among them people who contributed their time, means, and talents to the express task of securing equal opportunity, who were not afraid to demand explicitly full equality for all in our American society, regardless of race, color, or creed. And finally the expert legal staff that actually prepared the decisive material, and the humble contributors who made their work possible.

Now my aim here is not to pronounce an Independence Day panegyric for all these good men and true, these heroes living and dead. Others can do that job more effectively than myself. I do want to emphasize their motives, the fact that these people, with no exceptions worth bothering about, acted from deep, intense conviction. They believed that certain things were right and certain things were wrong, with no if's or but's. They were liberals, yes; liberals in the most weighty sense of the word. As liberals, they believed that human rights inhered to the individual persons, and could not be entrusted to the whims of politicians or legislators. As liberals, they believed that it was a noble and a necessary thing for men to labor to secure these rights for their neighbor. Some of this action was highly reasoned, some of it instinctive, but in any case it was carried on by those who placed conviction before doubt. They were not the type of people who put their faith in "steadfast" skepticism. They questioned popular errors and misconceptions, but were entirely positive when it came to those basic notions upon which we have built the structure of our nation. Such people are not the most interesting type of liberal; they do not breed aphorisms or soothe wounded feelings. But they get things done.

Moreover, a sizable proportion of this army of workers were religious people; persons who looked upon their striving for justice as the logical corollary of their own religious beliefs. They believed that religion itself speaks with the voice of freedom: not some elaborately rationalized interpretation of religion, but a simple faith in the teachings of the Bible as they knew it, in the Law of Moses or the Gospel of Jesus Christ. Their personal liberalism derived no nourishment from an attitude of religious skepticism, however refined.

I have spoken of the plainer people, but these remarks apply to the scholars as well. Popular enthusiasm would have failed of its goal without the patient research of our own American scholarship. Learned people of every section and race contributed. Honest scholarship has paid great dividends for the general welfare in the past forty or fifty years by demolishing ethnic racism, analyzing historical and psychological causes of our current tensions, studying the effect of separatism upon the character, especially of the young, assaying methods of intergroup personality, and, in more recent times, examining the working of racial integration in our schools and communities.

Here again the burden and the heat of the day were carried largely by scientists, historians, and sociologists who were not satisfied with endless processes of dissolution and criticism. Their work is distinguished by its positive note. Such a note characterizes one of the most monumental pieces of research, the *American Dilemma* of Gunnar Myrdal, as well as more modest but painstaking jobs, like that of Kenneth Clark and his wife, cited in the recent decision.

The Supreme Court has closed serious debate on the constitutional issue on which it passed verdict. The elimination of a false solution clears the way now for a nationwide debate on a vastly larger issue; the myriadfold question of how we shall learn to live together in peace in all our institutions and communities throughout the nation, and by the same token with all the peoples of the world. With a moot point of law cleared up, the moot of human co-existence itself remains to be examined. By postponing to later months the consideration of any practical implementation of its decision, the Court indicated now was the time to begin this discussion. Those of the minority group who were most successful in bringing out the verdict have wisely proposed that the discussion be conducted everywhere upon the local level. Back of that recommendation is the belief that the people themselves can find answers to the most vexing questions of group relationships, provided the people who are immediately concerned can converse among themselves in their own neighborhood, without throwing the burden of decision upon experts and agencies from afar. Implicit in that recommendation is the belief that free discussion is precisely the best plan. Let us solve these questions, Negro leaders declared at Atlanta, in the "atmosphere of give and take." It was through half a century of free discussion that we created a climate of opinion which made possible the decision of May 17th. In that same atmosphere we shall perfect a climate of opinion which will make possible newer and more positively constructive decisions in the future. Such decisions are particularly urgent as we are obliged to sleep on our arms, in the face of what Cardinal Spellman recently referred to as "the narrowing circle of freedom."

II

What, then, is the role of the scholar in this future period of general debate? Evidently he will need to collect and assess the lessons of the past and evaluate various techniques for developing mutual understanding. Immediate difficulties can be solved at the local level, and locally the different groups can learn to work together for the common good. But the question still remains as to the nature of that common good. People will not stay content merely with one another's peculiarities, or to labor conjointly for the more immediate needs of daily life. They will seek a wider and deeper basis of cooperation, they will seek to know what is the destiny of the nation itself. They will ask what are we, all of us, here on earth for anyhow. They will inquire as to whether we are anything but an inexplicable accident, or are we beings who can make free decisions based on a concept of life's ultimate goals, if life, they ask, has an ultimate goal. They will want to know if it is reasonable to talk of ultimates at all, and if so, how far is language a significant medium for such discussion. They will inquire about the meaning of men's dialog with one another, and whether all human dialog may not resolve itself in the last analysis into a dialog with the God Who put us here. Sooner or later they will inquire whether there may not be two participants to that dialog, whether it is all Job speaking to God, or whether God may not be saying something to Job.

This might sound as if I were expecting that the scholars' role in the coming discussion should be that of pronouncing upon matters of religious doctrine. I believe the theologians will have much to say in the future as they have had in the past, but my proposal is more elementary, one that I make as I see it, in the interests of true liberalism. Scholarship of the future, as concerned with the debates of the future, should feel free to study and reappraise the connection between religion—including organized, dogmatic religion—and a liberal policy of universal human rights. Is this proposal unreasonable? Are we obliged to pose the problem of liberalism as a choice between two extremes (I believe artificially assigned extremes): either as uneasy suspicion that some miching mallecho is brewing whenever the theologian enters the universe of discourse; or else paternally and piously to evade the pressing questions of the social community. It would seem reasonable for the genuine liberal to go still further, and to seek to explain historically some of the reluctances that certain large groups of our population show when asked to subscribe to liberal causes. Historical scholarship recalls, for instance, the days when the Irish immigrant and the Catholic citizen—immigrant or old-line American alike—were cruelly lampooned by the same broad-minded elements who championed the cause of the ex-slave: the same broad-minded elements who a decade or so later forgot all about the ex-slave, when it became convenient to conclude a business deal with the renascent South.

In short, I see no reason why the liberal-minded scholar is obliged to assume that an organized or institutionalized religion is necessarily unrelated to a policy of human rights, whatever attitudes individuals may assume. If an eminent and much beloved liberal-minded scholar, in his table talk, expresses just such a complete abhorrence of theology and theologians, I am not particularly surprised. After all, that is the climate of opinion in which he moves, and I am not aware of just what human or religious phenomena he may have encountered. We are all free to express our pet attractions and repulsions, and for all I know, he may be just spoofing. People moreover have committed sins under the sacred name of religion, as they have under the venerated egis of science and scientific investigation. But certainly out of its own tenets science never devised the cruelties of Dachau or Buchenwald. Those horrors were hatched in the minds of individuals who used a good and noble thing for their own evil and ignoble ends. So, too, what certain people may have derived from the misuse of religious doctrine is not necessarily to be ascribed to the nature of religion itself, but rather to its use emotionally as a handy instrument.

III

Of late, critical historical scholarship seems more ready to upset certain misconceptions of this type. As, for instance, in the case of my fellow Rhode Islander, Roger Williams. Few, if any, in that terraqueous State subscribe today to Williams's peculiar doctrinal tenets, and none, I assume, are attracted by his cantankerous character. Yet a coolheaded scholar, Perry Miller, demonstrates that Roger Williams derived his ideas on the treatment of people of various faiths, as well as his benign attitude toward the Narragansett Indians, directly from his views on the proximately unrealizable ideal religious commonwealth. The point of the matter is not the validity of Williams's religious notions nor the soundness of his historically famous conclusions, but simply the significant fact that the two sets of ideas were connected. He was not tolerant *in spite* of his contempt for the New Jerusalem of the Massachusetts Bay Colony, but palpably *because* of it.

Mention of Roger Williams recalls to me the very different and quite benign person of another famous Rhode Islander, the Reverend Thatcher Thayer, of Newport, who died when I was a boy of fifteen. Visiting Europe around 1847 with the purpose of discovering, as he said, the true nature of both Popery and Calvinism, the Dominie, as he was called, reflected mournfully on Europe's social evils one lovely summer day as he sat in front of a little Catholic chapel on the slopes of Mount Chamonix, in Switzerland. He was annoyed by the opinion of one of his Geneva colleagues, who argued that social backwardness was due to religious superstitions, and he asked himself whether one might not discover the remedy to these same grave social evils, if men were to study, as he said, the social doctrine contained in both Protestantism and Popery. If more men in Europe had shared the wisdom of Dominie Thayer, it might have escaped the disastrous upheavals of the year 1948. Europe might not have fallen into the disastrous 19th century choice of economic, *laissez-faire* Liberalism, with a big "L," as the Common Good, in place of its direct opposite, the social liberalism taught by certain great Christian theologians. Such men held that "government must not be thought of as a mere guardian of law and of good order, but must rather put forth every effort so that through the entire scheme of laws and institutions . . . both public and individual well-being may develop spontaneously out of the very structure and administration of the State"; and that all citizens, without distinction, may have equal share in the goods of order, liberty, and opportunity.

These were a clergyman's speculations. But they also might have been the musings of a scientist as such. Some, of course will shy at any mention of causes or causation in these affairs; but as Gordon Allport remarks: "Methodologists who banish causation from the front door, often admit it surreptitiously at the back. . . . To my mind social science at its present stage of development will be concerned with causation, or else it will be concerned with nothing of consequence." If this scientist today were a truly reflective man, not bound too tightly by the methodology and the limits of his own particular specialty, a man of somewhat larger view and wider consciousness of the many strictly factual elements in human life that nonetheless cannot be mathematically weighed and measured—he might also wish to examine more closely the roots of liberalism in certain Judeo-Christian doctrinal ideas. He might suspect—with the blessing of Dominie Thayer—that, after all, some help and light from on high, some divinely inspired graces are needed, if political liberalism is to pass effectively from mere theory to practise in this world of intense political passions and mass pressure on human freedoms. The very fact of that mass pressure might suggest some types of theological speculation.

He might go still further, and consider that the liberal's most difficult combat today is not so much with the selfishness of the reactionary as with the terror of the mass mind. Governor Talmadge in the flesh presents a sizable but limited difficulty. But Governor Talmadge photographically and electronically multiplied *ad infinitum* is something else again. The magnificent forces which man's mind has liberated so far seem to work as readily for man's enslavement as for his freedom. A universe conceived in nebulae and light-years can remain, of itself, blankly walled off from the spiritual infinitudes while the four walls of a contemplative's cell may open wide upon the vistas of eternity. On this crucial question as to how to free man's spirit from the crushing weight of an unmanageable material liberation, the theologian has much to say. Whether we agree with his theory or not, it is not without pertinence to the practical problems of human freedom. Indeed, when the entire free world is caught in a stranglehold with an enemy who relentlessly contests the very groundwork of all free existence, it would seem rather difficult to shrug off all talk of ultimates as irrelevant mysticism.

IV

The experiences of the recent convulsed decades have made us cautious and skeptical. They have also increased our readiness to attribute objective worth to certain ancient landmarks of spiritual experience and philosophical thought. They make us also more ready to probe deeply into the age-old, but ever new questions of reality and being; more anxious to find a bridge between the irreconcilable elements in our disparate universe—a bridge which will unite but will not confound. The unified field theory has given us the atomic and the hydrogen bomb. It has enriched us with resources of nuclear energy which may save man's existence upon this planet. But like Joseph Wood Krutch, I see no reason for bowing down to it as a god. Social sciences, he observes, "will never help to solve our problems as long as they continue to go on the assumption that whatever is true of a rat is true of a man." We are by no means certain that such a restricted outlook will provide us with the key to permanent peace and freedom.

I believe that just as the great step taken by the Supreme Court has helped to reveal the true face of our country, so the growth in understanding which I expect to come out of these impending debates will express still more what the American people genuinely wish and feel; how they do business with one another and, I hope, eventually with the world. Precisely because of this belief on my part I take a more hopeful attitude than is frequently expressed toward the development of scholarship in the years immediately to come. Even from a purely pragmatic point of view, reasoned hope turns out to be stronger liberal medicine than does sustained and angry dissent. That we are facing a certain wave of anti-intellectualism and pure utilitarianism is evident enough. But I do not see why this trend should necessarily develop into a tidal wave to engulf all free thought and free inquiry. I see grounds for such extreme anxiety only in the case of those who have allowed themselves to become fascinated by the intoxication of total doubt and a dogmatically negative attitude toward all normal human moral and religious values. Their hypercriticism earned for them, it now appears, some strange ideological bedfellows. The American people, from my own experience as a worker over the years for certain great liberal principles, will listen and do listen to the voice of reason, when the arguments are presented intelligently and dispassionately. Prejudices may be inborn, a young African said to me the other day, as he was preparing to return to his native country, but in these matters, he insisted, people may be and frequently are born again. There may be giants in the path, but giants, too, are vulnerable, and sometimes flop helplessly in the face of a well aimed slingshot.

Says the biblical Wise Man in the Latin Vulgate version: "*os bilingue detestor*," which may be rendered as: "I have no use for a face that talks with a double tongue." The *os bilingue*, the double-talking face, has nothing in common with *le monde bilingue*—a world where men can talk straight to each other despite language barriers. It has also nothing in common with the traditional traits of the American people. Despite the clamor of many bitter and angry voices, our country, when it speaks for itself, does speak today, as it has in the past, with a tone of reverence for things holy and with humble respect for the needs of the least human being. I believe that scholarship will take increasing cognizance of this truth, and so play a powerful part in presenting to the world the true face of our country.

The Basis of Interracial Peace

DECEMBER, 1954

I F I WERE asked to mention the greatest changes that have taken place in the thought of the American people within the last five years, I would find none second to the general recognition of the need of interracial peace, that is to say, practical and harmonious relations between the different racial groups in this country. This would include, outside of the white majority, the largest of the non-white minorities with the Negroes, but also the other non-white groups as well, such as the largely increasing Spanish-speaking peoples both in the East and the southwest of the United States, the Orientals, and of course the American Indians. People may differ as to how this peace can be secured; but as for its need there is a general acceptance among all reasonable elements of our country.

We need domestic peace for the prosperity of our country itself. American industry requires manpower. In recent years we have discovered in the much neglected Negro population a vast reservoir of largely untapped manpower capable of being developed to skilled workmanship even of a highly technical variety. Our Armed Forces, which recently officially banned racial separation, likewise realize this need of manpower. But it is not available unless the races live in cooperation with one another.

We see this need also for the peaceable development of our expanding cities as the population moves out more and more into the growing suburbs. The pressure increases to obtain dwellings for newly founded families and accommodation for school children and other basic human needs. This expansion breeds the anxious problem of the ghetto. People shut up in rigidly segregated areas wish to escape into a larger freedom. At the same time they come in conflict with the very people who have moved into the country in order to escape from the crowded metropolis. If the situation is neglected, panic will produce depreciation of property, social dis-order follows and new ghettos mushroom breeding crime and delinquency. Yet no mechanical adjustments will suffice without a genuine spirit of interracial peace. The problem of our ever-increasing overcrowding is bound to produce in the end a terrible explosion. Interracial peace is necessary for the safety of our coun-try, for its unity, for its prosperity, and for the harmonious educa-tion of all its people.

The same lesson is enforced on us with still greater urgency when we cast our eyes abroad. Hardly a month passes that an American traveler reporting on the situation in the Middle or the Far East does not emphasize the decisive role of our domestic racial attitudes in the relations of our country to the largely non-white population of those regions. Obviously we can return their re-proaches and point out injustices some of them commit in the name of caste and class. Nevertheless our own situation is continually exploited by the Communists and by people affected by Commu-nist propaganda and dissatisfied, rightly or wrongly, with their former colonial rulers.

The question of interracial peace is urgent in view of the mis-sions of the Church itself. Our home missions to the minority groups, wonderful as is the effort they embody, are still handi-capped by the attitude of the white majority. The same applies with equal force to the Church's mission throughout the world. We insist upon the unity, the universality of the Church. Taking these words literally, the nations whom we strive to evangelize keenly scrutinize conditions here at home. When they witness un-Catholic and unjust practices in our own American churches, they will conclude there is something wrong with the Christian message.

It is easier to talk about interracial peace than to achieve it. Yet merely to wish for it, to hope that it will come in some magical way at some remote period is contrary to the whole spirit of our Faith. In so grave a matter we cannot be satisfied with a policy of drift, the vain hope that by merely letting things take care of themselves the evil will go away and good will somehow prevail. The good *will* prevail, it is true, but it is a tempting of Divine Providence, a sin of presumption to throw all the responsibility on the Creator and do nothing within our own sphere to carry out His plans. Experience has shown us repeatedly, where there are sharp tensions between different racial or religious or other social groups, that merely waiting for things to improve instead of making things better leads to even greater bitterness and misunderstanding. Social disorders must be met by thoughtful, positive and concerted action. What, then, is required?

I think we can summarize under three simple headings: First, a knowledge of the facts; secondly, a knowledge of the attitude of our Divine Saviour and Leader Jesus Christ, and thirdly, the courage and humility to put what we know into effect. Let us look at these three requirements.

First, *a knowledge of the facts.* There is no use working in the dark, especially in matters where human relations are concerned, where ignorance and blundering can lead to infinite harm. We need to know the general facts as to the whole interracial situation. Such knowledge will deal with the history of the various racial groups in this country, their distribution, their migration, especially in recent years, their economic situation, their distribution at the present time, their elements of achievement, their social problems, etc.

Beside this general knowledge we need to understand the conditions in one's own community. We are not dealing with abstract entities but with living human beings. How do they live? What are their actual daily family problems, and how do they express themselves on them? People readily theorize about racial questions without taking the trouble to interview the very people affected and hear their direct and simple expression. There can be no real reform of disordered social conditions without a corresponding change of heart, and such a change is effected much more by what people love and cherish than merely by what they theoretically know. Of late much attention in this country has been given to social psychology. Immense amount of analysis has been made of the crisis and conditions of prejudice. Much of this knowledge is valuable even if a certain amount is attended by exaggeration.

Human conduct, however, can never be a matter of mere adjustment. There is always a tension in human affairs. Indeed, a society which is without tensions would be a lifeless society. Deep moral and religious convictions are needed in order to overcome these tensions. In the conflict of racial attitudes there is always a point at which we need to ask ourselves is it right or wrong? How does this or that practice agree with the whole Christian tradition on justice and mutual responsibility? Someone, somewhere has to make a sacrifice, and in the vast majority of cases such sacrifice has to be made by both parties to the difficulty.

To be concrete, in the case of a Negro moving into a white neighborhood the white person has to sacrifice his own selfishness, his own desire for a completely excluded neighborhood in order to do justice to his neighbor who has a genuine right both in ethics and in our American society to find a home for himself and family. On the other hand, the member of the minority group cannot dispense himself from making the necessary sacrifices, in order to conform to decent living standards and accommodate himself to the reasonable wishes of his neighbors; to be, in the full sense of the word, a *good*, constructive, helpful neighbor. Such truly neighborly conduct on everybody's part is a matter of conscience and there can be no interracial peace without the formation of an interracial conscience.

If such a conscience is to be a live affair and we are to put into practice what we think or know is right and wrong, we will consider as Christians first and foremost what would Christ, Our Lord, think: a question which takes us into the heart of the life and works of the Saviour of mankind. The teaching of Jesus is explicit and detailed on human relations. It is as fresh and pungent as when delivered nearly 2000 years ago.

The question of race relations is no mere accidental part of the Saviour's earthly career. It underlies His conflict with His own people, His own incessant pleadings and their angry and bitter response. His struggle with them on their racial prejudices developed with fearful intensity during the last two years of His life. His own experience parallels to an uncanny degree many an issue affecting interracial peace in our own day. Indeed it is true for the whole world what Archbishop Owen McCann of Capetown, South Africa, recently said, that the attitude towards those of another race must be the attitude "that Our Lord Jesus Christ would take," and, as the Archbishop points out, this applies to both or all parties in the conflict.

Looking still more deeply we find that the very death of Christ on the cross, as explained by the great Apostle St. Paul, was itself the breaking down of the barrier between the races, the end of that cruel separation between the chosen people and the gentile world that had lain like a pall over the world since the beginning of mankind. The Resurrection of Jesus Christ, as St. Paul reminds us, was a triumphant vindication of His mission to all men. It is in the Risen Person of Christ that all races are united. The institution that Christ established, the Church, embraces all races in Christ, an idea which was gloriously expressed in the first encyclical of our present Holy Father in 1939, the *Summi Pontificatus*.

To come finally to a crucial point. To channel these spiritual forces into reality is not just a pious aspiration on the part of a few zealous souls. It is a searching test of genuine Catholic virtue. As the great St. Peter Claver, S.J., apostle of the Negroes, the 300th anniversary of whose death was celebrated on September 9, 1954, used to say: "Deeds come first, then the words." This, as I have already indicated, applies to no one party in the question but to all concerned. Courage and humility are required. A widespread educational program fortified by courage and humility will acquaint people with the facts, will explain to them the moral and religious issues involved and will inspire them with love and enthusiasm for a pluralist community in which all men, honestly respecting their various characteristics, work together for the common good. Such an educational program mean hard work and study; it means frequently going counter to one's instincts of vanity and human respect. It cannot be passed off by either party upon the other.

The best form of interracial education, as many active American communities have demonstrated, is effected when whites and blacks, forgetting their racial consciousness, plan and labor together for practical welfare projects in their own neighborhood.

Last but not least, there is the element of prayer. As our Holy Father has reminded us on each of the great occasions in his pontificate such as the Holy Year and the Marian Year, our prayers must be offered not just for our own limited personal needs but for the good of the whole world, for the peace and unity of all men.

I see no nobler way of honoring Our Lady and expressing the deepest significance of the Marian Year than to work for a cause so dear to her and to her Son, which is such a perfect expression of that Holy Spirit who spoke through her and whose graces she is privileged to dispense. Our Lady in her famous apparitions laid down no easy program for the peace of the world, no passive remedy. She insisted that men must walk the hard path of much prayer, much penance and self-denial. There is no panacea for interracial peace, no single formula. It is neither more nor less than the expression of our total Christian life in a fashion peculiarly adapted to the urgent situation of the present moment. Certainly the Mother of God will bless and assist any effort we may make in this direction.

Christianity and the Negro

SEPTEMBER, 1955

THE AMERICAN NEGRO knows no country but the United States. His entire past over two centuries is inexorably bound up with our country's history in peace and in war, and there is no conflict of our nation from the Revolution of 1776 to Korea in which Negroes have not shed their blood for our freedom. Like the Indian, the Negro is in a peculiar and special sense that much-talked-about being, the one hundred percent American.

In the New World American Negro slaves were completely cut off from their ancient tribal heritage, language and customs. It was not until the beginning of the 18th century that some attempt was made by the Protestant church bodies to teach them about Christianity. Later, the widespread conversion of Negroes to Christianity was largely the effect of a wave of active Methodist and Baptist missionary endeavor that swept the slave states shortly before the American Revolution. Since that time the majority of Negro Christians have belonged to churches affiliated with one or the other of these two major evangelical sects.

Strongly fundamentalist Protestantism with its emphasis on the utter vanity of all things worldly and the glowing hope of glory beyond the grave provided a never ceasing source of consolation for a people who were utterly powerless to do anything to improve their own human condition. Once they found that the Negroes could be kept quiet and contented by concentrating their religious worship on the life to come, white masters looked with favor upon the Negro ministers' vivid pictures of the rewards and punishments of the future life. The same white masters likewise were not unfriendly to the noisy, shouting, highly emotional type of worship and religious assent which the revivalist missionaries brought to the Negro from the countrysides and the Protestant churches and chapels of England and Wales.

As for immediate release, the liberation that the slave could not obtain here and now from outward bonds he could derive to a certain extent in psychological fashion through a highly emotionalized type of worship. All humbled and oppressed peoples can enjoy a certain degree of inner escape through exuberant, demonstrative action, especially when it is done in common as an expression of a common hope and belief. Out of this tumultuous worship came the precious cultural gift of the Negro Spirituals—about which James Weldon Johnson, who did so much to interpret Negro folk-made music to the American people, remarks:

"The thought that the Negro might have refused or failed to adopt Christianity—and there were several good reasons for such an outcome, one being the vast gulf between the Christianity that was preached to him and the Christianity practiced by those who preached it—leads to some curious speculation. One thing is certain, there would have been no Negro Spirituals. His musical instinct would doubtless have manifested itself; but is it conceivable that he could have created a body of songs in any other form so unique in the musical literature of the world and with such a powerful and universal appeal as the Spirituals? Indeed, the question arises, would he have been able to survive slavery in the way in which he did? It is not possible to estimate the sustaining influence that the story of the trials and tribulations of the Jews as related in the Old Testament exerted upon the Negro bards, and they sang, sang their hungry listeners into a firm faith that as God saved Daniel in the lion's den, so would He save them; as God preserved the Hebrew children in the fiery furnace, so would He preserve them; as God delivered Israel out of bondage in Egypt, so would He deliver them."

When a Negro sang: "Joshua was de son of Nun. He never stopped till his work was done," he referred of course to the sinner who was beginning his conversion and should keep up the job of self-reformation until he was in the ranks of the elect. But behind the biblical allusion was the thought that another work was to be done for the whole race and people, the work of freedom, and they should never stop till they should enter the Promised Land. It is sheer legend that the Spirituals represented simply and solely a naive, childlike faith. On the contrary, they were sophisticated in the best sense of the word, conveying an underlying meaning, a symbolism, far beyond that of the rather grotesque images in which some of them were clothed.

Suffering is easier when endured in common, and Negro Protestantism helped to make things easier by its emphasis on community worship. In later years this led to the development of a great variety of social activities in the Negro Protestant church. These activities followed the curve of Protestant religious trends in the country generally, for religion here has always been shaped, to a certain extent, by the varying patterns of American culture. As a primitive appeal, shouting and singing lost their attraction. But the churches kept their hold upon the new generations by programs of all kinds of activities for young and old. As Deacon or Lady Chairman of a committee, an individual member, snubbed and a nobody in ordinary public life, became a person of no slight importance and was able to wield a little authority within a narrow but important sphere.

In this way the Protestant churches helped to form real leaders in the struggle for liberation and self-advancement. From being a local religious leader, the Protestant Negro minister in many instances developed into a leader on a regional or a national scale in his people's struggle for freedom. Many great leaders of the race found their start in church activities.

This became particularly evident in the field of education, the churches taking a prominent part in founding and conducting Negro colleges and universities and various institutions of secondary education. Many of these schools featured theological faculties. Lincoln University in southeastern Pennsylvania, the first Negro university in the United States and the only one established north of the Mason-Dixon line, is still the training ground for Presbyterian clergy through its Department of Theology.

With all their imperfections and compromises in handling the racial problem, the major Protestant denominations in the United States deserve a lasting credit for instructing vast numbers of the

American Negro people in certain basic doctrines of Christianity. They gave them the hope of the Scriptures and the knowledge of the Savior as well as the Sacrament of Baptism; they sustained their spirits in times of dire affliction and trained them in educational and in some cases social and political leadership. Finally, especially in later years, the various Protestant national religious organizations, including the Quakers, developed a galaxy of men and women from among their white membership dedicated to the work of promoting better race relations.

Protestantism's weakness as a social force lay in its lack of any central spiritual authority. This laid it open to numberless divisions and schisms as well as to passivity in the face of lay church leaders whenever they were determined to maintain a rigid pattern of white supremacy. Negro Protestantism would naturally reflect the atmosphere of the epoch for better or worse. Present-day stress on social benefits and social activities is paralleled by a corresponding increase of such activities in the more "progressive" Negro denominations. The prevailing atmosphere of secularism and of contempt for higher supernatural motives is paralleled, according to reports of various Protestant church bodies, by a corresponding impatience of Negro youth with the other-worldly philosophy that so moved the older generation.

For the Negro who has been more or less actively affiliated with Protestant denominations, conversion to the Catholic Church means in many instances a break with certain greatly cherished values, certain precious associations. Unless his vision is wide enough to rise to a plane where his new ideals and their ideals are fused, the convert feels no longer as close as he did to the generations of brave men and women who by their lives and sacrifices wove the great fabric of Negro liberation in the United States. He misses a multitude of intimate features of today's close knit Protestant religious community, those which appeal particularly to simpler people. If the convert is of the more educated group it is not always easy for him to take up life anew, among his Protestant neighbors who know little or nothing about the saints and martyrs.

What, then, does attract the Negro to Catholicism? The only

satisfactory answer to that question is: the grace of God. Certainly nothing would be more mistaken than to believe that any one formula has been, or could be devised, that would serve as *the* prevailing approach of the American Negro to Catholicism. Zealous missionaries have tried to devise such formulae, basing their speculations on Negro psychology, on the attraction of the Protestant worship, and so on. But the individual Negro is led to the Church in his own way, and generalizations are always misleading.

A zealous Negro convert friend of mine could not rest content until he should bring his old friend to the nearby rectory to talk to a Catholic priest and learn something of the Catholic faith firsthand. The idea was a good one, but unfortunately both pastor and assistants were away at the moment. Their place was taken by a somewhat crusty visiting clergyman, a total stranger to the place and surroundings. Uncomfortable and alarmed at this unexpected inquiry, he invited the inquirer and his anxious sponsor to leave the premises as soon as possible, which they promptly did. In utter dejection, my convert friend walked with his rebuffed companion in total silence. "You know what I think?" asked the companion after a few blocks had been passed. "Oh, I know what you think," grumbled my friend. "Let's not talk about it." "Here's what I think," repeated the companion. "That there man, he spoke with *conviction*. That's what I want in religion: I want conviction. He's convinced of the true church and I'll look into it."

Not only conviction but the sense of identification also plays its part, as was indicated in the experience of a young man, now in business in the North, with whom I talked recently. To my query as to what led to his conversion, he replied as follows:

"I can't say any one thing, Father. It just seemed to shape up that way. I grew up with all kinds of religious practice around me. But at college we all thought the only thing to do was to talk atheism. We did plenty of that, but it didn't make me feel any happier. Then I joined the Marine Corps, just to escape from myself. I ran into everything, good and bad, you can think of there. But I did notice one thing about those Catholic fellows. Whatever their behavior was, they did seem to have a sense of Deity—they could always come back to it, after things went wrong. God was there, waiting for them. I couldn't put my finger on any single item. But I felt something drawing me and I picked up first one idea, then another. Finally I had to decide. Usually when you make an important decision, you put it off for some months. But all the parts fell right together; I was as completely sure as anyone could be.

"It was strange when I first went to Mass. Nobody in the church seemed to be paying any attention to what was going on at the altar. Everyone was busy with his own thought and his books. Each one just talked to God, and went his own way. This seems so different from what we had in the Protestant service, where we all worshiped in common. But one thing has made a tremendous impression on me. You are at home everywhere in the Catholic Church. You have *identification*, and every fellow wants to be identified with something. When I was at Oak Bluffs the other day, that suddenly struck me. Here I am, I said to myself, in a completely strange town. Yet I could slip into confession in that local Catholic church; hear Mass and receive Holy Communion the next morning; and that would be the same anywhere in the whole wide world. I was identified not with this preacher or that parish, but with the whole world of God's Church."

The Negro brings to the Church something that is in danger of disappearing from its life in this country, and thereby putting American Catholicism out of touch with the rest of the great universal suffering world—a keen sense of social justice. In the past, the American Catholic Church built up its strength in great measure from multitudes of immigrant people, carrying in their veins a deep sense of social justice. They sought America to escape from cruel oppression, to worship God and raise their children in freedom. That belief in social justice nerved them to immense tasks, including the creation of parishes, dioceses, schools, colleges and universities, institutions and organizations of every description. It imparted a tremendous dynamism to the growing American Catholic Church. Today, we still need men and women in whom this spirit of social justice is alive.

The unfortunate element in the American situation is that so

much of the Negro's spiritual courage, resourcefulness and energy
has had to be employed in simply combating various inequities—
qualities which could have been used, and should still be used, for
the building up of Church and country. "One's heart is sickened,"
says the forthright American Negro author J. Saunders Redding,
"at the realization of the primal energy that goes undeflected and
unrefined into the sheer business of living as a Negro in the United
States—in any one of the United States. Negro-ness is a kind of
superconsciousness that directs thinking, that dictates action, and
that perverts the expression of instinctual drives which are salutary
and humanitarian—the civic drive, for instance, so that in general
Negroes are cynically indifferent to politics; the societal drive, so
that ordinarily the Negro's concern is only for himself as an individual; and even the sex and love drive, so that many Negroes
suffer sexual maladjustments and many a Negro couple refuse to
bear children who will inevitably grow up under a burden of
obloquy and shame that would daunt and degrade a race of angels!"

It is difficult to convey a sense of this waste to those who have
not themselves experienced it. It may and frequently does mean
tangible loss, such as exclusion from paying jobs for parents of
families, from decent housing where it is available for others than
those of the minority group; and so on. Even more consuming of
human patience, initiative and self-respect are the innumerable
intangibles, those that confront a mother who must explain to her
children why they cannot buy an ice cream cone or a bottle of pop
in a drugstore, why they cannot play or swim in a public park on
a hot day, why they must be careful not to crowd up to the communion rail in church until the whites are duly retired from it. In
numberless other places they will not meet all or any of these
things, but any of them *may* be met, and most unexpectedly. Mean-
while, such an experience is wasteful of human life, and is a standing encouragement to seek compensation in literal waste and irre-
sponsibility.

The Negro therefore is faced with a spiritual problem: whether
to resign himself to this situation or to fight against it. Holy men
and women have become saints by putting up with humiliations in

heroic fashion. Pierre Toussaint did this for a lifetime. Countless humble souls lay these spiritual offerings upon the altar of sacrifice. Sometimes this is ignored, sometimes they are eloquently praised for their wonderful humility. A veteran French missionary from Africa said of his flock to me, "Ah, those are the *real* Catholic Negroes. They have no foolish American idea of trying to better their condition. They are dear to Our Lord's Heart."

Yes, they are dear to Our Lord's Heart; but are they dear for the precise reason that Père X assumed? Such saintly Negroes as I have personally encountered—and there are many of them—accepted their troubles for the simple reason there was no other clear course open to them. Inwardly they were acutely grieved by the conflict between the Church's clear doctrine and the un-Christian actions of some of her members. The thoughtful and pious Negro finds it, as a rule, difficult to understand how it is that in the question of discrimination Catholics are supposed to conform with rigid exacti-tude to the prevailing social pattern, while in other instances they are enjoined to follow a bold non-conformity to current usage—in economic or family morals, in the field of education, in the observ-ance of Friday abstinence, and so on. Holy and humble souls can absorb, as it were, this contradiction and offer it up as a holocaust to the Creator, but when viewed from the outside, this same ambi-guity has long been a solid roadblock to a generalized embracing by the American Negro of the Catholic Faith.

Hence the perplexity, where the Negro, who would like to identify himself first and foremost with the Universal Church, finds not the Church, not her Supreme Pontiff nor her hierarchy, but so many of her members continuing to identify him first and above all with an accident of racial origin: not through ill will, it is true, but through a widespread and not inculpable ignorance. This, as I said, gives rise to a basic spiritual problem, the problem of a man who finds evasiveness where he is entitled to love, who finds that while the one Church of Christ claims his soul with abso-lute authority, at the same time so many of its members warn him not to take her teachings too universally, too seriously.

The way out of this dilemma is through a great spiritual ideal, the ideal of interracial justice, in the full moral and theological sense of the words: the way of a total and adequately motivated, adequately implemented love. But neither the white man nor the Negro can set this ideal in motion alone. It is a joint effort in which each must do his laborious part. Here the two apparent contraries, humility and militance, fuse into one harmonious whole, which is the integral following of Our Lord Jesus Christ, in the fellowship of His Mystical Body and in the role that Mystical Body is called to play in fighting injustice and bringing peace to the modern world. It will mean struggle, and it will mean humiliations, for nothing worthwhile is accomplished without pain: certainly nothing within the master-plan of Christ's Redemption; and by both races a general examination of conscience must be made. The fact that the Negro is not to blame for his present situation does not excuse him from the arduous task of trying to better his condition both with and without the help of the more fortunate majority.

Resentment can turn the wrong way. Like the scarring radiations of Hiroshima, it can burn deep into a closed soul and leave wounds that take generations to heal. But the transcending of resentment can be the portal through which the soul of a liberated people can pass into the sanctuary of a higher fraternity. Experience has led the Negro people to a concrete understanding of certain fundamental teachings of the Christian faith, teachings supremely necessary for our time. These are the great *ethical* truths of social justice and the Natural Law with its corollary of universal human rights and duties, and the great *religious* truths: the unity of all men in the Kingdom of Christ and the corollary of universal charity toward all men in the house of the Father, the Church of the Redeemer.

Christians and Catholics, it is true, accept these doctrines without question. But acceptance is one thing; inward realization is another. The white Catholic is likely to consider them more as speculative opinions, often quite remote from daily life. Misuse of natural-rights teachings by some of the nineteenth-century Liberals created a rather lasting suspicion of these teachings among Catholics, even when they were proclaimed under authoritative auspices. But the

Negro Catholic who has grasped these truths finds in them an immediate application to his own concrete situation.

It is not enough to protest rhetorically against the absorption of the individual by a this-worldly technological mass culture. If we wish to counteract its subtle influence we need a stronger weapon. This is the unadulterated natural-rights teaching of Christianity applied to all, to men of all classes and condition without fear or favor.

The most important field for realizing this idea is the interracial parish, where different races worship and pray and work as part of one religious community. In more and more localities of the United States it has become apparent that the once so honored separate racial parish is not and cannot be a solution. No matter how devotedly, how yearningly the pastor shepherds his monoracial flock, the deadly ambiguity still remains. It is exposed at every step, every time a parishioner makes a move in the larger community. The ambiguity can be removed only when all members of the parish, *in all that pertains to the parish*, unite in wholehearted cooperation and equality—whether this be at worship, in the school, at recreation, or in parish organizations. It is only an evasion when a "mixed" parish is still administered on a separatist plan.

In some instances, the interracial parish has originated by deliberately abandoning the old separatist parish scheme. In other instances, it is the natural result of population shifts when the once "blessedly" homogeneous neighborhood is invaded by "outside" groups. The pastor in such a case can tolerate this change as a calamity, patiently doing the best he can under the circumstances. Or he can regard it as a God-given opportunity to prove right the Church's mission program to the world. Thank God that so many Catholic pastors in this country today are of this latter category.

Paradoxically enough, identification with his racial group is in some respects an asset rather than a liability to the Negro in his dealings with the white man. Were all prejudice and discrimination suddenly to disappear, thinks Professor Arnold Rose of the University of Minnesota, "it is doubtful whether this group identification would last long." But as long as this decrease is gradual, the trend toward group identification at least for a time persists. In Dr. Rose's opinion it has given the Negroes great self-assurance and helped them to build effective protest organizations and political power. It has also made them aware of events throughout the country and throughout the world which affect them. The positive and helpful, therefore, as well as the purely negative and depressing aspects of group identification make it all the more necessary for the Negro not merely to be *accepted by*, but positively to *identify himself with* the higher unity both of Church and country.

From the preceding follows a deeply practical consideration that points to a special mission of the Negro people in our country and in our time. No pious exhortations to patience or humility can conjure away the Negro's deep-rooted instinct to press for equal status. This urge is all the more significant since it is part of a world trend. As the Negro people of America advance in education, they are increasingly conscious of similar aspirations among other nonwhite peoples of the globe. The question in this instance is not how to change this sentiment, but rather to consider what direction it is going to take, and on this answer depends in great measure the spiritual future of our Negro fellow citizens.

The universality of the Church—the all-embracing nature of the supernatural Kingdom of Christ—is for the Negro a very real guarantee of his own place in the Kingdom.

The spirituality of the American Negro is in a very special sense the spirituality of the Church militant and the Church universal: a spirit which he has acquired not by any inherited tribal magic, but through the long, hard school of experience. Those who have come to the Church from without have brought to it certain deep spiritual insights which their ancestors acquired even under the meager spiritual fare with which they were nourished. It took, and it still takes, a virile act of faith to identify oneself with a Church which does not in every instance seem particularly friendly.

Here in the United States, the Catholic Negro is a minority (some 500,000) within the total (some 15,000,000) of his own racial group, as the entire group is a "minority," though the largest "minority," among the ethnic bodies of the nation. But as a member of the Universal Church, he is spiritual kin to millions of non-white Catholics around the globe: their affairs, their advances, their hierarchy, priests and religious and outstanding lay men and women, are for him a subject of legitimate pride. He is a citizen of an immense and noble city. The respect that his person and his voice enjoy abroad, especially among the vast and diverse non-white peoples, is in inverse proportion to the indifference which he has only recently been starting to overcome at home. The voice of the American Catholic Negro has an honored place today among the councils of his own race and is becoming increasingly heard abroad. It is particularly effective when heard in conjunction with voices of other races, speaking not in isolation but in true fellowship, on whatever level and for whatever high and holy cause men choose to associate.

Our Christian spirituality reflects a purely individual phase, concerning the private relations of each individual with his Creator. But there is also a communal and an outgiving phase. In the complete Christian picture the two blend into one, not confusing those things which are distinct but coordinating them in one whole as the different aspects of the human personality are coordinated into the entire man in Christ. The long background of the Negro's past offers to him today a ready entrance into this communal and outgoing phase of the spiritual life. Its expression is not a matter for facile rhetoric but for patient study and for fervent, humble prayer and meditation.